HIS

Final Days

AND

Triumph

HIS

Final Days

AND

Triumph

JEFF NEVILLE

CFI
An imprint of Cedar Fort, Inc.
Springville, Utah

ISBN 13: 978-1-4621-4111-1

Published by CFI, an imprint of Cedar Fort, Inc.
2373 W. 700 S., Springville, UT, 84663
Distributed by Cedar Fort, Inc., www.cedarfort.com

Library of Congress Control Number: 2021949115

Cover design by Courtney Proby
Cover design © 2022 Cedar Fort, Inc.

Printed in the United States of America

10 9 8 7 6 5 4 3 2 1

Printed on acid-free paper

"We must never lose our sense of awe and profound gratitude for the eternal sacrifice of the Son of God. The Savior's Atonement cannot become commonplace in our teaching, in our conversation, or in our hearts."

—Dieter F. Uchtdorf

CONTENTS

THE WEIGHTIER MATTERS

T he Savior once said to the Jewish rulers, "Ye have neglected the weightier matters of the law" (Matthew 23:23). I submit to you that not all knowledge, not all truth in this world is of equal value. Some truths are *more weighty*, more important than others. Out of all of the truths in the universe, what truths would be considered the weightiest?

The prophet Alma declared, "Behold, there is one thing which is of more importance than they all—for behold the time is not far distant that the Redeemer liveth and cometh among his people" (Alma 7:7). Alma then went on to teach about the Savior's atoning sacrifice.

In the modern age, the Prophet Joseph Smith declared, "The fundamental principles of our religion are the testimony of the Apostles and Prophets, concerning Jesus Christ, that He died, was buried, and rose again the third day, and ascended into heaven; and all other things which pertain to our religion are only appendages to it."[1] Of all the truths pertaining to our religion, of all the truths relating to the plan of salvation, the atoning sacrifice, death, and resurrection of Jesus Christ stands supreme. It is the greatest message, the greatest truth, the greatest story ever told. Of those events Gordon B. Hinckley wrote, "When all is said and done when all of history is examined, when the deepest depths of the human mind have been explored, there is nothing so wonderful, so majestic, so tremendous as this act of grace."[2]

Concluding the Last Supper, the Savior traveled with His disciples to the Garden of Gethsemane. When they reached the Mount of Olives, the Savior looked toward heaven and offered His great intercessory prayer. As He prayed, He declared, "And this is life eternal, that they might know thee the only true God, and Jesus Christ, whom thou has sent" (John 17:3). The highest priority in our lives, the most important knowledge we can ever obtain in mortality and in eternity, for that matter, is a knowledge of Heavenly Father and His Only Begotten Son, Jesus Christ. According to John 17:3, our eternal life in the world to come hinges on that knowledge. We should note that in Greek, the tense of the verb *know* in this passage suggests to "know continually." Thus, knowing God and Christ in a way that leads to eternal life is not to be a one-time experience but a continual, lifelong effort.[3]

Our Father in Heaven wants us to know Jesus Christ, whom He has sent. Why? Because as David O. McKay explained, "What you sincerely in your heart think of Christ will determine what you are, will largely determine what your acts will be. No person can study this divine personality, can accept his teachings without becoming conscious of an uplifting and refining influence within himself. . . . Members of the Church of Christ are under obligation to make the sinless Son Man their ideal . . . by choosing him as our ideal, we create within ourselves a desire to be like him."[4] The more we study and learn about the divine personality of Jesus Christ, the greater that uplifting and refining influence will be in our lives. The more we learn of Him, the greater our desire will be to become like Him, the more we learn of Him, the more we will trust Him.

Neal A. Maxwell likewise noted, "One's realization about Jesus' role may commence with only an acknowledgment of Him, and ripen into real appreciation, then into deep admiration and finally into reverent emulation. Our ultimate praise, therefore, is to pattern our lives after His."[5] If we really want to change and become godlike, it is paramount that Christ and His atoning sacrifice become a 'weighty matter' in our life. Our current happiness and future happiness is directly connected to that one supreme reality.

During His mortal ministry the Savior extended the invitation, "Come unto me, all ye that labour and are heavy laden I will give you rest. Take my yoke upon you and *learn of me* for I am meek and lowly of heart; and ye shall find rest to your souls" (Matthew 11:28–29; emphasis added). In this dispensation the Lord said to the Prophet Joseph Smith, "*Learn of me*, listen to my words, walk in the meekness of my Spirit and you shall have peace in me" (D&C 19:23; emphasis added). The Lord's invitation in both of these verses of scripture is for us to learn of Him. President Howard W. Hunter once said to the members of the Church, "We must know Christ better than we know him, we must remember him more often than we remember him; we must serve him more valiantly than we serve him."[6]

On a personal note, one paragraph from my patriarchal blessing reads, "While yet in the premortal world you accepted the Master as your personal Savior and Redeemer. . . . I now commend Him to you, my beloved young brother, as your Exemplar, and admonish you *to earnestly study His flawless life*, to make Him central in your life. By doing so, you will establish a personal relationship with Him which will transcend any other value, and you will learn how to live your own life more perfectly." Years ago, when I was reading that paragraph, the word *earnestly* jumped off the page. I had read that blessing many times, but on that occasion the word *earnestly* made a powerful impression upon my mind and heart that has remained with me. The message for me was clear. I was not to just study the life of the Savior—I was to *earnestly* study it. My patriarchal blessing was a wake-up call for me to focus and increase my effort to search out and consume the weightier matters.

I believe the Lord expects more out of us in gospel scholarship and in our study of Christ today than He has of those in previous dispensations. Why? "For of him unto whom much is given much is required" (D&C 82:3). Take a moment and consider how much truth about Christ we have been given.

We are living in the dispensation of the fulness of times. A composite of all truth from all other previous dispensations has been and will be revealed and restored in our day. In our dispensation we have additional truths that have never been revealed until now (see D&C 128:18). It is not just the quantity of new scripture revealed but the quality and depth of the doctrine that can take our study and gospel knowledge to a deeper level.

Never in the history of the world have we had so much organized information about the gospel of Jesus Christ at our disposal. Because of technology we have massive amounts of gospel resources at our fingertips. With so much information at our disposal, it can be overwhelming. How do we know where to spend our time studying? We have to prioritize and first focus on the weightier matters.

During a mission president training seminar, Jeffrey R. Holland encouraged new mission presidents to do just that: "to have an eternal love affair with the life of the Son of God." He continued, "I pray that you will . . . love everything He did, everywhere He went, everything He said, and everything He is. I would walk on broken glass to find one more word, one more phrase, one more doctrine, any parable that anyone could give me of the life of Christ the living Son of God. The doctrine of Christ means everything to me."[7] May we likewise follow the counsel of Elder Holland and have an eternal love affair with life of the Son of God and make Him our ideal. May His life and teachings mean everything to us.

As we prayerfully and earnestly study the life and atoning sacrifice of the Savior, we will have a mind-enlightening, soul-stretching experience. Through such a study our understanding and vision of Christ and His sacrifice will expand, and with that vision will come increased motivation—motivation to change and become a more dedicated disciples of Christ, for we become like those things we habitually love, admire, and worship.

The Holy Ghost is the greatest asset we have in learning about and coming to know the Savior. The Prophet Joseph Smith taught, "The best way to obtain truth and wisdom, is not to ask it from books, but to go to God in prayer, and obtain divine teaching."[8] As we seek and ask, Heavenly Father, through the Holy Ghost, will reveal Himself and His Only Begotten Son to us. However, the Holy Ghost often needs something in our minds and in our hearts to work with. There is a reason the Lord admonishes us to "treasure up in your minds continually the words of life" (D&C 84:85). It is difficult for the Holy Ghost to bring things to our remembrance if there is nothing in our minds to remember. The memory is often the pulpit where the Holy Ghost preaches.

Therefore, we have been commanded to study and seek words of wisdom and learning out of *the best books* (D&C 88:118; emphasis added). What are some of the best books that will help us in our search to learn of and know Christ? The Savior said, "Search the scriptures, for in them ye think ye have eternal life; and they are they which testify of me" (John 5:39). The scriptures are unequivocally the very best books. They are the standard that should serve as our foundation.[9]

NARROWING OUR STUDY OF CHRIST

As we prioritize and narrow our study of Christ, what specific books of scripture should we focus on? The answer that first comes to mind is the four Gospels found in the New Testament. The Gospels focus directly on the life and mission of Jesus. Third Nephi in the Book of Mormon is sometimes referred to as the fifth Gospel. It gives an account of the ministry of the resurrected Lord among the Nephites. These books should be read and reread again and again.[10]

As we consider the mortal life of the Jesus, how many actual days of His thirty-three-year life do the Gospel writers make mention of? Some Biblical scholars have suggested that number is somewhere between thirty-one and thirty-five days. A full account will most likely have to wait until the peaceful time of the Millennium. One-third of what the Gospel writers wrote of Jesus were dedicated to the last week of His life and more specifically to His last twenty-four hours. They considered this to be the 'weightiest matter' of all. The Lord specifically preserved that portion of the record. The last week of the Savior, and more specifically the last twenty-four hours of His life and His triumphant resurrection, will be the focus of this book.

ENDNOTES

1. Joseph Smith and Joseph Fielding Smith, *Teachings of the Prophet Joseph Smith* (Salt Lake City: Desert Book, 1958/1977), 121. The Apostle Paul wrote to the Corinthians, "For I delivered unto you *first of all* that which I also received, how that Christ died for our sins according to the scriptures; And that he was buried, and that he rose again the third day" (1 Corinthians 15:3–4; emphasis added). The phrase that the King James translators rendered as "first of all" (en protois) can also be translated as "the most import things." Paul also makes it clear that the most important element of his teachings was first and foremost the Savior's atoning sacrifice and triumphant resurrection.

2. Gordon B. Hinckley, "The Wondrous and True Story of Christmas," *Ensign*, Dec. 2000.

3. On another occasion President Hinckley taught, "When all is said and done, when all the legions of the ages have passed in review . . . above all stands the lone figure of Jesus Christ, the Redeemer of the world, the Savior of mankind, the living Son of the living God, the Prince of Peace, the Holy One"[3] (Gordon B. Hinckley, "A Glorious Season," *New Era*, Dec. 2007).

4. President James E. Faust declared, "Our salvation depends on believing in and accepting the Atonement. Such an acceptance requires **a continual effort** to understand it more fully. . . . Any increase in our understanding of His atoning sacrifice draws us closer to Him" (James E. Faust, "The Atonement: Our Greatest Hope," October 2001 general conference).

5. David O. McKay and Clare Middlemiss, *Cherished Experiences, from the Writings of President David O. McKay* (Salt Lake City: Deseret Book, 1976), 24.

6. Neal A. Maxwell, *One More Strain of Praise* (Salt Lake City: (Salt Lake City: Bookcraft, 1999), 52.

7. Howard W. Hunter, "He Invites Us to Follow Him," *Ensign*, Sept. 1994.

8. Sheri L. Dew, *Amazed by Grace* (Salt Lake City: Deseret Book, 2015), 58.

9. Joseph Smith and Joseph Fielding Smith, *Teachings of the Prophet Joseph Smith* (Salt Lake City: Deseret Book, 1958/1977), 191.

10. As noted above Joseph Smith taught, "The best way to obtain truth and wisdom, is not to ask it from books, but to go to God in prayer, and obtain divine teaching." That being said, Joseph Smith studied and poured over the scriptures. He meticulously went over every single verse of the entire Bible, seeking divine guidance regarding its true meaning. From that study, he received revelation on at least 3,410 of those verses. We now have the Joseph Smith Translation of the Bible, the best Bible in the world. Joseph Smith once said, "I know the scriptures and understand them." One of the many reasons Joseph could make that statement about the scriptures was that he had prayerfully and earnestly studied them.

11. Gordon B. Hinckley likewise admonished, "Let us establish in our lives the habit of reading those things which will strengthen our faith in the Lord

Jesus Christ, the Savior of the world. He is the pivotal figure of our theology and our faith. Every Latter-day Saint has the responsibility to know for himself or herself with certainty beyond doubt that Jesus is the resurrected, living Son of the living God." President Hinckley went on to recommend a program of reading, his invitation was to read, "A chapter a day of the Gospels—that is, Matthew, Mark, Luke, and John in the Bible, and Third Nephi in the Book of Mormon, particularly beginning with the eleventh chapter of Third Nephi where is found the account of Christ's visit among the Nephites" (Gordon B. Hinckley, "Fear Not to Do Good," April 1983 general conference.

CHAPTER 1

PALM SUNDAY

S ix days before His death, Jesus left His beloved town of Bethany and descended the Mount of Olives. He stopped at the
village Bethphage to mount a donkey. He then triumphantly
entered into the city of Jerusalem and into the temple courtyard to
jubilant shouts of "Hosanna," with people waving palm branches.

Why the use of palm branches? Since the Hasmonaean period,
the waving of branches has been a symbol of Jewish patriotism and
triumph over foreign oppressors. Bruce R. McConkie taught, "The
palm branch is the symbol of joy and triumph."[1]

As the Savior entered the city, the people shouted, "Hosanna!"
The word *hosanna* means "save us, we beseech thee!" or "save us now!"
Similar shouts of hosanna to the Lord have occurred throughout
history. [2] Gospel scholar Truman G. Madsen explained, "Anciently,
crying 'Hosanna!' with palm branches raised up was, in effect, a
two-way reaching. On the one hand it was a plea: 'O, save us'—a
plea for redemption. On the other hand—as it was in the hearts
of those who welcomed Jesus triumphantly into Jerusalem—it was
a plea that he enter, that he come; it was an invitation that Christ
accept and visit his holy house."[3] We should note that Jesus' Triumphal Entry into the city ended with Him going into the temple, His
house, the house that saves.

Matthew wrote: "A very great multitude spread their garments
in the way; others cut down branches from the trees, and strawed
them in the way. And the multitudes that went before, and that
followed, cried, saying, *Hosanna to the Son of David*: Blessed is he

that cometh in the name of the Lord; Hosanna in the highest" (Matthew 21:8–9; emphasis added). The people did not just shout "hosanna" but shouted, "Hosanna to the Son of David." The phrase "Son of David" is a royal and messianic title that the people were familiar with. They were declaring Christ to be their long-awaited Messiah.

As Jesus entered the Holy City on Psalm Sunday, He deliberately chose to ride a donkey. Riding a horse would have symbolized strength, war, and an attempt to conquer. If Jesus had ridden a horse into the Holy City, His actions could have appeared to the Roman soldiers to be a symbol of opposition and aggression against the Roman occupiers. It may have triggered bloodshed.

Riding a donkey was a sign of humility and peace. However, there is more to the interpretation than just peace. In 1 Kings, David instructed his servants, "Cause Solomon my son to ride upon mine own mule and bring him down to Gihon" (1 Kings 1:33). David had Solomon purposely ride upon his mule in front of all the people. James E. Talmage explained, "The ass has been designated in literature as the ancient symbol of Jewish royalty."[4]

Anciently donkeys were often the conveyance of Old Testament kings and were especially used by King David. Thomas Wayment wrote, "In ancient Israel following the introduction of kingship in about 1000 BC and continuing until the Babylonian exile in 586 BC the Israelites celebrated an annual re-enthronement ritual of their king. Among the many rituals that constituted this re-enthronement ceremony, the king rode into the holy city on a donkey and was crowned again as the legal and just king of the land."[5] To ride upon white asses or ass-colts was the privilege of persons of high rank, princes, judges, and prophets. The scriptures point out that the donkey on which Jesus rode had never been ridden before, a further sign of royalty.

As Jesus entered the city on a donkey He attested to all of the Jews that He was their rightful king. It was a bold statement of royalty that the vast majority of the people understood. A prophecy from the Old Testament provides a prophetic backdrop for the Triumphal Entry: "Rejoice greatly, O daughter of Zion; shout O daughter of Jerusalem: behold thy *King* cometh unto thee: he is just and having salvation; lowly, and riding upon a colt" (Zechariah 9:9; emphasis added). Many watching Jesus enter Jerusalem would have called this verse of scripture to mind.

The Savior's entrance into Jerusalem was therefore no ordinary entrance. It suggested the fulfillment of the prophecy that Israel would once again have a king like David and that this future king would usher in a new dispensation of peace. Up to this point in His ministry Jesus had never made any personal claims to kingship. Earlier, when He appeared at Jerusalem during the Feast of Tabernacles, Jesus went into the Temple of Herod and spoke publicly of Himself in Messianic terms (see John 7:14–39). It was the role of the king to read the law and speak from the temple during the Feast of Tabernacles. Jesus may have been seen here by some as usurping a royal prerogative under Jewish law. However, a specific public claim of that royalty waited until the day of the Triumphal Entry. Jesus had now formally declared Himself to be a king.

John records, "When they heard that Jesus was coming to Jerusalem [they] took palm trees, and went forth to meet him and cried, Hosanna: Blessed is the *King of Israel*" (John 12:12–13; emphasis added). The people understood the Savior's actions and in agreement proclaimed Him to be their King. Whether the Jews believed that the future king was also to be the Messiah is a matter of debate, but Jesus and many of His followers had now openly declared both.

In preparation for the Passover, Jerusalem was overflowing with people. Great crowds had gathered to welcome Jesus as the Messiah and King of Israel. "The record suggests that the composition of this huge crowd was mostly made of the Savior's own constituency. Here were the hundreds he had healed, along with their neighbors, and friends."[6]

John gives us another reason for the crowds gathering to see Jesus: "The people therefore that [were] with him when he called Lazarus from the dead bare record. For this cause the people also met him, for that they heard that he had done this miracle" (John 12:17–18). Hundreds had gathered and come based on faith because they had heard that Jesus had raised Lazarus from the dead. Up to this point, it was the greatest miracle in His ministry. The people may have been stirred by what Jesus might do next.

As mentioned, the crowds shouted, "Hosanna," which means, "save us now." The people may have wanted immediate action. The Jews of the first century believed that the Messiah would physically save them from their political oppressors by military conquest. Maimonides, a famous early authority on Judaism (1135–1204 A.D.), summarized the teachings of the rabbis concerning the Messiah: "If there arise a king of the house of David **who . . . fights** the battles of the Lord, then one may properly assume that he is the Messiah."[7]

Perhaps on Palm Sunday the Jews expected Jesus to proceed directly to the Roman headquarters, the Antonia Fortress, and physically expel the occupiers and reestablish the kingdom of Israel. It appears that even His disciples, who had been warned that this was to be the beginning of the end, were, for the moment, carried away by the tide of enthusiasm. However, instead of going to the Antonia fortress Jesus proceeded to the temple.[8]

Of the Triumphal Entry Dieter F. Uchtdorf observed, "Perhaps [even] the disciples thought this was a turning point—the moment when the Jewish world would finally recognize Jesus as the long-awaited Messiah. But the Savior understood that many of the shouts of praise and acclamation would be temporary."[9] Hosanna, "save us now." Jesus had come to save them from something far greater than their political oppressors. He had come to save them from sin, Satan, hell, and death. The events soon to follow in Gethsemane, Golgotha, and at the Garden Tomb would signal the greatest Independence Day, the greatest day of liberation and saving in all history.

As the Triumphal Entry proceeded and the people were rendering Messianic honors and proclaiming Jesus to be the King of Israel, "the Pharisees therefore said among themselves, perceive ye how ye prevail nothing? the world is gone after him" (John 12:19). The Pharisees, unable to check the surging enthusiasm of the multitudes, unable to silence the joyous acclamations, made their way through the throngs until they reached Jesus. "And some of the Pharisees . . . said unto him, Master rebuke thy disciples. And he answered and said unto them, I tell you that, if these should hold their peace, the stones would immediately cry out" (Luke 19:39–40). Within a few days, immediately following the death of Jesus the stones would indeed cry out in agony.

Jesus accepted the acclamations that He was their long-anticipated Messiah and King. The time had come to publicly proclaim both. The Triumphal Entry was in essence a move that clarified the identity of both those who opposed Jesus and those who believed in Him. Such a clear and bold declaration sent His enemies into a maddened frenzy. His entry into the city revealed that Jesus was more popular and had far more followers than His enemies ever imagined. Jesus' popularity in Galilee now extended into Jerusalem and was even making inroads into the Jewish hierarchy. John wrote, "Among the chief rulers also many believed on him, but because of the Pharisees they did not confess him [why?], lest they should be put out of the synagogue" (John 12:42). While some of the rulers were afraid to make their belief known, many in the crowd were not.

Among the crowds that gathered during that last week, many questioned whether Jesus would appear publicly in Jerusalem during the feast. The plan of the Jewish hierarchy to take Jesus into custody was no secret. After Lazarus was raised from the dead, the Jewish leaders concluded they had to act. From that moment on, they were conspiring to get Christ out of the way.

The courage displayed during the Triumphal Entry by many of the followers of Jesus stood as an obstacle that His enemies now faced in removing Him. Because of the pro-Jesus crowds, the enemies of Jesus, particularly the Jewish hierarchy, could no longer oppose Him openly. It became abundantly clear that Jesus would have to be taken by stealth. They now had to work quickly, secretly, and illegally to isolate, arrest, and kill Him before His followers could muster a defense. In the Gospels, the Jewish leaders are shown to be fearful that arresting Jesus would cause a disturbance. They would have to take Jesus at night, subtly, using a guide who could report His whereabouts before His supporters could gather. The plot to kill Jesus was finalized by the Jewish leaders on Wednesday, just three days following Psalm Sunday with Judas agreeing to betray Jesus. The Triumphal Entry of Jesus had hastened the process that would result in His death.

In ancient Rome, a sign was attached to each cross indicating the criminal charges for which a person was being crucified. What was the inscription on the Savior's cross? "Jesus, The King of the Jews." Jesus was formally condemned for claiming to be the King of the Jews, not for declaring Himself to be the Jewish Messiah or even Jehovah.

The Triumphal Entry appears to have been the final tipping point for the enemies of Jesus, the act that would push them over the edge. Ironically, what some have taken to be only a humble act of submission, by riding in on a donkey, was also a bold move on the part of Jesus. Through this act, He publicly testified of His own mission as the long-awaited Messiah and true King of Israel.

Despite the joyful reception Jesus received at the Triumphal Entry, within a few days the crowds would demand His death. Maybe, some of their initial enthusiasm had faded when Jesus did not come as the physical, political deliverer they had long hoped for. We should also note that it is very possible that the people in the crowd that welcomed and embraced the Savior at the Triumphal Entry were different from the crowd a few days later that called for His death. The crowds calling for Jesus' death were led and inspired by the Jewish leaders, the enemies of Jesus. Perhaps because of the secrecy and speed of the arrest, and the illegality of the trials, the supporters of Jesus did not have sufficient time to gather in large numbers. Let's give His followers the benefit of the doubt.

The Triumphal Entry marked a glorious moment in Christ's ministry. But with due respect to the adoring crowd, this was a very little parade compared to what the Master deserved and would soon deserve. The Triumphant Entry of Jesus into Jerusalem on Palm Sunday was, in truth, but a prelude to the greatest day of triumph ever to be, just a few days distant.

ENDNOTES

1. Bruce R. McConkie, *Doctrinal New Testament Commentary*. Vol. 3 (Salt Lake City: Bookcraft, 1965), 495.
2. The Hosanna Shout was performed during the Jewish Feast of Tabernacles. When the resurrected Savior appeared to the Nephites at the Bountiful temple, the shout was given. It appears the shout memorialized the

pre-earthly council in heaven, when all the sons and daughters of God shouted for joy. John Taylor said, "Indeed the shout was . . . older than the everlasting hills . . . aye, older than the earth. . . . For was not this the shout which shook the heavens before the foundations of the earth were laid, when, 'the morning stars sang together and all the sons of God shouted for joy'?" (B. H. Roberts, *The Life of John Taylor*, 366.) The shout was also performed after the closing prayer of the Kirtland Temple dedication and all temple dedications since.

3. Truman G. Madsen, *The Temple: Where Heaven Meets Earth* (Salt Lake City: Deseret Book, 2008), 110.

4. James E. Talmage, *Jesus the Christ* (Salt Lake City: Deseret Book, 1915/1982), 480.

5. Thomas A. Wayment, "The Triumphal Entry," *The Life and Teaching of Jesus Christ*, vol. 2 (Salt Lake City: Deseret Book, 2006), 402.

6. W. Cleon Skousen, *Days of the Living Christ* (Ensign Publishing Co., 1992/2018), 431.

7. Gershom Gerhard Scholem, *The Messianic Idea in Judaism* (Schocken Books, 1971), 28.

8. The Joseph Smith Translation of Mark reads, "And Jesus entered into Jerusalem, and into the temple. And when he had looked round about upon all things, and *blessed the disciples*, the eventide was come; and he went out unto Bethany with the twelve" (JST, Mark 11:11; emphasis added). The significance of the Joseph Smith Translation is that Jesus blessed His disciples. They were most likely blessed against the day when Jerusalem would be destroyed. Two days later during the Olivet Discourse Jesus discussed with His disciples the impending abomination of desolation that was coming, future scenes of death, and destruction that caused Jesus to weep (see Matthew 24:12).

> In 66 A.D., the Jews, believing that the Messiah would come and battle for them, revolted against the Romans. In 70 A.D., the Roman legions under Titus laid siege on Jerusalem. During the fighting the Jewish rebels took refuge within the walls of Jerusalem. The famine and hunger that followed was so severe that some resorted to cannibalism. Any Jew caught trying to escape the city was crucified in front of the walls of the city for all to see. Eventually the entire city was destroyed, the temple was burned to the ground and leveled, and all of Jerusalem was plowed as a field. Over 1,100,000 Jews were slaughtered, and 97,000 were taken captive. In all, the Romans destroyed 987 towns in Palestine and slew 580,000 men, while still larger numbers perished through starvation, disease, and fire. Jesus, having foreseen all of this, wept on at least two occasions for His people.

9. Dieter F. Uchtdorf, "The Way of the Disciple," April 2009 general conference.

CHAPTER 2

THE FINAL PASSOVER AND LAST SUPPER

With the plot to kill Jesus finalized on Wednesday, we turn our focus to Thursday. It was Thursday evening as we reckon time, but the beginning of Friday according to the Jewish calendar. It was the last twenty-four hours of the mortal life of Jesus, the day before Jesus was to be crucified. According to Matthew, Mark, and Luke, the Passover celebration had begun. This would be the final approved Passover meal at Jerusalem. The great and last sacrifice was about to be offered. It was to be the Passover of all Passovers.

There were two main reasons for the celebration of the Passover. First and foremost, it was a time to remember that during the very first Passover in Moses's day the angel of death passed over the homes and flocks of Israel, preserving their firstborn males. A second purpose was to remember Jehovah, the Great Deliverer of Israel. He had delivered them in the past and would deliver them in the future. All ceremonial rituals in the festivities centered on these two themes.

According to Matthew, Mark, and Luke, at the very hour that Jesus and His disciples met in that upper room, sacrificial lambs were being offered up in the temple. We should note that John's chronology of the Passover differs from the other Gospel writers. In John's account Jesus would have celebrated the Passover with His disciples in advance, a day prior to the formal holiday. According to

9

John, Jesus died on the cross at three o'clock, the very moment the first Passover lamb was sacrificed.

How long had the Lord's followers been sacrificing lambs? Since Adam. Why lambs? All in similitude of the great and last sacrifice of God's Only Begotten Son, the Lamb of God. Ever since the first Passover (just prior to the Israelites' exodus from Egypt), thousands of paschal lambs had been slain each year for some 1,500 years to usher in the Passover celebration. In his classic *The Life of Christ*, gospel scholar and historian Fredrick Farrar has written that in total some 260,000 lambs were slain during the Passover feast.[1] That was a lot of sheep being sacrificed each Passover. Think of the millions of lambs that had been offered up over the years, all in anticipation of what was about to take place.

Jesus came not only as a lamb but also as a lion. In the book of Revelation, the Apostle John first refers to Jesus as the "Lion of the tribe of Judah, the Root of David" (Revelation 5:5). Christ was from the tribe of Judah and descended from King David. As mentioned, on the day of the Triumphal Entry Jesus in essence proclaimed Himself to be the lion, the King of Israel. It is interesting to note that that's the only reference to the Savior as a lion in the book of Revelation. In the next verse John does not see a lion. He sees "a lamb as it had been slain" (Revelation 5:6). Paradoxically, the lion mentioned turned out to be a "lamb," the first of twenty-nine references to Jesus as a lamb in the book of Revelation. Why does John repeatedly stress a lamb? Jesus did not come as a military, political conquering king. He came meekly as a willing, loving sacrifice for all mankind. He came as the suffering servant. The messianic king would not come to slay the wicked Jewish occupiers and oppressors, but as John had seen to be slain Himself.

Prior to coming to earth the Lamb was considered as having already been slain. John noted "the Lamb slain from the foundation of the world" (Revelation 13:8). The prophet Enoch likewise taught, "The Lamb is slain from the foundation of the world" (Moses 7:47). The atoning sacrifice of Jesus Christ was put into effect long before this world came into existence, and the Lamb was foreshadowed even then. It was by that power that the war in heaven was won.

John wrote, "For they have overcome him [Lucifer] by *the blood of the lamb*" (Revelation 12:11; emphasis added). The Atonement of our Savior is infinite in time and is retroactive. It was the blood of the lamb that saved us during our premortal life. It was by that power Satan was banished. It was also by the blood of the lamb that we were cleansed of our sins during our first estate and born clean into this world.

THE SETTING

We go with the Savior to an upper room in Jerusalem with His Twelve Apostles. Tradition holds it was either the dwelling place of His disciple John Mark or the home of John Mark's parents. Just prior the last supper preparations were made. Luke recorded, "And he [Jesus] sent Peter and John, saying, go and prepare us the Passover that we may eat" (Luke 22:8). Peter and John went as instructed and prepared for their Passover meal. At some point, they returned from the temple with their slain lamb. Lying on the table during the Last Supper was the roasted lamb they would eat, symbolizing the very Lamb of God who would soon be sacrificed. One can only wonder what thoughts our Savior had as He looked at that lamb.

Leonardo da Vinci, Carl Heinrich Bloch, and other artists have given us magnificent portraits of the Last Supper. As beautiful as these paintings are, the artists take artistic freedom with the actual details. In those renditions the participants are seen sitting in chairs. In Jesus's day small, short tables were used. Sometimes they hung them from the ceiling so as not to touch the floor and be defiled. It was the custom, as Jewish law directed, for free men to occupy a separate pillow or cushion and recline at a table. They were to lie on their left side and lean on their left hand, their feet stretching back-ward, toward the outside. "The rabbis explained that this pose represented the fact that Israel had been delivered from bondage (from the Egyptians) and could now eat in a relaxed, reclined position as was the custom of all free men in ancient times."[2]

As they were taking their selected seats contention arose among the disciples, "there was also a strife among them, which of them should be accounted the greatest" (Luke 22:24). The disciples were competing and comparing two major sins of pride that most of us struggle with. They were men of passion, with weaknesses and challenges like the rest of us. The contention initially arose over precedence in the seating arrangements. Among the Pharisees and Jews of the time, the rank and place of each person at the table was a matter of great concern. It was a Jewish custom for the host of the Passover feast to have his choicest friends, those who were considered the greatest and most worthy, reclined next to him. Who sat next to the Savior during the meal? From the reading we learn that John, the youngest Apostle, "the disciple whom Jesus loved," received the second place of honor and was seated on the right side of the Savior, and Judas in all probability was at His left. Judas had obtained the chief seat. We can surmise that Judas was most likely at the root of the trouble.

Who should have been closest to the Savior? Peter was the chief Apostle, and his place was certainly next to the Savior. We can only imagine how the argument might have gone between Judas and Peter. The Savior responded to the strife by stating, "The kings of the Gentiles exercise lordship over them; and they that exercise authority upon them are called benefactors. But ye shall not be so: but he that is greatest among you, let him be as the younger, and he that is chief, as he that doth serve. For whether is greater, he that sitteth at meat, or he that serveth? Is not he that sitteth at meat? But I am among you as he that serveth" (Luke 22:25–27).

The Savior's response to the disputing disciples was to serve. The Prophet Joseph Smith taught, "If any person will build up others; benefit, bless and permanently aggrandize others he in turn will be aggrandized eternally, [and] that is the only principle or plan upon which it can be done and remain forever."[3] If we truly want to get ahead in the sight of God, we must strive to help others get ahead. We must serve as Jesus did. After the admonition of the Savior I am guessing Peter backed down, and knowing his nature, he probably took the least respected seat at the table.

WASHING OF THE FEET

During the feast, without saying a word, John recorded that Jesus "riseth from supper, and laid aside his garments; and took a towel, and girded himself and began to wash the disciples' feet" (John 13:4–5). Their feet would have been dirty because the disciples wore sandals as they walked along dusty, dirt roads. Jesus tied a towel about Him for two reasons. One was for a practical purpose, so that He might have it in readiness to dry the feet of His disciples after He had washed them. Second and more important, by girding Himself with towel Jesus took upon Himself the role of a servant. "To be girded with a towel was to be acknowledged as a servant or slave. Slaves washed the feet of their masters and, as a courtesy, the feet of their master's guests."[4] After washing the feet of the disciples Jesus said to them, "I have given you an example, that you should do as I have done to you" (John 13:15). The Savior had just taught them by precept about serving. True to His form, He then taught by example. He taught them a lesson in humility and service they would never forget. No service was to be beneath them, no soul was to be unworthy of their ministrations.

As Jesus washed the disciples' feet, He said to them, "What I do thou knowest not now, but thou shalt know hereafter" (John 13:7). The Savior explained that at some point in the future the Apostles would understand the full significance of what He had just done. This act was much more than mere service and an object lesson on humility. Through this act of washing the feet, Jesus reinstituted a sacred ordinance that would be performed by legal administrators among true disciples from that day forward.

During my two-year mission I vividly recall sitting at a table during a zone conference and eating lunch with Elder Vaughn J. Featherstone of the Quorum of the Seventy. During the lunch he asked us if we had any gospel questions. One of the missionaries I sat with asked him if the ordinance of the washing of the feet was still practiced today. He assured us that it is still practiced and then proceeded to talk about it during our zone conference the next hour.

In this dispensation, the command to reinstitute the ordinance of the washing of the feet was given in Doctrine and Covenants 88:

"And ye shall not receive any among you into this school save he is clean from the blood of this generation. And he shall be received by the ordinance of the washing of feet for unto this end was the ordinance of the washing of feet instituted. And again, the ordinance of washing feet is to be administered by the president or presiding elder of the church. It is to be commenced with prayer; and after partaking of bread and wine, he is to gird himself according to the pattering given in the thirteenth chapter of John's testimony concerning me. Amen" (D&C 88:138–141). In compliance with the command, Joseph Smith first performed this ordinance in the School of the Prophets, on January 23, 1833. During the first year, members were admitted to the School of the Prophets only after participating in the ordinance of the washing of the feet. After the first year, Joseph Smith waited until the temple was completed to continue performing the ordinance.

Joseph Smith explained, "The house of the Lord must be prepared . . . and in it we must attend to the ordinance of washing of feet. It was never intended for any but official members. It is calculated to unite our hearts, that we may be one in feeling and sentiment, and that our faith may be strong, so that Satan cannot overthrow us, or have any power over us here."[5] Jesus washing the feet of His disciples would serve to strengthen, fortify, and unite them for the difficulties of the coming night and prepare them for their future missions. President Howard W. Hunter explained, "There the Master sought to fortify His special witnesses against the snares of the evil one by laying aside his outer garment, girding Himself with a towel and washing the Apostles' feet."[6]

JUDAS

The final Passover supper proceeded under conditions of intense sadness. The Savior's heart was heavy. His impending sacrifice lay just ahead of Him. In addition, one of those closest to Him was about to betray Him. We should note, the Savior also washed Judas's feet. What more could Jesus have done to help move Judas with compassion and swerve him from his dark intent than kneeling before him in this humblest of all service? But it was to no avail. Judas had already surrendered his will to another master.

As they began eating, the Savior explained, "The hand of him that betrayeth me is with me on the table" (Luke 22:21). Once Jesus made this declaration, the disciples "were exceedingly sorrowful, and began every one of them to say unto him, Lord, is it I?" (Matthew 26:22). Why didn't the disciples nudge one another and say, "I bet it is Judas"? I think it reflects something of their stature and character. From the remark "Lord, is it I?" we learn some wonderful lessons from these disciples. We should never disregard counsel from our leaders. We should always look inward and ask ourselves where we need to improve and where we need to change.

Dieter F. Uchtdorf explained,

> I wonder what each of us would do if we were asked that question by the Savior. Would we look at those around us and say in our hearts, "He's probably talking about Brother Johnson. I've always wondered about him," or "I am glad Brother Brown is here. He really needs to hear this message"? Or would we, like those disciples of old, look inward and ask that penetrating question: "Is it I?" In these simple words, "Lord, is it I?" lies the beginning of wisdom and the pathway to personal conversion and lasting change . . . being able to see ourselves clearly is essential to our spiritual growth. If our weaknesses and shortcomings remain obscured in the shadows, then the redeeming power of the Savior cannot heal them and make them strengths . . . a first step on this wondrous and fulfilling path of true discipleship starts with our asking the simple question: "Lord is it I?"[7]

Is this a question we could ask ourselves? Do we have the humility and courage to follow the early Apostles, and ask "Lord, is it I?"

During the meal Peter asked John to find out from Jesus who would betray Him (see John 13:24). The Savior responded, "He it is to whom I shall give a sop when I have dipped" (John 13:26). What does it mean to give a sop? "In areas of the world where table utensils are not used at mealtime, it was and is common practice to place both broth and meat in a dish in the center of the table. Thin pieces of bread, often shaped to make a spoon, are used to extract both meat and broth from the dish. The bread thus dipped becomes a 'sop.' It was the mark of great honor for two friends to dip from the same sop dish and an even greater mark of respect for one to dip for a friend and present the sop to him."[8] The Savior presented Judas with a sop. By that act Jesus presented Judas with an offer of friendship, giving him another opportunity to look inward, receive His love, and abandon his planned betrayal.

Only after the Savior had given Judas the sop did Judas finally ask, "Master is it I? [Jesus answered], Thou has said" (Matthew 26:25). Have you ever wondered why the others didn't stop Judas or at least say something to him? Judas was seated to the left of Jesus and could have asked Him quietly while the feast was in progress, and Jesus in a like manner could have whispered the response. John, sitting closest, would have most likely heard the private conversation and then later recorded it.

The other possibility is that the private conversation started earlier. Peter may have beckoned to John discretely, to ask the Savior who would betray Him, without the others noticing. Jesus then could have whispered to John and explained, "He it is to whom I shall give a sop" (John 13:27). Only Peter and John would have known. John then recorded, "After the sop Satan entered into him." Is this to be taken literally? Perhaps. "Then said Jesus unto him, That though doest, do quickly" (John 13:27). The other disciples probably assumed Judas had gone to buy bread and take care of business associated with the Passover. Judas had not gone to get bread, but to betray the Bread of Life.

We should note that Judas had not acted in ignorance. His was an act of open rebellion. Judas ignored multiple warnings from the Savior, including the one given that night during the supper. During the meal the Savior had warned, "Woe unto that man whom the Son of Man is betrayed! It had been good for that man if he had not been born" (Matthew 26:24). Some have suggested that the Savior needed Judas to betray Him and that it was predestined. Judas always had a choice; he always had his agency. No one was foreordained to fail or to be wicked. Had Judas made the choice not to betray the Savior, another way would have been opened up for

Jesus to be arrested and crucified. "The works and the designs, and the purposes of God cannot be frustrated, neither can they come to naught" (D&C 3:1). The Savior's atoning sacrifice would occur with or without Judas' involvement.

The Joseph Smith Translation in Mark 14 adds an interesting insight into the betrayal: "And he said unto Judas Iscariot . . . what thou doest, do quickly: But beware of innocent blood. Nevertheless Judas . . . went unto the chief priests to betray Jesus unto them; for he turned away from him and *was offended because of his* [Jesus'] *words*" (see JST Mark 14:10 and the complete inspired version of Mark 14:28; emphasis added). In this verse, the Savior gives Judas an additional warning. He was betraying innocent blood. We also learn that one of the reasons Judas turned away from Jesus was because he was offended because of Jesus' words. The Prophet Joseph Smith explained, "Judas was rebuked, and immediately betrayed his Lord into the hands of His enemies, because Satan entered into him."[9] Apparently chastised by Jesus for something he had said or done, the defensive young Apostle rejected the correction, and refused to confess his error and repent.

His prideful reaction lead to his demise. Is there a lesson in this for us? It is a choice to be offended; it is not a condition inflicted or imposed upon us by someone or something else. We determine how we will act, how we will respond. One sign of true humility is to learn to accept correction and to accept it cheerfully. [10]

THE SACRAMENT IS INTRODUCED

Once Judas left the room, the Savior proceeded to introduce the sacrament. Of this sacred moment J. Reuben Clark likewise concluded, "The institution of the Sacrament . . . occurred, I feel, after Judas has left the chamber to arrange to betray the Master."[11] Why would the Savior wait until Judas was gone to introduce this ordinance? Sometimes great spiritual experiences will occur only after Satan and his servants leave the premise. I think of Adam and Eve being taught by angels only after Satan was cast out from among them. In the first chapter of Moses we read of an encounter between

Moses and Satan. Once Satan was cast out, Moses not only beheld the glory of the Lord, but had one of the greatest visions of all time (see Moses 1:22–40). After Judas was gone, the depressive, dark atmosphere changed to hope, love, and light.

Gospel scholar Susan Easton Black explained, "The final Passover was, in reality, two events rather than one: a formal celebration of the annual Passover supper and the first observance of the Lord's Supper in commemoration of the atoning act of Jesus Christ."[12] The Last Supper, therefore, was not only the last meal Jesus had as a mortal, but more specifically, it was the last Passover supper to be recognized by God. A new ordinance was introduced to take its place.

The Passover meal in Jesus' day called for the devout worshipers to break bread, to bless both bread and wine, and to eat and drink. Jesus took the symbols of the past and gave them a new meaning for the future.[13] Just as the Passover had pointed hearts and minds forward to the great and last sacrifice, the emblems of the sacrament would point hearts and minds back to the events that would shortly occur in Gethsemane and at Golgotha. "The Passover signified deliverance from death; the sacrament not only signified deliverance from death but also signified new life."[14]

Regarding this occasion Bruce R. McConkie has written, "No single account of the institution of the sacrament of the Lord's Supper, standing alone, contains enough to let us know the reality and the glory and the wonder of what happened in that upper room as the Paschal supper died and the sacramental supper was born. Nor for that matter do all the biblical accounts taken together reveal the glorious mystery of it all."[15] A full and complete knowledge of this event may have to wait for a future Millennial day. Yet one thing is clear: that Thursday evening in the upper room the Paschal supper died and the sacramental supper was born. In the closing of the Judean ministry of the Savior, there was a new beginning.

There was also a new beginning on April 6, 1830. The ancient Church of Jesus Christ was organized anew and restored to the earth. Those in attendance on that historic day partook of the sacrament. The sacrament was one of the first ordinances to be restored in this new gospel dispensation. An early member of the Church, Zebedee Coltrin, commenting on what took place in the School of the Prophets, wrote, "At every meeting, the washing of feet was attended to, the sacrament was also administered at times when Joseph appointed, after the ancient order; that is, warm bread to break easy [sic] was provided and broken into pieces as large as my fist and each person had a glass of wine and sat and ate the bread and drank the wine; and Joseph said that was the way that Jesus and his disciples partook of the bread and wine. And this was the order of the church anciently until the church went into darkness."[16]

As we consider this restored ordinance today, there are at least three things fundamentally important with the sacrament that we might think about and engage in when we partake of it. First, we could use the time for self-discernment and introspection. As we reach out to take the bread and water, we usually are the ones who determine whether we should partake of it or not. It could be a time to examine our own personal worthiness, a time to reflect on the conduct of our previous week, a time to ask the question, "Lord is it I?" Second, we could use the time to pray, ponder, and commune with the Father. Third, it is a time when we renew and recommit to live our baptismal covenant. That covenant includes the promises to take His name upon us, to keep His commandments, and to always remember Him. In both sacramental prayers, remembering Christ is a key element. There are thirty-three verses in the standard works that specifically describe the ordinance of the sacrament. The word *remember* or *remembrance* is used twenty-three times in those verses.

The Passover that was celebrated once a year had been replaced by the ordinance of the sacrament. Meeting once a year to partake of the sacrament was not going to be enough for the Lord's disciples. They soon began administering it on a weekly basis so they would never forget what their Master had done. They did it to keep Jesus and His sacrifice in the forefront of their minds and hearts. They would strive to always remember Him.

Jeffrey R. Holland taught, "Since that upper room experience on the eve of Gethsemane and Golgotha, children of the promise have been under covenant to remember Christ's sacrifice in this newer, higher, more holy and personal way."[17] Why such a focus on remembering? Remembering the Savior and His sacrifice can serve as a motivating force that will help us to change and become more like Him.

As we partake of those sacred emblems in remembrance of the Savior, we should be aware of what the Joseph Smith Translation of Matthew 26:26–28 clarifies: the bread and wine are not changed into Christ's literal body and blood. However, as we partake of those sacred emblems, hopefully we are changed. The sacrament is the only ordinance in which we eat, drink, taste, and swallow. This might suggest what we are to do with His offering. The Savior's Atonement has the power to literally change our very nature, to purge out the natural man within us and serve to make us "new creatures" in Christ (see Mosiah 27:26).

For that change to occur, Melvin J. Ballard taught,

> We must come, to the sacrament table hungry. . . . We must come hungering and thirsting for righteousness. . . . Who is there among us that does not wound his spirit by word, thought, or deed, from Sabbath to Sabbath? . . . If there is a feeling in our hearts that we are sorry for what we have done . . . then repair to the sacrament table where, if we have sincerely repented and put ourselves in proper condition, we shall be forgiven, and spiritual healing will come to our souls. It will really enter into our being. You have felt it. I am a witness that there is a spirit attending the administration of the sacrament that warms the soul from head to feet; you feel the wounds of the spirit being healed, and the load is lifted.[18]

I will never forget the first time I blessed the sacrament as a young sixteen-year-old priest. For weeks I had practiced saying the sacrament prayers out loud in the solitude of my bedroom. I did not want to be the priest who had to redo it four times. I was nervous, to say the least. In our ward, we always had four priests prepare the sacrament. The two priests who sat in the middle would say the prayers. I made it a point to sit on the outside when I prepared the sacrament and had for a time avoided giving voice to the prayers.

One Sunday, I once again found my regular seat on the outside, but that day one of my fellow priests wouldn't have it. He was a kid you just did not argue with. With my pulse racing and my heart pounding, I said the prayer on the water. After saying the prayer, I looked up to our bishop. He nodded in the affirmative. To my great relief, I had managed to get it right the first time. Then the miracle happened. When I sat down, I experienced what Melvin J. Ballard taught. The Spirit engulfed me, warming my soul from the crown of my head to the soles of my feet. I felt a healing, a cleansing, and a burden lifted. That day I learned that through the ordinance of the sacrament we can access and apply the Savior's atoning sacrifice.

The ordinance of the sacrament served to strengthen and prepare the Savior for His pending sacrifice. By instituting the sacrament, Jesus had also prepared and fortified His Apostles against the spiritual tribulation and onslaught of the adversary that was soon to come upon them. If we likewise are going to successfully meet the challenges that lie ahead of us, if we are to become the men and women God wants us to become, it is vital that the ordinance of the sacrament become a priority in our lives.

SACRED MUSIC

The final act of the Savior and His disciples following the Passover meal, Last Supper and instructions was the singing of a hymn. "And when they had sung a hymn, they went out into the Mount of Olives" (Matthew 26:30; Mark 14:26). It was customary to end Passover by singing. They would sing what was called the *Hallel Psalms* from Psalms 113–118. These sacred lyrics were indeed prophetic, for they include the phrases, "The Lord is on my side; I will not fear: what can man do unto me? . . . The stone which the builders refused is become the head stone of the corner. . . . This is the Lord's doing; it is marvelous in our eyes" (Palms 118:6–7, 22–23). Sacred music serves to bring spiritual strength.

They may have done more than just sing a hymn. A very early apocryphal work, known as the Acts of John (written about A.D. 130), portrays Jesus and His Apostles forming a circle to pray together before His arrest and trials: "[Jesus] gathered all of us together and said: Before I am delivered up unto them let us sing a hymn to the Father, and so go forth to that which lieth before us. He bade us therefore make as it were a ring, holding one another's hands, and himself standing in the midst he said, 'Answer Amen unto me.' He began, then, to sing [or recite] a hymn and to say: Glory be to thee, Father. And we, going about in a ring, answered him: Amen.'"

To prepare Himself and the disciples for the difficulties that they lay ahead the Savior and his disciples were united in faith, prayer, and song and were possibly connected in a sacred circle.

JOHN 17: THE GREAT INTERCESSORY PRAYER

Sometime after they had sung a hymn, the Savior led the eleven Apostles to the Mount of Olives, just outside of Jerusalem, where He lifted up His eyes to heaven and gave what is known as the Great Intercessory Prayer. Of this prayer David O. McKay wrote, "The greatest, most impressive prayer ever uttered in this world is found in John 17:14–22."[19]

"Intercessory" refers to the pleadings of Jesus to His Father in behalf of His disciples and for those who would believe on their words (see John 17: 20–26). During this prayer the Lord acted as a mediator for the disciples and for those who would believe on them.

This prayer is also known as "The Great High Priestly Prayer." This title referred to His future sacrifice for the sins of the world (see Hebrews 3:1). Once each year in ancient Israel, the presiding high priest entered into the holy of holies, the most sacred place within the tabernacle. There he would perform certain rites in connection with the Day of Atonement, a day set aside for national humiliation and contrition.

The priest, having first bathed himself and then dressed in white linen, would present before the Lord a young bullock and two young goats as sin offerings, and a ram as a burnt offering in behalf of his sins and those of the people. The high priest's role was that of mediator, or one who interceded with the Lord in behalf of the people. His role, of course, was but a type of the great mediating role of the Savior in our behalf. Thus, when Jesus pleaded to the Father for all those who believed on Him, He did so as our Intercessor, or Great High Priest.[20] Thus, as a priest sacrificing a lamb, Jesus would perform the sacrifice. And as a Lamb, He became His own victim. [21]

FIRM AND STEADFAST

A week prior to the Last Supper, Jesus "took unto him the twelve, and said unto them, Behold, we go up to Jerusalem, and all things that are written by the prophets concerning the Son of man shall be accomplished" (Luke 18:31). Just prior to instituting the Last Supper He said to His disciples, "I have desired to eat this Passover with you before I suffer" (Luke 22:15). Concluding the Last Supper John explained, "Jesus knew that his hour was come that he should depart out of this world" (John 13:1). These verses make it clear that as the Savior went to Gethsemane it was with total awareness of what lay ahead. He knew He was going to Gethsemane to suffer; He knew He was going to Calvary to freely lay down His life.

Gordon B. Hinckley shared similar sentiments when he stated,

I like occasionally to open the New Testament and read of the Last Supper. I think I can envision in my mind the gathering together of the Twelve in the Upper Room. I think maybe they came in very happily, very jauntily. They were all brethren and they probably shook hands with one another and said, "How are you doing, Peter?" "How are things going, John?" and a few such things as that. But I think when the Lord came in, He was sober and quiet and thoughtful and sad. *He knew what was coming.* They could not seem to understand it. But *He knew what was coming*, that He would have to give His life in pain and terrible, unspeakable suffering if He were to accomplish the mission out-lined by His Father for the redemption of mankind.[22]

Jesus knew what was coming. He knew what lay ahead for Him.

On a similar note Brigham Young declared that before the hour of the atoning sacrifice "Jesus had been with his Father, talked with Him, dwelt in His bosom, and knew all about . . . the transgression of man, and what would redeem the people, and that he was the character who was to redeem the sons [and daughters] of earth, and the earth itself from all sin that had come upon it." [23]

Prior to the Last Supper, Jesus said, "Now is my soul troubled; and what shall I say? Father, save me from this hour: but for this cause came I unto this hour" (John 12:27). Jesus foresaw and began to feel the weight of the coming burden long before He entered Gethsemane. Following the Last Supper, the Savior said, "Arise, let us go hence" (John 14:31). Go where? To Gethsemane. Jesus and His disciples "walked on under the moonlight . . . with an awful dread brooding over their spirits, [Jesus] walked before them with bowed head on the way to the garden of Gethsemane."[24]

Once again, Jesus knew what Gethsemane meant for Him. Knowing the burden and sacrifice that lay ahead, Jesus courageously, without hesitation moved forward. As I consider the determination of the Savior I am reminded of the words of Isaiah, "I set my face like flint" (Isaiah 50:7). Flint is a very hard, firm rock. The Savior was always firm and steadfast in the course He was to follow. He was determined to do His Father's will, never hesitating, never wavering. A lifetime—no, an eternity—of preparation had come down to this night and this moment for Jesus in Gethsemane.

ENDNOTES

1. Fredric Farrar, *The Life of Christ*. (London, England: Cassell and Company, 1874), 554. Jewish historian Josephus wrote the number of slain lambs during Passover on one occasion was around 256,500 (Flavius Josephus, *The Wars of the Jews*. Edited by Ernest Rhys, vol. 6 (J. M. Dent), 1936), section 9:3.
2. Richard Neitzel Holzapfel and Thomas A. Wayment, *From the Last Supper through the Resurrection: The Saviors Final Hours* (Salt Lake City: Deseret Book, 2003), 89.
3. Oliver B. Huntington, *Diary of O. B. Huntington*, 2 vols. (Provo, UT: Brigham Young University, 1942), 2:212. Brigham Young likewise taught, "We will grow in knowledge of the truth when we impart knowledge to others. . . . Wherever you see an opportunity to do good, do it, for that is the way to increase and grow in the knowledge of the truth" (*Journal of Discourses* 2:267)

4. Susan Easton Black, *400 Questions & Answers about the Life and Time of Jesus Christ*, (American Fork, UT: Covenant Communications, 2010), 189.

5. Joseph Smith, *History of the Church*. Edited by B H Roberts, vol. 2 (Salt Lake City, UT: Deseret Book, 1842/1976), 309.

6. Howard W. Hunter, "His Final Hours," April 1974 general conference.

7. Dieter F. Uchtdorf, "Lord, Is It I?" October 2014 general conference. An example of early Apostles in our dispensation asking, "Lord, is it I?" occurred in the days of President Brigham Young. Sometime after the Saints arrived in Utah a spirit of complacency took hold upon many within the Church. Lorenzo Snow related: "When President Young was aroused to call upon the people to repent and reform . . . , he talked very strongly as to what ought to be done with some people—that their Priesthood ought to be taken from them, because of their failure to magnify it as they should have done. The brethren who lived in those days will remember how vigorously he spoke in this direction. Well, it touched Brother Franklin's heart, and it touched mine also; and we talked the matter over to ourselves. We concluded we would go to President Young and offer him our Priesthood. If he felt in the name of the Lord that we had not magnified our Priesthood, we would resign it. We went to him, saw him alone, and told him this . . . There were tears in his eyes when he said, 'Brother Lorenzo, Brother Franklin, you have magnified your Priesthood satisfactorily to the Lord. God bless you"[8] (Lorenzo Snow, *The Teachings of President Lorenzo Snow* (The Church of Jesus Christ of Latter-Day Saints, 2012), 117).

8. "Sop," Harper's Bible Dictionary (HarperCollins, 1959).

9. Joseph Smith and Joseph Fielding Smith, *Teachings of the Prophet Joseph Smith* (Salt Lake City: Deseret Book, 1958/1977), 67.

10. I am reminded of Elder Orson Hyde, who once gave a sermon in which he unknowingly preached some false doctrine. Following the meeting as they were dining, the Prophet Joseph Smith turned and said to Elder Hyde that he was going to offer some corrections to his sermon. Orson immediately responded, "They [your corrections, Joseph] shall thankfully be received" (Hyrum Mack Smith and Janne M Sjodahl, *Doctrine and Covenants Commentary* [Salt Lake City: Deseret Book, 1972], 812–13). In humility Orson Hyde received the correction cheerfully without taking offense. The result of Joseph's corrections became section 130 of the Doctrine and Covenants.

11. J. Reuben Clark, *Behold the Lamb of God* (Salt Lake City: Deseret Book, 1991), 342.

12. Susan Easton Black, *400 Questions & Answers about the Life and Time of Jesus Christ* (American Fork, UT: Covenant Communications, 2010), 185.

13. Bruce R. McConkie, *Doctrinal New Testament Commentary*. Vol. 1 (Salt Lake City: Bookcraft, 1965), 720. Elder Bruce R. McConkie has written extensively on what usually took place during the Passover meal: (1) The first cup was blessed and drunk. (2) The hands were washed while a blessing was said. (3) Bitter herbs, emblematic of the sojourn in Egypt, were partaken of, dipped in sour broth made of vinegar and bruised fruit. (4) The

son of the house asked his father to explain the origin of the observance. (5) The lamb and the flesh of the thank offerings (chagigah) were placed on the table, and the first part of the Hallel sung (Psalms 113, 114). (6) The second cup was blessed and drunk. (7) Unleavened bread was blessed and broken, a fragment of it was eaten, then a fragment of the thank offerings, then a fragment of the lamb. (8) Preliminaries being thus ended, the feast proceeded at leisure till all was consumed. (9) The lamb being quite finished, the third cup, the cup of blessing, was blessed and drunk. (10) The fourth cup was drunk, and meanwhile the second part of the Hallel (Psalms 115–118) was sung. Of the cup which Jesus blessed and passed among them, Dummelow comments: "Since it was taken after supper, and is expressly called by the latter the 'cup of blessing' (1 Cor. 10:16), it was clearly the third cup of the paschal supper, called by the rabbis the 'cup of blessing.'"

14. W. Jeffrey Marsh, *His Final Hours* (Salt Lake City: Deseret Book, 2000), 85.

15. Bruce R. McConkie, *The Mortal Messiah: From Bethlehem to Calvary.* Vol. 4, (Deseret Book, 1979), 57; emphasis added.

16. "Statement of Zebedee Coltrin," *Minutes*, 3 October 1883, Salt Lake School of Prophets, LDS Church Archives, Salt Lake City, Utah, 56–57.

17. Jeffrey R. Holland, "This Do in Remembrance of Me," October 1995 general conference.

18. Melvin J. Ballard, "The Sacrament and Spiritual Growth," *Improvement Era*, Oct. 1919, 1025–1028.

19. David O. McKay, *Pathways to Happiness* (Salt Lake City: Bookcraft, 1957), 345.

20. See Church Education System, *The Life and Teachings of Jesus and the Apostles.* 2nd ed., The Church of Jesus Christ of Latter-Day Saints, 1978, 171.

21. See D. Kelly Ogden and Andrew C. Skinner, *Verse by Verse: The Old Testament* (Salt Lake City: Deseret Book, 2013), 299–300.

22. Gordon B. Hinckley, *Teachings of Gordon B Hinckley* (Salt Lake City: Deseret Book, 1997), 561–562.

23. Brigham Young, *Journal of Discourses*, vol. 3, The Editorium, 2013, 206.

24. Frederic William Farrar, *The Life of Lives: Further Studies in the Life of Christ* (Cassell and Company, 1900), 478.

CHAPTER 3

GETHSEMANE

O f the Savior Bruce R. McConkie declared, "The most transcendent event in his entire eternal existence, the most glorious single happening from creation's dawn to eternity's endless continuance, the crowning work of his infinite goodness—such took place in a garden called Gethsemane."[1] I would add, the greatest act of love in all of human history and perhaps in all eternity took place in a garden called Gethsemane. With the deepest and most profound reverence we go with Jesus and His disciples to the Garden of Gethsemane.

John makes it clear that the company crossed "over the brook Cedron [Kidron], where [there] was a garden" (John 18:1). Following the Last Supper, a widely held opinion suggests that the company made the trek to Gethsemane by traveling through the temple complex and out of the city through the east gate, crossing the Kidron Valley on one of the two bridges that spanned the gorge. The Kidron Valley contained tombs in Jesus's time, as it does today. The valley was deeper in ancient times and hence in shadow much of the day. The walk through the Kidron to Gethsemane evokes the scripture, "I walk through the valley of the shadow of death" (Psalm 23:4). The shadow of death had now fallen over the Savior.

Gospel historian Adam Clarke explained,

> Cedron is a very small rivulet, about six or seven feet broad, nor is it constantly supplied with water, being dry all the year, except during the rains. It is mentioned throughout the Old Testament: 2 Sam 15:23; 1 Kings 15:13, 2 Kings 23:4: and it

appears the evangelist only mentions it here to call to remembrance what happened to David, when he was driven from Jerusalem by his son Absalom, and he and his followers obliged to pass the brook Cedron on foot. All this was a very expressive figure of what happened now to this second David, by the treachery of one of his own disciples . . . *it being the place into which the blood of the sacrifices, and other filth of the city, ran.* It was rather, says Lightfoot, the sink, or *the common sewer, of the city,* than a brook.[2]

In Jesus' day, the Kidron river was used for the disposal of waste blood from the temple sacrifices. Perhaps that very evening, blood from the 260,000 Paschal lambs sacrificed during the Passover was flowing into it. For centuries that blood had served as a type and shadow of the blood that would be spilt by Jesus that night in the Garden of Gethsemane.

Jesus often retired to Gethsemane for meditation, solitude, and prayer with His disciples. "Judas knew the place" (John 18:2). Judas knew where to find to find Jesus.

The owner of the land was not a stranger to Jesus and may have been a disciple. Some have speculated that the sight was the country villa of Mary, the mother of John Mark, and that the lightly clad young man mentioned in Mark 14:51–52 was actually Mark himself, who had been roused from bed by the commotion on the chilly night.[3] The Joseph Smith Translation of Mark 15:51 clarifies that the young man was indeed a disciple of Jesus.

Biblical scholar and historian Alfred Edersheim wrote that the entrance to Gethsemane may have led through a building with an oil press and that eight of the Apostles were left there.[4] "Then cometh Jesus with them unto a place called Gethsemane, and saith unto the disciples, Sit ye here, while I go and pray yonder. And he took with him Peter and the two sons of Zebedee, and began to be sorrowful and very heavy. Then saith he unto them, My soul is exceeding sorrowful, even unto death: tarry ye here, and watch with me" (Matthew 26:36–38). Jesus left eight of His Apostles at the entrance, which was either a gate or building and took Peter, James, and John and went deeper into the garden.

The record states "[they] began to be sorrowful and very heavy . . . then saith he [Jesus] unto them, my soul is exceeding sorrowful, even unto death" (Matthew 26:37, 38). Adam Clarke explained it was "exquisite sorrow, such as dissolves the natural vigor, and threatens to separate soul and body."[5]

Isaiah taught that Christ would be "a man of sorrows, and acquainted with grief . . . surely he hath borne our griefs, and carried our sorrows" (Isaiah 53:3–4). "Here, at this moment, while he prayed in this garden, was to be centered in him the agony and sorrow of the whole world. Sorrow is the child of sin, and as he took upon himself the sins of the world, he thereby bore the weight of the world's sorrows."[6]

According to Clarke, one translation of the Greek word used in Mathew 26:37 for "very heavy" means overwhelmed with anguish. The Greek denotes the most extreme anguish which the soul can feel—excruciating anxiety and torture of spirit.[7]

An alternative from the Greek for "sorrowful and very heavy" in verse 37 is "distressed" and "troubled." The Savior was overwhelmed with anguish. He was distressed and troubled. He knew He was about to do something infinitely hard.

Luke wrote that Jesus was "withdrawn from [His disciples] about a stone's cast" (Luke 22:41). The verb in Luke translated "withdrawn" can literally mean to "tear oneself away," indicating that Jesus found it difficult, even painful, to leave the company of His disciples. He sought human companionship in this desperate hour. Of this Edersheim wrote, "That in that last contest [Christ's] human soul craved the presence of those who stood nearest Him and loved Him best."[8] Before withdrawing from His three disciples Jesus asked them to watch with Him (see Matthew 26:38). It is interesting to note that it was customary for someone to stand watch on Passover night. They did this in symbolic remembrance of guarding against the angel of death that passed over Egypt to take the lives of all the firstborn sons in Moses's day.

Church history scholar Susan Easton Black explained, "His agony in Gethsemane hallowed the olive garden on the night of Seder. The night of Seder is called *Leil Shimurim*, meaning, '[the] night of the watchers.' On this night Jews were to stay awake and watch for God to save His people. *'Blessed is he that watcheth, and keepeth his garments'* was a common saying among the rabbis when speaking of temple guards who stayed awake at their posts on that night. If found asleep, guards were beaten, and their garments set on fire."[9] This night, Peter, James, and John would endeavor to stand and watch as Satan (the fallen angel of death) attempted to destroy Heavenly Father's firstborn Son. The three Apostles would attempt to stand and watch as Jesus would strive to save all of God's children from death.

The Greek translation for "watch" in Matthew 26:38 means "stay awake." Why did Jesus want His disciples to stay awake? As mentioned above, Jesus wanted them to support and stand with Him during His hours of suffering. The disciples may have needed to stay awake to fulfill the law of witnesses. This was the most important event that would ever transpire in the history of the world. There had to be witnesses of it, witnesses who could record and tell the story. The date of the Passover is determined by the cycles of the moon. According to the lunar and Jewish calendars, that night in Gethsemane there was a full Passover moon. Peter, James, and John would have had little difficulty witnessing the events that transpired.[10]

Besides *watching*, the Savior gave additional instruction to his three disciples. He said to them, "Watch and pray that ye enter not into temptation" (Matthew 26:41). Despite what Jesus was personally facing, He was concerned about the welfare of His disciples. He wanted them to be vigilant and prayerful lest they succumb to temptation and sin.[11]

What might the temptation be for the disciples? The Joseph Smith Translation of Mark 14:36–38 gives us one possible answer. "The disciples [all eleven] began to be sore amazed and to be very heavy, and to complain in their hearts, *wondering if this be the Messiah* . . . Jesus knowing their hearts . . . taketh with him Peter James and John, and rebuked them." Doubt had arisen in the hearts of all of the Apostles. They began to wonder if Jesus was truly the Messiah. Peter, James, and John were the ones rebuked; the Savior expected more from them. They were to be His future First Presidency that would lead the infant Church.

At this point, why would any of the Apostles complain, wonder, and doubt that Jesus was the Messiah? This was the first time the Apostles ever saw their Master struggle with a situation. His superhuman attributes seemed to be fading away. The Apostles could not believe what was happening. They were "sore amazed." They were "distressed and troubled."

I believe Satan used this to his advantage and filled the minds of the Apostles with doubt regarding Jesus and His mission. However great the Apostles were, they still had failed to fully comprehend what Jesus had taught them about His impending suffering and redemptive sacrifice. In the minds of the Jews, the Messiah was not supposed to suffer. After the Triumphal Entry and second cleansing of the temple, the Apostles were possibly still expecting that in the end Jesus would be the same kind of Messiah the rest of the Jewish people were looking for: a towering military conqueror and political deliverer.

While their Master suffered, when Jesus needed them most, these disciples fell short. They failed to watch with Him, failed to stay awake, and entered into temptation. It is easy for us to be critical of them. But, let us remember that Gethsemane is in view before the eyes of all of us. While we, like the disciples, cannot understand the full significance of what took place in that garden, we know enough. We know that in Gethsemane Jesus suffered an infinite burden, and to some degree we know why it was necessary. Yet, even with that knowledge, while viewing the scenes of the Master suffering, we in our weakness, like the disciples of old, have at times fallen asleep and failed to watch with Him. All of His disciples throughout history have on occasion needed to be woken up by the patient and gentle touch of the Master. Jesus did not condemn His three sleeping disciples. He did not give up on them, but in a tone of tender reproach admonished them to do and to be better. So it is with us. Jesus will never give up on us. Even in our worst moments, He is there always reaching out, trying to wake us up.

"And he cometh a third time and saith unto them, Sleep on now, and take your rest, *it is enough,* the hour is come, behold the Son of man is betrayed into the hands of sinners. Rise up, let us go" (Mark 14 :41–42; emphasis added). What did Jesus mean by sleep on now and take your rest? It was certainly not time to sleep. Judas and the band of men were quickly approaching. Soon Jesus had them up and moving. Jesus had also said, "It is enough." What was enough? The Savior had swallowed the bitter cup in Gethsemane. He had meekly submitted to the will of His Father and had done all that He needed to do in the garden. It was enough, and as a result of that, all of us could now sleep on and find rest in Him. In some ways Jesus was saying to them and to all of us, "I know you are mortals with weaknesses. I am here to save you; sleep on and find rest in me."

SLEEPING

Luke taught that "Jesus found them [Peter, James, and John] sleeping for sorrow" (Luke 22:45). According to Mark, the Savior had to wake His three disciples up at least three times.

Matthew records, "And he cometh unto the disciples, and findeth them asleep, and saith unto Peter, What, could ye not watch with me one hour?" (Matthew 26:40). Jesus specifically gets after Peter, His chief Apostle. He expected more from him.

The next thing we find in the record is, "The spirit indeed is willing, but the flesh is weak" (Matthew 26:41). The Joseph Smith Translation of Mark 14:38 reads, "And they said unto him, the spirit truly is ready, but the flesh is weak." According to the Joseph Smith Translation it was the three Apostles, not Jesus, who said, "The spirit is ready, but the flesh is weak." Maybe that was their excuse for falling asleep. It is important to note that they did not recognize the complete gravity of what had happened in Gethsemane or what was still going happen. It was late in the evening. No doubt the Apostles were tired by this time. It had been a long, difficult, emotional, and physical draining week for them, and it was customary to retire to bed early in the Middle East. At this late hour most people would have been asleep. Their flesh was weak.

The Joseph Smith Translation of Luke 22:45 reads, "He found them sleeping, for they were filled with sorrow." The disciples were feeling the oppressive gravity of the moment and were overwhelmed with sorrow. They were depressed in spirit. Their hearts ached as they watched their Master suffer. As gospel theologian Fredrick Farrar put it, "They were dim witnesses of an unutterable agony, far deeper than anything which they could fathom."[12] During times of great emotional distress and grief, the human body often copes by shutting down and retreating to sleep. In addition, this was a dark hour. It appears they were not alone. Satan and his legions were also present in the garden. Satan may have wanted them to sleep. He certainly did not want the Apostles to support their Master during His suffering. He surely did not want witnesses of the event.

The Savior asked Peter, James, and John to watch with Him. Each week, as we partake of the sacrament, we likewise are invited by the Lord to watch with Him, to stay awake and focus on Him, His life, His suffering, and His sacrifice. Have you ever fallen asleep during the sacrament? Has your mind wandered? Have you ever failed to be alert and attentive during that ordinance? I certainly have. Let's cut Peter, James, and John some slack and commit to do better as we watch with the Savior each week.

During the sacrament, when our eyes get heavy, when our mind starts to wander, fight it, and focus on Him. Stay alert and attentive, and remember Gethsemane and the admonition that was given to watch, and stake awake. Referring to the Savior's sacrifice and the sacrament Jeffrey R. Holland taught, "In as much as we contributed to that fatal burden, such a moment demands our respect."[13] After all Jesus has done for us, let us give Him our best effort and watch with Him during that sacred ordinance. Respecting that moment by focusing on Jesus allows Heavenly Father to more fully bless us, heal us, and fill us with His love and with the Spirit.

The sacrament and every ordinance of the gospel, for that matter, is given from God to man to foreshadow and typify the Savior and His atoning sacrifice. Even though His Atonement was wrought nearly two thousand years ago, its reality to us and its effect on us can be as great as though we had been contemporaries of the Savior living in Jerusalem. George W. Pace, a professor of religion at Brigham Young University has written, "Indeed, under the quiet workings of the Holy Ghost, we can stand as it were, in the Garden of Gethsemane, as witness of the Savior's agony; we can stand as it

were, at the foot of Golgotha and obtain an overwhelming awareness of the pain of the cross; we can receive in our hearts a measure, . . . as the Spirit can reveal it, of the tremendous pain, sorrow
and humiliation he suffered. We can in other words, experience in
part the majesty of the Atonement and make it the greatest event in
our lives."[14] Such can be our experience if we will receive the Savior's
invitation each Sabbath and watch with Him.

During his first mission in the state of Pennsylvania in March
of 1877, Elder Orson F. Whitney had a dream in which he found
himself inside the Garden of Gethsemane. He watched from behind
a tree, viewing the events that unfolded that night. A portion of
that vision included Peter, James, and John falling asleep and being
aroused by the Savior three times.

Elder Whitney recorded:

> I seemed to be in the Garden of Gethsemane, a witness of the
> Savior's agony. I saw Him as plainly as ever I have seen anyone.
> Standing behind a tree in the foreground, I beheld Jesus, with
> Peter, James, and John, as they came through a little wicket gate
> at my right. Leaving the three Apostles there, after telling them
> to kneel and pray, the Son of God passed over to the other side,
> where He also knelt and prayed. . . .
>
> As He prayed the tears streamed down his face, which was
> toward me. I was so moved at the sight that I also wept, out of
> pure sympathy. My whole heart went out to him; I loved him
> with all my soul and longed to be with him as I longed for noth-
> ing else.
>
> Presently He arose and walked to where those Apostles were
> kneeling—fast asleep! He shook them gently, awoke them, and
> in a tone of tender reproach, untinctured by the least show of
> anger or impatience, asked them plaintively if they could not
> watch with him one hour. There He was, with the awful weight
> of the world's sins upon his shoulders, with the pangs of every
> man, woman and child shooting through his sensitive soul—and
> they could not watch with him one poor hour![15]

Elder Whitney, who later became an Apostle, recorded the interpretation of this powerful dream. He said, "I saw the moral clearly.

I had never thought of being an Apostle, nor of holding any other office in the Church. . . . Yet I knew that those sleeping Apostles meant me. I was asleep at my post—as any man is who, having been divinely appointed to do one thing, and does another."[16]

Elder Whitney explained he was asleep at his post. Apparently, he was not completely, fully immersed in the work. Before the prophet Lehi died, his final admonition to his two oldest sons was, "O that ye would awake, awake from a deep sleep" (2 Nephi 1:13). Laman and Lemuel were asleep to the things of God, to the things of the Spirit. They were asleep at their post.

We would all do well to occasionally reflect and consider what the Lord has asked us to do. We can think about our Church callings, our responsibilities, and stewardships. Are we asleep at our post? Have we become casual in our sacrament worship, our prayers, our scripture study, our temple attendance, or in our ministering? I have been asleep at times.

Watching with the Savior means more than just staying awake, more than just going through the motions. The scriptures teach we are to be "anxiously engaged in a good cause" (D&C 58:27). The Savior, our perfect exemplar, went about doing good. Lehi told his sons not only to awake, but to arise. May we all awake and arise to the things of God and actively be involved in building His kingdom.[17]

THE SUFFERING BEGINS

The Apostle Paul taught that the Savior offered the Atonement, "with strong crying and tears" (Hebrews 5:7). Orson F. Whitney's vision affirmed that tears streamed down the Savior's face as he prayed and suffered. The Savior comprehends every tear we weep because He wept them first.

Gospel painters have given us portraits of Jesus on His knees in the garden. He may have started on His knees, but as the weight of the burden came, "he . . . fell on his face and prayed" (Matthew 26:39), the bitter cup crushing Him. The Hebrew word for Jesus's being "bruised" in the process of the Atonement means "to be crushed" (see Isaiah 53:5). As the weight of that burden pressed upon Jesus, "he . . . began to be *sore amazed*" (Mark 14:33; emphasis added). Gospel scholar Andrew Skinner explained that the Greek word translated as "sore amazed" means "terrified surprised, awestruck, astonished, extreme horror, a profound disarray, or an irresistible fright in the face of a terrible event."[18] The Savior moved far beyond being sorrowful and very heavy, far beyond being distressed and troubled.

Of this moment Neal A. Maxwell wrote, "Imagine Jehovah, the Creator of this and other worlds, 'astonished'! Jesus knew cognitively what He must do, but not experientially. He had never personally known the exacting process of an atonement before. Thus, when the agony came in its fullness, it was so much, much worse than even He with his unique intellect had ever imagined."[19]

As Jesus began to feel the weight and magnitude of the burden, not only was He astonished, but He was also terrified. Bruce R. McConkie declared, "There is no language known to mortals that can tell what agony and suffering was His while in the Garden."[20] It was beyond all description, beyond all finite comprehension.

The Savior learned some things in the garden that night. Being pure, holy, and perfect, He could not have known what sin and its effects felt like. It was a complete shock to His pure system. In the words of the Apostle Paul, God the Father "hath made him to be sin for us, who knew no sin" (2 Corinthians 5:21). He who was sinless became, as it were, "full of sin." We should note that Christ not only bore the eternal consequences of our sins but also the very sins themselves (see Mosiah 15:12, 26:23, Alma 7:13, 3 Nephi 11:11). In Gethsemane the Great Jehovah, the Eternal God of the Old Testament, the God of the Universe, learned things about sin and spiritual death that He had never fully known before.

THE BITTER CUP

In the garden the Savior prayed, "*Abba,* Father, all things are possible unto thee; take away this cup" (Mark 14:36; emphasis added). Abba is the most intimate Aramaic word meaning "Papa" or "Daddy." It is a form of address signifying the close, intimate, loving bond that develops between some fathers and their children. Of this moment, Elder Jeffrey R. Holland said, "This is such a personal moment it almost seems a sacrilege to cite it. A son in unrelieved pain, a Father His only true source of strength, both of them staying the course, making it through the night—together."[21]

The Greek word translated as "cup" (*poterion*) also means "a person's lot," as in lot in life. Adam Clarke explains,

> The word, "cup" is frequently used in the sacred writings to point out sorrow, anguish, terror, [and] death. It seems to be an allusion to a very ancient method of punishing criminals. A cup of poison was put into their hands, and they were obliged to drink it. To death, by the poisoned cup, there seems to be an allusion in Hebrews 2:9. . . . Jesus Christ, by the grace of God, TASTED death for every man. The whole world is here represented as standing guilty and condemned before the tribunal of God; into every man's hand the deadly cup is put, and he is required to drink off the poison—Jesus enters, takes every man's cup out of his hand, and drinks off the poison, and thus tastes or suffers the death which every man otherwise must have undergone.[22]

The Savior has made it clear that Heavenly Father is the one who gave and placed the infinite burden upon Him. He referred to it as "the cup which my Father hath given me" (John 18:11). He also declared, "I have drunk out of the bitter cup which the Father hath given me" (3 Nephi 11:11). Only a God with infinite power could place such a burden. Bruce R. McConkie likewise taught that while in the garden, "Upon his suffering servant [Christ], the great Elohim there and then placed the weight of all the sins of all men of all ages. . . . This was the hour when all eternity hung in the balance."[23] In the Garden of Gethsemane, the Savior would experience what the scriptures call "the winepress of the fierceness of the wrath of the Almighty God" (D&C 76:107, 88:106).

Matthew records that at least three times the Savior plead, "If it be possible let this cup pass from me" (Matthew 26:39). Could the Father have let the cup pass from the Savior? Paul wrote, "Who in the days of his flesh, when he had offered up prayers and supplications with strong crying and tears *unto him that was able to save him from death,* and was heard in that he feared" (Hebrews 5:7; emphasis added). According to Paul, the Father was able to save Jesus from death. Just as the Father had placed the infinite cup, He had the power to remove it. Paul also taught that when the answer was heard, when Jesus learned His Father's will, as the burden approached Jesus *feared*, the magnitude of the bitter cup terrified Him. Once again, the infinite burden was so much worse than He had ever anticipated.

Gospel scholar Edwin Aldous has written, "Just as [the Father] can remove our pain, He could have spared His son that agony, indeed He had the power to remove the bitter cup from the Savior, but the consequences were unacceptable."[24] And so like Elder Holland taught, the Father "stayed the course" and refrained from removing the cup.

"If it be possible let this cup pass from me" (Matthew 26:39). Jesus repeatedly asked that question. Why? "He demonstrated the human impulse to look for a way out of the horrors and agonies of Gethsemane. The Savior's human nature wrestled with His divine nature." [25]

Of this prayer Obert C. Tanner offered this insight:

> Jesus knew that he was approaching a violent death long before he came to the end of the road. The temptation to save his life, by changing course . . . had long before been met and conquered. He had of his own free will, chosen the path of the cross. True, he was not oblivious to pain. He wanted to live. He enjoyed life. He wanted to postpone death as long as such a postponement was not a retreat from his teachings. But he was not afraid to die. Such a belief would be wholly inconsistent with his life, and with the fifteen hours of subsequent bravery and fortitude. For his was a courage before which hardened Roman soldiers involuntarily bowed in awe and respect; a fortitude on the cross that impelled a hardened criminal to worship him. . . . He was not tempted to save his life by running away from Jerusalem and retiring to his beloved Galilee. That temptation had been with him for three years. . . . Jesus in Gethsemane through his love for all the children of men, suffered in sorrow for all their sins, and prayed to

the Father, if it be possible, if there were some other way without hiding, without running away, without changing his message or his methods, by which he could continue in his work to save human souls, then let him remain. It was a spiritual struggle of soul, which only Jesus could experience in the full. And in his struggle for another way, he turned to his Father.[26]

I love that thought. Jesus was not running. He was not changing course. He wanted to know if there was another way to save everyone without drinking the bitter cup. In His darkest, most difficult hour Jesus turned to His Father. There is a lesson in that for us.

Perhaps it is possible to plead for deliverance, to plead for a miracle, and at the same time be perfectly submissive to God's will. I believe such was the case for the Savior. There may come a time in your life and in mine when we need a miracle, when we would like deliverance from a difficult situation. The God we worship is certainly a God of miracles. There is nothing wrong with asking in faith for a miracle. We know that with God all things are possible. With that in mind, the Savior, serving as our great exemplar, taught us in Gethsemane that part of the testing in mortality is learning to submit and accept the will of the Lord, whatever it might be.

Of the Savior's prayer in Gethsemane, Neal A. Maxwell has written, "Will we, too, trust the Lord amid a perplexing trial for which we have no easy explanation? Do we understand—really comprehend—that Jesus knows and understands when we are stressed and perplexed? The complete consecration which effected the Atonement ensured Jesus' perfect empathy; He felt our very pains and afflictions before we did and knows how to succor us. Since the most innocent one suffered the most, our own cries of Why? cannot match His. But we can utter the same, submissive word: *Nevertheless*' (Matthew 26:39)."[27] Elder Maxwell wrote from firsthand experience. For nearly eight years he suffered terribly and eventually died from leukemia. He may have asked the Lord "why?" He probably asked for a miracle. He certainly had the faith to be healed. But like the Savior, Elder Maxwell said, "Nevertheless," and submitted to the Lord's will. He also had the faith to not be healed.

The Savior asked if there was another way. Was there another way? Jeffrey R. Holland explained that "*it was the only way* that a saving, vicarious payment could be made for the sins of all His other children."[28] There was no back-up plan, no plan B, no second option. Drinking the bitter cup was the only option, and Christ was the only one in the universe who could do it. Similarly, King Benjamin taught, "There shall be no other name given nor any other way nor means whereby salvation can come unto the children of men" (Mosiah 3:16–17). Once again, in the Garden of Gethsemane Jesus was learning and growing. He grew from grace to greater grace. One thing He learned or was reminded of in the garden was that there was no other way to save us. He alone was our only hope.

I find it interesting that Matthew recorded Jesus saying the same prayer at least three times. Maybe initially He was not sure if it was God's will for Him to die at that time. When the answer did come and Jesus clearly understood His Father's will, it was not the answer He had hoped for. Sometimes it takes numerous prayers to receive an answer, and sometimes we will not receive the answers we hope for. Not all trials and difficulties will be taken from us during our mortal probation. Spencer W. Kimball explained,

> If all the sick for whom we pray were healed, if all the righteous were protected and the wicked destroyed, the whole program of the Father would be annulled and the basic principle of the gospel, free agency, would be ended. No man would have to live by faith. If joy and peace and rewards were instantaneously given the doer of good, there could be no evil—all would do good but not because of the rightness of doing good. There would be no test of strength, no development of character, no growth of powers, no free agency, only satanic controls. Should all prayers be immediately answered according to our selfish desires and our limited understanding, then there would be little or no suffering, sorrow, disappointment, or even death, and if these were not, there would be also be no joy . . . if we were to close the doors upon sorrow and distress, we might be excluding our greatest friends and benefactors. Suffering can make saints of people as they learn patience, long-suffering, and self-mastery.[29]

I am reminded of the Apostle Paul, who, on three separate seasons of countless prayers, prayed that a thorn in his flesh might be removed. Paul, like the Savior, did not receive the answer He wanted. So, it may be for us at times. When that occurs, we need to remember that it is certainly not evidence that God does not love us. Never did a father love a son more than at this pivotal moment of suffering in Gethsemane.

True, the Savior asked if there was another way, but He did not hesitate to press forward and perform His atoning sacrifice once He received an answer. He said, "Nevertheless, glory be to the Father, and I partook" (D&C 19:19). "Nevertheless," the choice to submit, was made carefully, intentionally, and thoughtfully. In Gethsemane Jesus was perfectly submissive and obedient to His Father's will. That submission was the hallmark of His entire life. The Savior had submitted to the will of the Father long before He ever uttered those famous words in Gethsemane, "Not my will, but thine, be done" (Luke 22:42). On one occasion Jesus said, "The Father hath not left me alone; for I do always those things that please him" (John 8:29). The resurrected Savior declared to the Nephites, "I have suffered the will of the Father in all things *from the beginning*" (3 Nephi 11:11; emphasis added). From when? From the beginning, which I believe means during His pre-earth life, from the time of His spirit birth. It was Jesus's full obedience that fully ransomed us all.

In Gethsemane never was a father more pleased with a son. Jesus was completely dedicated to doing the will of His Father. Isn't that the main purpose of prayer? Jesus taught us that we pray to learn the will of the Father and then submit to it and move forward in faith, trusting the Lord knows more than we do. Elder Maxwell taught, "The submission of one's will is really the only uniquely personal thing we have to place on God's alter. . . . It is the only possession which is truly ours to give."[30]

C. S. Lewis wisely observed, "There are only two kinds of people in the end: those who say to God, 'Thy will be done!' And those to whom God says in the end, 'Thy will be done.' All that are in Hell, choose it. Without that self-choice there could be no hell."[31] The Lord will never force us into heaven. Ultimately we are "free to choose liberty and eternal life through the great Mediator of all men, or to choose captivity and death" (2 Nephi 2:27). In Gethsemane Jesus chose liberty and eternal life for Himself and opened that possibility for all of us by freely submitting to the will of His Father.

THE NATURAL MAN

Regarding the choice Jesus made, Jeffrey R. Holland offered this insight:

> Christ's final triumph . . . came not because he had a divine parent (although that was essential to the victory over death) and not because he was given heavenly authority from the beginning (although that was essential to his divine power) but ultimately because he was, in his own mortal probation, perfectly obedient, perfectly submissive, perfectly loyal to the principle that the spiritual in his life must rule over the physical. That was at the heart of his triumph, and that is a lesson for every accountable man, woman, and child who ever lives. It is a lesson for which Abinadi—and Christ—were willing to die. It is the lesson which virtually every prophet has given his voice and his life: spirit over flesh; discipline over temptation: devotion over inclination; "the will of the Son being swallowed up in the will of the Father."[32]

Christ's divine nature triumphed over His human nature. The spiritual ruled over the physical. This was not only a test for Jesus but is a test for all of us. One of the primary challenges we face in mortality is between our divine nature and the carnal natural man. King Benjamin taught that we overcome the natural man and become a Saint by choosing to yield to the enticing of the Holy Spirit and by applying the atonement of Christ (see Mosiah 3:19). The Savior is the answer to overcoming the natural man. Because He overcame the flesh, we can too. As we come to Him and apply His sacrifice the Savior will change our very nature and help us become new creatures in Him. Through Him our bodies can be sanctified and we can receive His image in our countenance.[33]

AN INFINITE AND INCOMPREHENSIBLE SACRIFICE

The New Testament tells us about some of the events that occurred in the Garden of Gethsemane, but the Gospel writers are silent as to what caused the Savior's misery and suffering in Gethsemane and why it was necessary. The Book of Mormon and modern revelation explain the reason behind the atoning sacrifice of the Savior.

Three different writers in the Book of Mormon declare the magnitude of the bitter cup. The prophet Jacob wrote, "It must needs be an infinite atonement" (2 Nephi 9:7). Nephi wrote, "The atonement, which is infinite" (2 Nephi 25:16). And Amulek likewise wrote, "It must be an infinite and eternal sacrifice" (Alma 34:10).

Human nature makes us want to quantify and measure the atoning sacrifice. The Savior's sacrifice wasn't so much suffering for so much sin. It was not a quantifiable mass. It was off any scale, beyond all comprehension. Elder Maxwell explained, "The cumulative weight of all mortal sins—past, present, and future—pressed upon that perfect, sinless, and sensitive Soul! All our infirmities and sicknesses were somehow, too, a part of the awful arithmetic of the Atonement. . . . **His suffering was as it were, enormity multiplied by infinity.**"[34]

President Gordon B. Hinckley shared the following:

> I once sat in the shadow of an old olive tree in the Garden of Gethsemane and read of that terrible wrestling of the Son of God as He faced the certain future, sweating drops of blood and praying to the Father to let the cup pass if it might. . . . I had an overwhelming feeling that He wasn't making His plea, He wasn't facing that ordeal in terms of the physical pain He was about to face, the terrible, brutal crucifixion on the cross. That was part of it, I am sure. But in a large measure it was, I think, a sense of His part, His role in the eternal welfare of *all the sons and daughters of God, of all generations of time.*[35]

The Atonement of Jesus Christ encompasses all of God's children, of all generations, both past, present, and future in this world, and in every world He created. The Savior suffered for an infinite number of people, on an infinite number of worlds. He is the Redeemer of everything He had a hand in creating. Hence, He is the Redeemer of the entire universe.[36]

King David, in a Messianic psalm, prophetically described the Gethsemane and Golgotha experience of the Savior: "Reproach hath broken my heart; and *I am full of heaviness*: and I looked for some to take pity, but there was none; and for comforters, but I found none" (Psalm 69:20). Of that heaviness Elder Tad R. Callister has written,

> What weight is thrown on the scales of pain when calculating the hurt of innumerable patients in countless hospitals? Now, add to that the loneliness of the elderly who are forgotten in the rest homes of society, desperately yearning for a card, a visit, a call. . . . Keep on adding the hurt of hungry children, the suffering caused by famine, drought, and pestilence. Pile on the heartache of parents who tearfully plead on a daily basis for a wayward son or daughter to come back home. Factor in the trauma of every divorce and tragedy of every abortion. Add the remorse that comes with each child lost in the dawn of life, each spouse taken in the prime of marriage. Compound that with the misery of overflowing prisons, bulging halfway houses and institutions for the mentally disadvantaged. Multiply all this by century after century of history, and creation after creation without end. Such is but an awful glimpse of the Savior's load. Who can bear such a burden or scale such a mountain as this? No one, absolutely no one, save Jesus Christ, The Redeemer of us all.[37]

Gospel scholar Gerald Lund offered a similar insight into the size of the Atonement:

> If you look at the United States alone, there are now more than fifty murders committed every day (that's nearly nineteen thousand per year.) There are more than twenty-one thousand thefts reported every day, and more than fifty-five hundred reported cases of child neglect and abuse. Think of how many times on a single day adultery or some other violation of the law of chastity is committed somewhere in the world. How many cases of incest, child abuse, pornography, burglary, and robbery? How many

times in any one day is the name of God taken in vain? How many times are sacred things profaned? Then multiply these over the span of human history. And that takes into consideration only our world. We know that the Atonement extended to other worlds as well.[38]

This quantitative approach by Elder Lund and Callister helps us finite mortals in an attempt to wrap our minds around the heaviness and size of the load that Christ bore. But once again, His was an infinite sacrifice, it was not a quantifiable mass, it was off any and all scales of measurement, beyond all human comprehension.

In Alma 7, the prophet Alma gives some wonderful insights into the Savior's Atonement. Toward the end of his comments on the Savior's sacrifice Alma states, "Now the spirit knoweth all things" (Alma 7:13). Why did he say this? Because, try as he had, Alma knew his efforts to explain the Savior's Atonement were not sufficient. It takes Deity to fully understand how the Atonement was wrought and how it works. It takes a God to understand all of its implications. No mortal being can fully comprehend it. Hence, we sing in the Hymn "O God, the Eternal Father," "That sacred holy offering, by man least understood" (*Hymns*, no. 175).

Elder McConkie has written, "There is no mystery to compare with the mystery of redemption. . . . Finite minds can no more comprehend how and in what manner Jesus performed his redeeming labors than they can comprehend how matter came into being. . . . We may not intrude too closely into this scene. It is shrouded in a halo and a mystery into which no footstep may penetrate."[39] "There is no language known to the human tongue, there are no words that mortals can speak or write; there are no feelings that can fill the heart of an earthbound soul; there is no way by the power of the greatest intellect [or all intellects combined] to begin to portray the infinite power and eternal wonder of the atoning sacrifice."[40] "We do not know, we cannot tell, no mortal mind can conceive the full import of what Christ did in Gethsemane . . . We know in some way, incomprehensible to us, his suffering satisfied the demands of justice, ransomed penitent souls from the pains of sin, and made mercy available to those who believe in his holy name."[41] All of that being said, as incomprehensible as it is, we must strive to understand and apply it.

The Savior's Atonement is an active saving power in the universe. Hugh Nibley has written, "In its sweep and scope, the atonement takes on the aspects of one the of grand constants in nature—omnipresent, unalterable, such as gravity or the speed of light. Like them it is always there, easily ignored, hard to explain, and hard to believe in without an explanation. Also, we are constantly exposed to its effects whether we are aware of them or not. . . . Like gravity, though we are rarely aware of it, it is at work every moment of our lives, and to ignore it can be fatal. It is waiting for our disposal to draw us on."[42] I love that thought by Elder Nibley. The infinite Atonement is certainly difficult to explain, yet it is an active healing and saving power waiting for us to draw on. As our awareness of it increases we learn to appreciate it and apply it more and more.

HIS DIVINITY AND HUMANITY

In the Garden of Gethsemane, Jesus voluntarily let His humanity take precedence over His divinity. "Our Lord voluntarily . . . emptied himself of all of his divine power, or enfeebled himself by relying upon his humanity and not his Godhood, so as to be as other men and thus be tested to the full by all the trials and torments of the flesh."[43] On a similar note Tad Callister explained, "Somehow his sponge alone would absorb the entire ocean of human affliction, weakness and suffering. For this descent, he would fully bare his human breast. There would be no godly powers exercised that would shield him from one scintilla of human pain."[44]

By setting aside the fulness of His power and glory that He possessed, He was able to experience mortality in its fulness. As He took upon Him infinite suffering, He did it with only His mortal faculties with but one exception. What was the exception? Why would Christ need to tap into His divine Godly powers?

Mark taught that in Gethsemane, Christ's soul was "exceedingly sorrowful, *even unto death*" (Mark 14:34; emphasis added). King

Benjamin explained, "He shall suffer . . . even more than man can suffer, *except it be unto death*" (Mosiah 3:7; emphasis added). Death would have been an escape. Christ's godhood was summoned to hold off unconsciousness and death. He used His divine power not to soften the blow, but to keep Himself alive so He could drink a bigger, infinite cup. Bruce R. McConkie taught, "In this garden called Gethsemane, . . . was the greatest member of Adam's race, the One whose every thought and word were perfect, pleaded with his Father to come off triumphant in the most tortuous ordeal ever imposed upon man or God. There, amid the olive trees—the spirit of pure worship and perfect prayer—Mary's son struggled under the most crushing burden ever borne by mortal man."[45] Had Jesus not tapped into His divinity, He would have been crushed in an instant by the heaviness of the load. He suffered as only a God could suffer.

Of the Messiah the prophet Isaiah taught, "He hath no form nor comeliness and when we shall see him there is no beauty that we should desire him" (Isaiah 53:2). This simply means Jesus did not stand out in any distinctive physical way. Joseph Fielding Smith explained, "In appearance he was like men . . . he was not so distinctive, so different from others that people would recognize him as the Son of God. He appeared as a mortal man."[46]

His mortal body may have appeared like other men, but it was different. It was created by a mortal woman and an immortal, glorified God, and that certainly made His body different. Gospel scholar Craig J. Ostler explained,

> When the hour of the atoning sacrifice came, Jesus Christ called upon every lesson learned, ever power over the flesh He had attained. To the greatest extent, He submitted His tabernacle of clay to the pains of death and sin. . . . He knew intimately the reason that His mortal body must needs be sired by God. It was absolutely necessary that His physical body have a perfect organization of mortal matter, inherited by divine design, to suffer "more than man can suffer" (Mosiah 3:7). The material that made up His body was like that of His brothers and sisters, consisting of the dust of the earth. However, that body was "specifically prepared," taught John Taylor, "and being the offspring of God, both in body

and spirit, he stood preeminently in the position of the Son of God, or in the place of God, and was God, and thus the fit and only person capable of making an infinite atonement." Hence, we read: "Wherefore, when he cometh into the world . . . a body thou hast prepared me" (Hebrews 10:5). The body of flesh and blood that Jesus Christ inherited from God, His immortal father, and Mary, His mortal mother, fitted Him for the atoning sacrifice.[47]

The Savior's body was specially prepared by Deity to withstand death and the horrors of Gethsemane. Once again, this was not to soften the blow but to keep Him alive so He could drink the infinite bitter cup.

James E. Talmage wrote,

Christ's agony in the garden is unfathomable by the finite mind, both as to intensity and cause. . . . He struggled and groaned under a burden such as no other being who has lived on earth might even conceive possible. It was not physical pain, nor mental anguish alone, that caused Him to suffer such torture as to produce an extrusion of blood from every pore; but a spiritual agony of soul such as only God was capable of experiencing. . . . In some manner, actual and terribly real though to man incomprehensible, the Savior took upon Himself the burden of the sins of mankind from Adam to the end of the world.[48]

Fulfilling the prophecy of Isaiah, "His visage was so marred more than any man, and his form more than the sons of men" (Isaiah 52:14). Christ experienced mortality in its fulness. His humanity took precedence over His divinity. His divinity kept Him alive as He suffered the infinite burden, which caused His visage to marred more than any man.

THE OIL PRESS

Most scholars conclude that the name "Gethsemane" is derived from the Hebrew and Aramaic *gat semani,* meaning "oil press." Some have suggested that the location was so named for the presence of one or more oil presses used at the sight to make olive oil.

GETHSEMANE

Truman G. Madsen explained how the olive press in Jesus's time worked: "To produce olive oil, the refined olives had to be crushed in a press. The mellowed and seasoned olives were placed in strong bags and flattened on a furrow stone. Then a huge crushing circular rock was rolled around on top, paced by a mule or an ox and a stinging whip. Another method used heavy wooden levers or screws twisting beams downward like a winch upon the stone with the same effect: pressure, pressure, pressure—until the oil flowed."[49]

Of *Gethsemane* meaning "oil press," gospel scholar Stephen Robinson wrote, "What an appropriate name for the Garden where Jesus took upon himself the infinite weight of the sins and sorrows of the world and was pressed with that tremendous load until the blood flowed through his skin. Just as olives and grapes are squeezed in the press, so Jesus, the true vine, was squeezed in Gethsemane, 'the press,' until his richness, his juice, his oil, his blood, was shed for humanity. No wonder that the wine of the Last Supper and of the Christian sacrament is such a fitting symbol for the blood of Christ—they are obtained by the same process."[50] We should note that when olives are squeezed in a press its earliest product bears a red distinctive color.

Luke (who was a physician) informs us, "His sweat was *as it were* great drops of blood falling down to the ground" (Luke 22:44; emphasis added). The medical term for such a condition is hematidrosis. Under rare, extreme distress and pressure the capillaries can burst and hemorrhage into the sweat glands, the skin becoming fragile and tender. Luke said his "sweat was as it were great drops of blood." Did Christ really bleed from every pore? King Benjamin and modern revelation confirm that the Savior literally bled from every pore (see Mosiah 3:7, D&C 19:18).

B.H. Roberts wrote, "If it be true, and it is, that men value things in proportion to what they cost, then how dear to them must be the Atonement, since it cost the Christ so much in suffering that He may be said to have been baptized by blood-sweat in Gethsemane, before he reached the climax of his passion, on Calvary."[51]

The word "Messiah" in Hebrew and the word "Christ" in Greek mean "anointed one." When Christ emerged from Gethsemane, He was in the complete sense the Messiah, the Anointed One. He had been fully anointed with His own blood.

President John Taylor wrote, "Groaning beneath this concentrated load, this intense, incomprehensible pressure, this terrible exaction of Divine Justice, from which feeble humanity shrank, and through the agony thus experienced sweating great drops of blood, He was led to exclaim, 'Father, if it be possible, let this cup pass from me.' . . . He had struggled against the powers of darkness that had been let loose upon him there; placed below all things, His mind surcharged with agony and pain, *lonely and apparently helpless and forsaken, in his agony, the blood oozed from his pores.*"[52] John Taylor taught that for a time in the Garden of Gethsemane Jesus was alone and forsaken. It appears that in the Garden of Gethsemane the Father, to some degree, withdrew and that is when the blood oozed from Christ's pores.

Brigham Young likewise explained, "At the hour when the crisis came for him to offer up his life, the Father withdrew His spirit from His Son, at the time he was to be crucified . . . at the hour when the crisis came for him to offer up his life, the Father withdrew Himself, withdrew His Spirit, and cast a veil over him. That [also] is what made him sweat blood. If he'd had the powers of God upon him, he would not have sweat blood; but all was withdrawn from him, and a veil was cast over him."[53] Brigham Young's quote here is a little difficult to follow. At one moment he is talking about Christ on the cross, but a moment later he is talking about Jesus bleeding from every pore in Gethsemane. Like John Taylor, Brigham Young suggested that in Gethsemane the Father for a time withdrew, casting a veil between them both. Without His Father's sustaining power and influence, the blood flowed from every pore.

THE ANGEL

Bruce R. McConkie explained, "As near as we can judge, these infinite agonies—this suffering beyond compare—continued for some three to four hours."[54] It would appear that Jesus and the disciples spent a few hours in Gethsemane, and that during that time, one or many angels were present.[55]

Gospel scholar Paul Smith wrote that as Jesus prayed, "He knelt and lifted up His head and His arms toward heaven."[56] I am not sure where Brother Smith got that insight from, but it feels right to me. Such a plea for help from Adam and others with arms lifted up has at times brought heavenly messengers. As Christ prayed, we know an angel came during the ordeal, strengthening him. "And there appeared an angel unto him from heaven, strengthening him" (Luke 22:43). Artists Frans Schwartz and Carl Bloch have painted magnificent, sacred images of this moment in the garden. What an honor for this angel! What an assignment! Who could it have been? Bruce R. McConkie wrote, "If we might indulge in speculation, we would suggest that the angel who came into this second Eden was the same person who dwelt in the first Eden. . . . Adam, who is Michael, the archangel—the head of the whole heavenly hierarchy of angelic ministrants—seems the logical one to give aid and comfort to his Lord on such a solemn occasion."[57]

What was the purpose of sending the angel? The angel came not to remove His suffering, not to deliver Him, but most likely to give Jesus comfort and encouragement to press forward and endure. Maybe the angel came to remind Him that the success of the entire plan of salvation depended upon Him, that there was no other way, that there was no back-up plan, and that the only way to save us was for Him to drink the bitter cup.

The angel may have said something like, "Oh Jehovah, you do not have to do this unless you wish, but you should know that unless you fulfill this assignment, the Father will lose not only this family, this whole family, but the entire creation associated with them; the planets, the plants, the animals, everything that you laid your hands on to create will be lost to the Father and go back to the chaos from which it came." The angel may have expressed his faith that Jesus could do it and that He represented many of us, an infinite number of us, who believed in Him and were counting on Him. On the other hand, maybe the angel did not use words to communicate but reverently mourned with Jesus and sustained Him during the suffering.

THE CONFRONTATION IN GETHSEMANE

"And being in an agony he prayed more earnestly" (Luke 22:44). Jesus prayed "more earnestly." What a lesson! All prayers are not equal. The Savior taught us that some trials require more earnest prayer than others. This was the greatest trial of all time and eternity. The Savior prayed like He had never prayed, more intensely, more earnestly, with greater faith than He had ever prayed before.

"Of all prayers ever uttered, in time or in eternity—by gods, angels, or mortal men—this one stands supreme, above and apart, preeminent over all others. . . . It was at this hour that he, who bought us with his blood, offered the most pleading and poignant personal prayer ever to fall from mortal lips. . . . Here in Gethsemane . . . he poured out his soul to his Father with pleadings never equaled. . . . Perhaps like his coming prayer among the Nephites, the words could not be written, but could be understood only by the power of the Spirit."[58]

"And being in an *agony* he prayed" (Luke 22:44; emphasis added). The word "agony" in the Greek here means literally a contest, struggle, or fight, facing an opponent. Who did the Savior contend with, and face in the Garden?

Alfred Edersheim taught, "This night seems to have been the [night of the] power of darkness, when . . . Christ had to meet by Himself the whole assault of hell. . . . That night the fierce wind of hell was allowed to sweep unbroken over the Savior and even to expand its fury upon those that stood behind in His shelter."[59]

As mentioned earlier, John Taylor taught that in the Garden, "The powers of darkness had been loosed upon the Savior there." Adam Clark likewise explained, "His conflict in the garden was with [the] devil, who appeared in a bodily shape most horrible; and that it was through this apparition that he began to be *sore amazed and very heavy*, for as Satan assaulted the first Adam in the garden in a bodily shape, it is not unreasonable to conclude that in the same way he assaulted the second Adam in a garden."[60]

In the Garden of Gethsemane, the Savior was challenged on two fronts: the first was partaking of the bitter cup that His Father placed on Him, which included, among other things, suffering an infinite burden of sin and pain. Second was Satan's assault.

The Father's power and influence withdrew in its fulness when Jesus was upon the cross, but as mentioned above, it may have occurred first in Gethsemane for a time. Gospel scholar Andrew Skinner explained, "Two conditions resulted from the withdrawal of the Father's power and influence . . . from Jesus. First, he was engulfed by spiritual death and hell. Second, he became completely vulnerable to the powers of Satan."[61]

In the garden, Satan and his legions were unleashed upon the Savior in their full fury. It was a supreme contest with the forces of evil, a battle royal. Satan surely tried to get the Savior to back out and turn away from His appointed mission. The entire plan of salvation and everything in the entire universe depended upon the Savior in the garden that night.

Tad Callister surmised, "Part of the battle may have necessitated an invasion of Satan's turf, perhaps even an intrepid trespass into the dark abyss of the Devil's domain. . . . With merciless fury Satan's forces must have attacked the Savior on all fronts—frantically, diabolically seeking a vulnerable spot, a weakness, an Achilles heel through which they might inflict a mortal wound, all in hopes they could halt the impending charge."[62]

Alma explained that the Savior would go forth "suffering temptations of every kind" (Alma 7:11). Part of the Savior's atoning sacrifice included Him overcoming and refusing to yield to every temptation known to man.

Regarding temptation C. S. Lewis offered this insight:

No man knows how bad he is till he has tried very hard to be good. A silly idea is current that good people do not know what temptation means. This is an obvious lie. . . . After all, you find out the strength of an army by fighting against it, not by giving in. You find out the strength of a wind by trying to walk against it, not by lying down. A man who gives in to temptation after five minutes simply does not know what it would have been like an hour later. That is why bad people, in one sense, know very little about badness. They have lived a sheltered life by always giving in. We never find out the strength of an evil impulse inside us until we try to fight it; and Christ, because He was the only man who never yielded to temptation, is also the only man who knows to the full what temptation means—the only complete realist.[63]

It is important to remember that just like you and me, like everyone, Jesus was certainly capable of sinning and could have succumbed to temptation. The prophet Abinadi taught that the Savior "suffereth temptation, and yieldeth not to *the temptation*, but sufffereth himself to be mocked, and scourged, and cast out, and disowned by his people" (Mosiah 15:5; emphasis added). Abinadi seems to be referring to a specific temptation. "[He] yieldeth not to *the temptation*." What was the greatest temptation for the Savior?

Doctrine and Covenants 19:18 teaches that as the burden and suffering pressed itself upon the Savior, His initial reaction was that He "might not drink of the bitter cup and shrink." The possibility of Him shrinking and recoiling from horrors of Gethsemane, from the horrors of that infinite burden, was real. That I believe was "the temptation" of all temptations for the Master.

As the infinite burden pressed upon Him, Satan surely attempted to place doubt in Him as the Savior plead, "Father let this cup pass from me." Maybe, just for a moment Jesus wondered if He could really do it. Satan certainly then and a thousand times before had told Him He could not do it, that it was impossible.

Lorenzo Snow taught, "The atonement required *all* the power that [Jesus] had, *all* the faith that He could summon for Him to accomplish that which the Father required of Him."[64] Part of His power, part of His faith was not enough. Christ gave everything; He gave His all to drain the dregs of the bitter cup. It was the greatest act of faith ever demonstrated. He exercised all of His faith in His Father, faith in His Father's plan, and it is because of that faith we can be saved.

The Apostle Paul, in six different verses of scripture, testified that salvation comes because of the faith of Christ (see Romans 3:22; Philippians 3:9; Galatians 2:16, 20, 3:22; Ephesians 3:12). Paul's emphasis is not that righteousness and blessings come to us through our faith in Christ, but that it comes to us because of the faith of Christ. The prophet Lehi similarly taught his son Jacob, "I know that thou art redeemed, *because of the righteousness of thy Redeemer*" (2 Nephi 2:3; emphasis added).

We can have faith in Christ, we can become righteous, and we are ultimately saved because of the faith and righteousness of Jesus Christ. It was the faith He had in His Father, in His Father's plan, and the faith He had in Himself that saves. I believe that through the Gethsemane and Calvary experience somewhere in the back of His mind was the thought that the Father completely trusted and believed in Him. He held on to that thought, and that faith not only saved Him but ultimately can save an infinite number of us.

The Prophet Joseph Smith explained that faith is the foundation of all righteousness, that it is a principle of action in all intelligent beings, and that it is the principle of power that existed in the bosom of God.[65] The Savior's faith was both a principle of action and of empowerment that He tapped into as He worked out the Atonement.

As the battle raged in the garden, Tad Callister taught, "The Savior pressed forward . . . until every prisoner was freed from the tenacious tentacles of the Evil One. This was a rescue mission of infinite implications. Every muscle of the Savior, every virtue, every spiritual reservoir that could be called upon would be summoned in the struggle. No doubt there was an exhaustion of all energies, a straining of all faculties, and exercise of all powers."[66]

According to the song "Gethsemane" written by Melanie Hoffman, it was "the biggest battle that ever was won, this was done by Jesus, the fight was won by Jesus." James E. Talmage concluded, "In that hour of anguish Christ met and overcame all the horrors that Satan . . . could inflict. . . . From the terrible conflict in Gethsemane, Christ emerged a victor."[67]

After enduring forty-six days and nights of debilitating chemotherapy treatment for leukemia, Neal A. Maxwell was asked by David A. Bednar what lessons he had learned from his suffering and illness. Elder Bednar reported, "I will remember always the precise and penetrating answer he gave. 'Dave,' he said, 'I have learned that not shrinking is more important than surviving.'"[68]

Elder Maxwell would later teach, "As we confront our own . . . trials and tribulations, we too can plead with the Father, just as Jesus did, that we 'might not . . . shrink'—meaning to retreat or to recoil (D&C 19:18). Not shrinking is much more important than surviving! Moreover, partaking of a bitter cup without becoming bitter is likewise part of the emulation of Jesus."[69]

During His farewell discourse to His Apostles the Savior declared, "The prince of darkness who is of this world cometh, but he hath no power over me" (JST, John 14:30). Satan and His legions came, and Jesus, true to His word, withstood and overcame the onslaught. They had no power over Him. John wrote, "For this purpose the Son of God was manifested, that he might destroy the works of the devil" (1 John 3:8).

Of this confrontation in the garden, Boyd K. Packer said, "No mortal watched as evil turned away and hid in shame before the light of that pure being. All wickedness could not quench that light. When what was done was done and the ransom had been paid. Both death and hell forsook their claim on all who would repent. Men at last were free. Then every soul who ever lived could choose to touch that light and be redeemed."[70]

In the Garden of Gethsemane, Jesus pressed forward until He had safely secured the glorious eternal possibilities of every child of Heavenly Father. The seed of the woman, the light of the world, crushed the head of the prince of darkness. Satan's head was crushed by the very heel that he had bruised. Because of that victory, we now can be redeemed by that light, by the seed of the woman, that destroyed the works of the devil. We can press forward on to eternal life because Jesus pressed forward against Satan and drank every drop of the bitter cup, because He refused to shrink (see 2 Nephi 31:20).

The hymn "Come Thou Fount of Every Blessing" by Robert Robinson reads,

Come thou fount of every blessing
Tune my heart to sing Thy grace
Streams of mercy never ceasing
Call for songs of loudest praise
Teach me some melodious sonnet
Sung by flaming tongues above
Praise the Mount I'm fixed upon it
Mount of Thy redeeming love
Here I raise my Ebenezer
Hither by Thy help I come
And I hope by Thy good pleasure
Safely to arrive at home
Jesus, sought me when a stranger
Wandering from the fold of God
He, to rescue me from danger
Interposed His precious blood
O to grace, how great a debtor
Daily I'm constrained to be
Let Thy goodness like a fetter
Bind my wandering heart to Thee
Prone to wander, Lord, I feel it
Prone to leave the God I love
Here's my heart, Lord, take and seal it
Seal it for Thy courts above.

Years ago, when I first heard this song, I had no idea what the phrase "here I raise my Ebenezer" referred to. Later I learned it comes from 1 Samuel 7. In that chapter the stone of Israel, Jehovah, had interceded and saved all of the Israelites from the Philistines. Following their deliverance, Samuel raised up a stone as a monument "and called the name of it, Ebenezer saying, hither has the Lord helped us" (1 Samuel 7:12). In this verse the English translation of the Hebrew text "Ebenezer" means "stone of help." The Ebenezer stone raised up by Samuel represented Jehovah's help. He was the Israelites' only hope of deliverance. In our modern-day battles with the Philistines, Jehovah is our stone of help, our only hope of deliverance, who will rescue us from danger because He interposed His precious blood.

MOTIVATION

As Jesus was working out the Atonement, He always had a choice. He had the power within Himself at any time to withdraw and stop the suffering. Why didn't He?

Before the Creation Jesus had covenanted to perform the Atonement and to be our Redeemer. During our pre-earth life when Jesus learned the Father's will and knew He was needed, He stepped forward and said, "Here am I, send me" (Abraham 3:27). Neal A. Maxwell said, "It was one of those special moments when a few words are preferred to many. Never has one individual offered, in so few words, to do so much for so many as did Jesus when He meekly proffered Himself as ransom for us, billions and billions of us!"[71]

Amulek explained that Christ would perform the Atonement because "the Lord God hath spoken it" (Alma 34:8). His word was His bond. He explained, "For as I the Lord God liveth even so my words cannot return void, for as they go forth out of my mouth they must be fulfilled" (Moses 4:30, 5:15). Abraham likewise wrote, "There is nothing that the Lord thy God shall take in his heart to do but what he will do it" (Abraham 3:17). Christ had taken it into His heart to be our Redeemer. His word was His bond. He would not fail us.

The love that Jesus had for His Father served as His greatest motivation. During His farewell discourse Christ said to His disciples, "That the world may know that I love the Father; and as the Father gave me commandment even so I do" (John 14:31.) Jesus would not disappoint his Father. James E. Talmage explained that through His entire mortal life, "the accomplishment of the Father's will was never lost sight of as the object of the Son's supreme desire."[72]

Abinadi likewise taught, "The will of the Son being swallowed up in the will of the Father" (Mosiah 15:7). "Being 'swallowed up' means being totally enveloped-without question, protest, reservation, or resentment. It is 'all the way,' not halfway."[73] It was the will of the Father that the bitter cup be swallowed. Jesus was all the way in. He would swallow every drop of the bitter cup. Never was there a more obedient son.

We should note that from the beginning Heavenly Father had complete and total faith in His Firstborn Son. He knew Jesus could and would do it. "Thousands of years before He came upon earth, the Father had watched His course and knew that He could depend upon Him when the salvation of worlds should be at stake, and He was not disappointed."[74]

Who else knew they could depend on the Savior to perform an atoning sacrifice? All of us born into mortality. During our pre-earth life, as the war in heaven raged, we rallied beside the Savior, raising our voice in testimony, declaring our belief that Christ would indeed be true to His word, be true to His covenant and do the Father's will.

John the Beloved explained that the war in heaven was won and Satan was overcome by "the blood of the Lamb and *by the word of their testimony*" (Revelation 12:11; emphasis added). By the word of the combined testimony of faithful the battle was one. That testimony included yours. It should be noted that in the pre-earth life faithfulness varied. Some were more faithful and valiant to the cause of Christ than others.

When it came to performing His atoning sacrifice, the Savior was motivated because of His love for all of mankind. Everything He did was prompted by His unselfish, infinite love for all of us. Nephi taught, "The world, because of their iniquity, shall judge him to be a thing of naught; wherefore they scourge him, and he suffereth it; and they smite him, and he suffereth it. Yea, they spit upon him, and he suffereth it, [why?] because of his loving kindness and his long-suffering towards the children of men" (1 Nephi 19:9). Of all of Jesus's perfect attributes, His loving kindness and longsuffering equipped Him to accomplish the Atonement.

While the scriptures attest that the atoning sacrifice of our Savior was made for all mankind, they also teach that the Savior performed the Atonement specifically for those who would believe on His name and apply His sacrifice. Speaking of the faithful,

Abinadi taught, "For these are they who sins he has borne; these are they for whom he has died" (Mosiah 15:11–12). The resurrected Lord likewise said regarding the faithful, "For such have I laid down my life" (3 Nephi 9:22).

In Proverbs we read, "Where there is no vision, the people perish" (Proverbs 29:18). President Lorenzo Snow explained, "When Jesus went through that terrible torture on the cross, He saw what would be accomplished by it; He saw that His brethren and sisters—the sons and daughters of God—would be gathered in, with but few exceptions—those who committed the unpardonable sin. The sacrifice of the divine Being was effectual to destroy the powers of Satan. I believe that every man and woman who comes into this life and passes through it, that life will be a success in the end."[75] The Savior foresaw what would come because of His sacrifice, and that vision served to motivate Him, that vision saved us from perishing.

Because of the Atonement of Christ, all men and women (save the sons of perdition) will eventually be raised up to a better condition. The Savior knew this and focused on it as He suffered. The Apostle Paul explained that Christ "who for the joy that was set before him endured the cross" (Hebrews 12:2). One reason Christ endured the bitter cup was that He knew the eventual joy that would come because of it. Joy that would come to Him, joy that would come to His Father, and joy that would come to an infinite number of us. He focused on that potential joy while He suffered. Russel M. Nelson said, "Think of that! In order for Him to endure the most excruciating experience ever endured, our Savior focused on joy."[76] Is there a lesson in that for us during our suffering?

One Messianic psalm reads, "When he maketh inquisition for blood, he remembereth them" (Psalm 9:12). As the blood fell from His pores, He remembered you, He remembered me. Isaiah Messianically wrote, "When thou shalt make his soul an offering for sin, he shall see his seed" (Isaiah 53:10). In addition to remembering us, it appears that as Savior suffered, He saw us, He had a vision of all of the sons and daughters of God He suffered for, and that vision motivated Him. Merrill J. Bateman taught, "In the Garden and on the Cross Jesus saw each of us."[77] The Savior saw all of us as He suffered, and that vision motivated Him. With you and countless others before Him, He refused to shrink and forged ahead in Gethsemane.

Elder Bateman continued:

For many years I thought of the Savior's experience in the garden and on the cross as places where a large mass of sin was heaped upon Him. Through the words of Alma . . . Isaiah and other prophets . . . my view has changed. The Atonement was an intimate, personal experience in which Jesus came to know how to help each of us. The Pearl of Great Price teaches us that Moses was shown all the inhabitants of the earth, which were numberless as the sand upon the seashore. (Moses 1:28). If Moses beheld every soul, then it seems reasonable that the Creator of the universe has the power to become intimately acquainted with each of us. He learned about your weaknesses and mine. He experienced your pains and suffering. He experienced mine. I testify that He knows us. He understands the way in which we deal with temptations. He knows our weaknesses. But more than that, more than just knowing us, He knows how to help us if we come to Him in faith.[78]

The Atonement was not only infinite but intimate and personal. It is and was about people, an infinite number of people. Through the experience of Gethsemane and Calvary Jesus perfectly came to know how to help each of us, how to succor us in our infirmities. His sacrifice was tailor made for each and every one of us. The Savior's atoning sacrifice is infinite in reach and perfectly intimate in its effect.

As C. S. Lewis put it, "[Christ] has infinite attention to spare for each one of us. He does not have to deal with us in the mass. You are as much alone with Him as if you were the only being He had ever created. When Christ died, He died for you individually just as much as if you had been the only man [or woman] in the world."[79] Not only did the Savior see each one of us, but He became each one of us as He suffered God's wrath in our place.

It has been borne upon my soul that the Savior's love was such that if it was just you, and just you alone, the Savior would have suffered and offered the same sacrifice. That is how great the worth of your soul is to Him. Never underestimate your self-worth. He hasn't. You were His motivation.

PRIVATE AND PUBLIC BATTLES

Gethsemane was a private garden where a private battle occurred for the Savior. As He suffered, His disciples may have had some small glimpse and understanding of what was taking place, but their knowledge was extremely limited. It was a private experience that would not make the local news. The world knew nothing of what was taking place and of its eternal significance and importance. In all reality, even today we know very little about the private battle the Savior experienced in Gethsemane.

Ezra Taft Benson taught, "Great battles can make great heroes and heroines. We will never have a better opportunity to be valiant in a more crucial cause than in the battle we face today and in the immediate future. Some of the greatest battles we will face will be fought within the silent chambers of our own souls."[80] All of us will have our own private battles—battles and challenges that few will know about. Battles that we will fight within the silent chambers of our own souls. "The greatest conflict that any man or women will ever have . . . will be the battle that is had with self."[81]

Everything that followed Gethsemane—the betrayal, the illegal trials, the scourging, and the cross at Calvary—represented a public battle for Jesus that concluded on a public hill. They were battles and challenges that occurred in the open with many eyes watching. Like the Savior, the day may come when we encounter public battles—challenges that will occur in the open, in front of others.

Stephen R. Covey explained that when we confront our battles first in private, it gives us "the opportunity to live out our public battles in our minds and in our hearts before we ever come to them. We can, in the unseen presence of God, deal with all of our unrighteousness. . . . Gethsemane was the place where [the Savior] renewed and deepened his internal commitment or covenant, with His Father to complete His atoning mission. . . . Christ's [public battle] Calvary was successful partly because Gethsemane [His private battle] was successful."[82]

What a wonderful insight. We will not be successful in our public battles if we don't first win our private battles. May we in the unseen presence of others courageously face and address our own unrighteousness. May we be honest with ourselves and pray to have the eyes to see our sins, weaknesses, and inadequacies for what they truly are and see them as God sees them. As we come to Christ, He will show us our weaknesses (see Ether 12:27). Only then can we fully address our unrighteousness and follow Moroni's admonition to "deny ourselves of all ungodliness" and put off the natural man (see Moroni 10:32).

The people of King Benjamin did just that. "They had viewed themselves in their own carnal state, even less than the dust of the earth" (Mosiah 4:2). That self-awareness served as a catalyst for change. "Just as man does not really desire food until he is hungry, so he does not desire the salvation of Christ until he knows why he needs Christ."[83] By viewing themselves properly, the people of King Benjamin spiritually speaking became hungry. They knew they needed the Bread of Life. As a result, they applied the atoning blood of Christ and were changed. They declared, "The Spirit of the Lord Omnipotent . . . has wrought a mighty change in us, or in our hearts, that we have no more disposition to do evil, but to do good continually (Mosiah 5:2).

President Benson testified, "Christ lived on earth and was subject to all manner of temptation, but he won every battle. He is the most successful warrior that ever walked the earth, and He wants to help us win every battle, be it personal or public. When we fall short His atonement will compensate for us on conditions of our repentance."[84]

Through it all, from Gethsemane (His private battle) to the Cross (His public battle), Christ remained true. True to His commitment, true to His covenant, true to His Father! He refused to shrink and came off the victor, and because He remained true, with His help, we can remain true. Because of Him we can overcome and win both our private battles and our public battles. With the help of the Master we can, like Him, overcome the world.

ENDNOTES

1. Bruce R. McConkie, "The Purifying Power of Gethsemane," April 1985 general conference.
2. Adam Clarke, *The New Testament of Our Lord and Saviour Jesus Christ* (Abingdon), 641.
3. Richard Neitzel Holzapfel and Thomas A. Wayment, *From the Last Supper through the Resurrection: The Saviors Final Hours* (Salt Lake City: Deseret Book, 2003, 142.
4. Alfred Edersheim, *The Life and Times of Jesus the Messiah*. Vol. 2 (Eerdmans Pub. Co., 1971), 538.
5. Adam Clarke, *The New Testament of Our Lord and Saviour Jesus Christ* (Abingdon), 257.
6. Bruce R. McConkie, *Doctrinal New Testament Commentary*. Vol. 1, (Salt Lake City: Bookcraft, 1965), 775.
7. Adam Clarke, ibid.
8. Alfred Edersheim, ibid.
9. Susan Easton Black, *400 Questions & Answers about the Life and Time of Jesus Christ*, (American Fork, UT: Covenant Communications, 2010), 192.
10. Richard Neitzel Holzapfel and Thomas A. Wayment, ibid., 149.
11. Who would tempt the disciples in the Garden of Gethsemane? Satan not only attacked and tried to destroy the Savior in Gethsemane, but I believe he also turned his furry upon Jesus's disciples and tempted them. With Christ there were no boundaries; Satan had complete access to Him. With the disciples it was different. There were bounds set that Satan could not pass. I have had it borne upon my soul that the Savior protected and defended His disciples that night in the Garden of Gethsemane from Satan and His legions. He was an impenetrable rock that held Satan in check.
12. Frederic W. Farrar, *The Life of Christ*. (Salt Lake City: Bookcraft, 1995), 634.
13. Jeffrey R. Holland, "Behold the Lamb of God," April 2019 general conference.
14. George W. Pace, "The Very Heart," *The Gift of the Atonement* (Salt Lake City: Deseret Book, 2002), 64.
15. Ivan J. Barrett, "'He Lives! For We Saw Him,'" *Ensign*, Aug. 1975.
16. Orson F. Whitney, *Through Memory's Halls. The Life Story of Orson F. Whitney* (Zions Print and Pub. Co., 1930), 82–83.
17. Of this experience in the garden President Spencer W. Kimball wrote, "That brings to my thought, am I asleep; are you asleep? Are you taking for granted all of the joys and blessings of this world without thinking of the eternities that are to come beyond? Are we asleep? Are we his disciples called by him to serve and to teach and to train, and are we asleep? That question always reaches into my heart" (Spencer W. Kimball and Edward L. Kimball, *The Teachings of Spencer W. Kimball* [Salt Lake City: Deseret Book, 1982], 152). Elder Bruce R. McConkie suggested an alternative explanation for

the disciples sleeping that needs to be mentioned: "Perhaps the very reason Peter, James, and John, slept was to enable a divine providence to withhold from their ears, and seal up from their eyes, those things which only God's can comprehend" (*Moral Messiah* 4:124).

18. Andrew C. Skinner, *Gethsemane* (Salt Lake City: Deseret Book, 2002), 58.
19. Neal A. Maxwell, "Willing to Submit," April 1985 general conference.
20. Bruce R. McConkie, "The Purifying Power of Gethsemane," April 1985 general conference.
21. Jeffrey R. Holland, "The Hands of the Fathers," April 1999 general conference.
22. Adam Clarke, *The New Testament of Our Lord and Saviour Jesus Christ* (Abingdon), 258.
23. Bruce R. McConkie, "Why the Lord Ordained Prayer," *Ensign*, Jan. 1976.
24. Edwin W. Aldous, "A Reflection on the Atonement's Healing Power," *Ensign*, Apr. 1987.
25. Andrew C. Skinner, *Gethsemane* (Salt Lake City: Deseret Book), 2002, 63.
26. Obert C. Tanner, *The New Testament Speaks* (Department of Education of the Church of Jesus Christ of Latter-Day Saints, 1947), 485–487.
27. Neal A. Maxwell, *If Thou Endure It Well* (Salt Lake City: Bookcraft, 1996), 52. Elder Maxwell taught further that "[Jesus] partook voluntarily of the bitter cup in the awful, but for Him avoidable, Atonement; we must therefore, drink from our tiny cups. I thank Him for likewise not interceding on our behalf, even when we pray in faith and reasonable righteousness for that which would not be right for us" (Neal A. Maxwell, "Jesus of Nazareth, Savior and King," *Ensign*, Dec. 2007).
28. Jeffrey R. Holland, "The Hands of the Fathers," April 1999 general conference. John Taylor likewise explained that Jesus's doing the will of the Father "was a hard thing for Him to do. . . . He exclaimed, 'Father, if it be possible let this cup pass.' But it was not possible. It was the decree of God" (*Journal of Discourses* 24:34).
29. Spencer W. Kimball, "Tragedy or Destiny," *The Improvement Era*, Mar. 1966.
30. Neal A. Maxwell, "Swallowed Up in the Will of the Father," October 1995 general conference.
31. C. S. Lewis, *The Great Divorce* (HarperOne, 2015), 72.
32. Jeffrey R. Holland, *Christ and the New Covenant* (Salt Lake City: Deseret Book, 2006), 193.
33. D&C 84:33; Alma 5:14.
   Joseph Smith taught, "As the Holy Ghost falls upon one of the literal seed of Abraham, it is calm and serene; and his whole soul and body are only exercised by the pure spirit of intelligence; while the effect of the Holy Ghost upon a Gentile, is to purge out the old blood, and make him actually of the seed of Abraham. That man that has none of the blood of Abraham (naturally) must have a new creation by the Holy Ghost. In such a case, there may be a more powerful effect upon the body, and visible to the eye, than

upon an Israelite, while the Israelite at first might be far before the Gentile in pure intelligence" (Joseph Smith and Joseph Fielding Smith, *Teachings of the Prophet Joseph Smith* [Salt Lake City: Deseret Book, 1958/1977], 149). Brigham Young taught, "You dare not quite give up all your hearts to God, and become sanctified throughout, and be led by the Holy Ghost. . . . This arises from the power of evil that is so prevalent upon the face of the whole earth. It was given to you by your father and mother; it was mingled with your conception in the womb and it has ripened in your flesh, in your bones, so that it has become riveted in your very nature. If I were to ask you individually, if you wished to be sanctified throughout, and become pure and holy as you possibly could live, every person would say yes; yet if the Lord Almighty should give a revelation instructing you to be given wholly up to Him, and to His cause, you would shrink, saying, 'I am afraid he will take away some of my darlings.' That is the difficulty with the majority of this people. It is for you and I to wage war with that principle, [the natural man] until it is overcome in us, then we shall not entail it upon our children. It is for us to lay a foundation so that everything our children have to do with will bring them to Mount Zion" (Young, Brigham. *Journal of Discourses*, vol. 2, *The Editorium*, 2013, 134).

34. Neal A. Maxwell, *If Thou Endure It Well* (Salt Lake City: Bookcraft, 1996), 73.

35. Gordon B. Hinckley, *Teachings of the Presidents of the Church: Gordon B. Hinckley* (The Church of Jesus Christ of Latter-Day Saints, 2016), 325.

36. Marion G. Romney, "Jesus Christ, Lord of the Universe," *Improvement Era*, Nov. 1968.

37. Tad R. Callister *The Infinite Atonement* (Salt Lake City: Deseret Book, 2000), 105.

38. Bruce A. Van Orden Bruce and Brent L. Top, editors. *Doctrines of the Book of Mormon* (Salt Lake City: Deseret Book, 1991), 86.

39. Bruce R. McConkie, *The Mortal Messiah: From Bethlehem to Calvary*. Vol. 4 (Salt Lake City: Deseret Book, 1979), 124.

40. Bruce R. McConkie, *A New Witness for the Articles of Faith* (Salt Lake City: Deseret Book, 1985), 621.

41. Bruce R. McConkie, "The Purifying Power of Gethsemane," April 1985 general conference.

42. Hugh Nibley, *Approaching Zion* (Salt Lake City: Deseret Book, 1989), 603.

43. Bruce R. McConkie, *The Mortal Messiah: From Bethlehem to Calvary*. Vol. 3 (Deseret Book, 1979, 88.

44. Tad R. Callister, *The Infinite Atonement* (Salt Lake City: Deseret Book, 2000), 96.

45. Bruce R. McConkie, "Why the Lord Ordained Prayer," *Ensign*, Jan. 1976.

46. Joseph Fielding Smith, *Doctrines of Salvation*. Vol. 1, (Salt Lake City: Bookcraft, 1954), 23.

47. Paul H. Peterson, et al., editors. *Jesus Christ, Son of God, Savior* (Brigham Young University: Religious Studies Center, 2002), 219.

48. James E. Talmage, *Jesus the Christ* (Salt Lake City: Deseret Book, 1915/1982), 613.
49. Truman G. Madsen, "The Olive Press," *Ensign*, Dec. 1982.
50. Stephen Edward Robinson, *Believing Christ: The Parable of the Bicycle and Other Good News* (Salt Lake City: Deseret Book, 1992), 119.
51. B. H. Roberts, "The Seventy's Course in Theology, Fourth Year: The Atonement," *Deseret News*, 1911, 126.
52. John Taylor, "Mediation and Atonement," *Deseret News*, 1882/1998, 151.
53. Brigham Young, *Journal of Discourses*, vol. 3, *The Editorium*, 2013, 206.
54. Bruce R. McConkie, "The Purifying Power of Gethsemane," April 1985 general conference.
55. Bruce R. McConkie, *The Mortal Messiah: From Bethlehem to Calvary.* Vol. 4, (Salt Lake City: Deseret Book, 1979), 124.
56. Paul Thomas Smith, *This Is the Christ*, (American Fork, UT: Covenant Communications, 2010), 80.
57. Bruce R. McConkie, *The Mortal Messiah: From Bethlehem to Calvary.* Vol. 4, (Salt Lake City: Deseret Book, 1979), 124.
58. Bruce R. McConkie, "Why the Lord Ordained Prayer," *Ensign*, Jan. 1976.
59. Alfred Edersheim, *The Life and Times of Jesus the Messiah.* Vol. 2 (Eerdmans Pub. Co., 1971), 535.
60. Adam Clarke, *The New Testament of Our Lord and Saviour Jesus Christ* (Abingdon), 492.
61. Andrew C. Skinner, *Gethsemane* (Salt Lake City: Deseret Book, 2002), 100.
62. Tad R. Callister, *The Infinite Atonement* (Salt Lake City: Deseret Book, 2000), 129–130.
63. C. S. Lewis, *Mere Christianity* (HarperCollins, 2001), 142.
64. Lorenzo Snow, *The Teachings of Lorenzo Snow: Fifth President of the Church of Jesus Christ of Latter-Day Saints* (Salt Lake City: Deseret Book, 1998), 98.
65. Larry E. Dahl, et al., *The Lectures on Faith in Historical Perspective* (Brigham Young University: Religious Studies Center, 1990), 31.
66. Tad R. Callister, *The Infinite Atonement* (Salt Lake City: Deseret Book, 2000), 130–131.
67. James E. Talmage, *Jesus the Christ* (Salt Lake City: Deseret Book, 1915/1982), 614.
68. David A. Bednar, "That We Might 'Not . . . Shrink.'" CES Devotional for Young Adults. Mar. 3, 2013.
69. Neal A. Maxwell, "Apply the Atoning Blood of Christ," October 1997 general conference. Like the Savior, Elder Maxwell did not shrink from the bitter cup that was given to him, but pressed forward with a steadfastness in Christ as he suffered for eight years with leukemia, enduring faithfully to the very end of his life. What an example! What a disciple! He would not shrink from doing God's will, even if it meant death.
70. Boyd K. Packer, "Atonement, Agency, Accountability," April 1988 general conference.
71. Neal A. Maxwell, "Meekly Dressed in Destiny," BYU Devotional. Sept. 5, 1982.

72. James E. Talmage, *Jesus the Christ* (Salt Lake City: Deseret Book, 1915/1982), 614.

73. Neal A. Maxwell, *That Ye May Believe* (Salt Lake City: Deseret Book, 1992), 2–3. On another occasion Elder Maxwell taught, "In considering consecration, it is well to remember . . . that nothing is held back-whether turf, attitude, or hobbies. One's will is to be swallowed up in the will of God-just as occurred with Jesus . . . the will of the Son being swallowed up in the will of the Father. . . . Most forms of holding back are rooted in pride or are prompted by the mistaken notion that somehow we are diminished by submission to God. Actually, the greater the submission, the greater the expansion!" (as quoted by Henry B. Eyring in *On Becoming a Disciple Scholar*, 61–62).

74. Lorenzo Snow, *The Teachings of President Lorenzo Snow. The Church of Jesus Christ of Latter-Day Saints*, 2012, 110.

75. Brian H. Stuy, *Collected Discourses: Delivered by President Wilford Woodruff, His Two Counselors, the Twelve Apostles, and Others*. Vol. 3, B.H.S. Pub., 1988, 364.

76. Russell M. Nelson, "Joy and Spiritual Survival," October 2016 general conference.

77. Merrill J. Bateman, "The Power to Heal from Within," April 1995 general conference.

78. Ibid., "A Pattern for All," October 2005 general conference.

79. Jerry Root, and C. S. Lewis, *The Quotable Lewis*. Edited by Wayne Martindale (Tyndale House Publishers, Inc., 1989), 248.

80. Ezra Taft Benson, "In His Steps," *Ensign*, Sept. 1988.

81. Melvin J. Ballard, "Struggle for the Soul," *New Era,* May 5, 1928.

82. Robert L. Millet, editor. *The Redeemer: Reflections on the Life and Teachings of Jesus the Christ* (Salt Lake City: Deseret Book, 2000), 90.

83. Ezra Taft Benson, *A Witness and a Warning* (Salt Lake City: Deseret Book, 1988), 33.

84. Ibid., "In His Steps," *Ensign*, Sept. 1988.

CHAPTER 4

THE MEANING OF HIS SUFFERING

W hen it comes to Jesus in Gethsemane, the Bible is vague. "Most Christian denominations regard Christ's prayer in Gethsemane as merely a plea to the Father to strengthen Him for the imminent suffering of Calvary rather than a central act of His atoning Sacrifice."[1] Gethsemane played a central role in the Savior's Atonement. Our Lord's suffering in the garden was not simply an awful anticipation of Calvary, but it was redemptive in nature. We turn to modern-day scripture and revelation to understand more fully what happened in Gethsemane and why it was necessary.

Restored scripture makes it clear that an atonement for sin was needed because God governs the universe by laws. Eternal laws are essential for our progression and ultimate happiness. God instituted a system of fixed and immutable laws and has given us our agency so He can bless us. The Lord has said, "That which is governed by law is also preserved by law and perfected and sanctified by the same. That which breaketh a law, and abideth not by law . . . willeth to abide in sin and . . . cannot be sanctified by law. . . . Therefore, they must remain filthy still" (D&C 88:34–35). According to these verses we are preserved, perfected, and sanctified as we exercise our agency and keep God's laws. We also learn that sin is the willful breaking of God's laws (see D&C 130:20–21; 2 Nephi 2:5, 13). None of us have always and unfailing chosen to be perfectly obedient to God's laws. "For all have sinned, and come short of the glory of God" (Romans 3:23).

One aspect of God's nature is perfect justice. He "cannot look upon sin with the least degree of allowance" (D&C 1:31). God is a just God, a God who abides by law. When God's laws are broken there are consequences. Justice requires a payment (see 3 Nephi 28:35) That payment involves suffering. Alma explained there is a punishment affixed for every broken law. A punishment must be paid for every sin, for every broken law (see Alma 42:14–22). Dallin H. Oaks taught, "According to eternal law, the consequences that follow from the justice of God are severe and permanent. When a commandment is broken, a commensurate penalty is imposed. This happens automatically."[2]

Gospel scholar Cleon Skousen has written,

> Our Heavenly Father cannot be unjust or "he would cease to be God." He cannot allow his compassion or love of mercy to rob the demands of justice, or "he would cease to be God" . . . He "cannot look upon sin with the least degree of allowance," or he would cease to be God. This vividly establishes an iron clad principle of Godhood: The Father must accomplish his purposes within very strict parameters that ensure the trust and love of those He governs, or He would 'cease to be God.' This tells us that when Jesus asked the Father if it were possible for the Father to take us back into his presence without the atoning sacrifice, He received the most explicit of all answers. "No." The Father did not have that option.[3]

God cannot act any way He pleases to bless and save us, for He Himself is governed by law.

Of the Savior's sacrifice B.H. Roberts explained,

> Let the severity of Christ's Atonement for man's sins bear witness, for it required all that the Christ gave in suffering and agony of spirit and body, to lay the grounds for man's forgiveness and reconciliation with God. The severity of the Atonement should impress men with the fact that we live in a world of stern realities, that human actions draw with them tremendous consequences that may not be easily set aside if the actions in which they have their origin are wrong. . . . Suffering is the consequence or the penalty of violating divine, moral law, and the penalty must be paid, either by [the] one sinning or by another who shall suffer vicariously for him."[4]

As explained, a penalty must be paid for each and every sin. Justice demands it. During our mortal existence we alone cannot fully appease justice. No amount of suffering on our part is sufficient; the debt is too great. Elder Ronald E. Poleman explained, "Throughout the repentance process we have feelings of regret, remorse, and guilt, which cause us to suffer. However, our individual suffering does not satisfy the demands of justice which follow disobedience to divine law. We [alone] cannot pay the price for our own sins [in mortality]."[5]

There are many things in this life that we simply cannot overcome on our own. For example, on our own we can never overcome Satan, sin, and death. We cannot repair and restore all of the consequences of our poor choices and sins. There are wounds we have caused or received that we simply cannot heal. There are things that we break and cannot fix. It is impossible for us to become clean from our sins on our own. Yet such a cleansing is necessary if we are to live again with God. In addition, on our own we cannot overcome the natural man and become sanctified and holy. It is all far beyond our mortal capacity to fix and change these things. In essence, man has fallen into a pit and cannot climb out. At the end of the day, we are all in need of help: we need mercy, we need grace. However, the scriptures are clear; mercy cannot rob justice (see Alma 42:25). According to the rules that frame the universe, the full consequences of transgressed laws cannot be dismissed or overlooked. Justice must be satisfied. Hence the need for a mediator, one who will offer himself as a sacrifice for sin to answer the ends of the law and appease the demands justice (see 2 Nephi 2:7; Alma 42:15). Therefore, as Russell M. Nelson explained, "Jesus Christ came to pay a debt He didn't owe because we owed a debt we couldn't pay."[6]

Marion G. Romney likewise taught, "Since we suffer this spiritual death as a result of our own transgressions, we cannot claim deliverance therefrom as a matter of justice. Neither has any man the power within himself alone to make restitution so complete that he can be wholly cleansed from the effect of his own wrongdoing. If men are to be freed from the results of their own transgressions and brought back into the presence of God, they must be the beneficiaries of some expedient beyond themselves which will free them from the effect of their own sins. For this purpose, was the atonement of Jesus Christ conceived and executed."[7]

Because of Jesus Christ we become the beneficiaries of some expedient beyond ourselves. Jesus did for us what we could not and cannot do for ourselves. He was and is our only hope. We are saved only "through the merits, mercy and grace of the Holy Messiah" (2 Nephi 2:8). Because of Christ's merits (His atoning sacrifice), He can grant us mercy and grace. Mercy signifies an advantage greater than is deserved. The Savior does this for us by withholding deserved punishments and by granting underserved benefits and blessings.

The Savior's grace saves us. Grace is a gift; it is an enabling power offered mercifully by Christ through His atoning sacrifice. His grace allows men and women to receive strength, assistance, and blessings that they otherwise would not receive if left on their own. His grace not only heals but lifts and can change our very nature and over time transform us into someone truly godlike. His grace not only will justify us but eventually sanctify us and, in the end, save us.

President Boyd K. Packer taught,

> Each of us lives on a kind of spiritual credit. One day the account will be closed, a settlement demanded. However, casually we may view it now, when that day comes and foreclosure is imminent, we will look around in restless agony for someone, anyone, to help us. And, by eternal law, mercy cannot be extended save there be one who is both willing and able to assume our debt and pay the price and arrange for the terms for our redemption. Unless there is a mediator, unless we have a friend, the full weight of justice untempered, unsympathetic, must positively fall on us. The full recompense for every transgression, however minor or however deep, will be exacted from us to the uttermost farthing. But know this, Truth glorious truth proclaims there is such a Mediator. 'For there is one God, and one mediator between God and men, the man Christ Jesus' (1 Tim. 2:5). Through Him mercy can be fully extended to each of us without offending the eternal law of justice. This truth is the very root of Christian doctrine. . . . The extension of mercy will not be automatic. It will be through covenant with Him. It will be on His terms, His generous terms, which include, as an absolute essential, baptism

by immersion for the remission of sins. All mankind can be protected by the law of justice, and at once each of us individually may be extended the redeeming and healing blessing of mercy.[8]

The Atonement of Jesus Christ is the means by which justice is served and mercy is extended, thus, giving hope to all of us and giving life to the entire plan of Salvation.[9] Jesus perfectly unites justice and mercy so He can save us from our sins.

"IT IS EXPEDIENT THAT AN ATONEMENT SHOULD BE MADE" (ALMA 34:9)

What would have happened had the Savior failed and there was no atonement made? We turn once again to modern-day scripture and revelation for answers. Without an atonement, we would be permanently stained by sin and remain filthy. We would be forever shut off from the presence of God. Without the Savior's atoning sacrifice there would be no resurrection. As a result, we would remain as spirits without physical bodies indefinitely, and become subject to the devil (see 2 Nephi 9:7–8). Alma taught that without the Savior's Atonement we would "unavoidably perish, becoming hardened, fallen and forever lost" (Alma 34:9). Jacob explained that not only would we become subject to the devil, but we would become his subjects, his angels, and endure never-ending torment. Without the Savior's Atonement we ultimately would be lost to perdition (see 2 Nephi 9:9).[10]

Therefore, without the Atonement of Jesus Christ all of our good choices, in the end, would be meaningless. We would be in Satan's grasp regardless of our best efforts to be good and do good. The Savior, in essence, purchased our agency with His sacrifice. Our good choices to follow God's laws now actually mean something. Those choices help us qualify to inherit the Savior's merciful blessings, blessings that cleanse, sanctify, and lift us in spite of own shortcomings. Because of the Savior's Atonement we, like Jesus, can overcome Satan, hell, and death.

Paul declared, expansively, that "in [Christ] all things hold together" (Revised Standard Version, Colossians 1:17). "Jesus' role as the creator of the cosmos and His rescuing and emancipating atonement reflect how

He holds all the everlasting things together."[11] The hymn "While of These Emblems We Partake" reads, "That else were this creations doom" (*Hymn no. 174*). I believe the entire creation that is held together by Christ would have been doomed had the Savior failed to perform His atoning sacrifice. Everything that had been organized by the Savior which includes this earth, worlds without number, and the universe itself would have become unglued. Entropy, the second law of thermodynamics, would have taken over and everything would have gone into disarray.

Therefore, Alma declared, "Behold, there is one thing which is of more importance than they all—for behold the time is not far distant that the Redeemer liveth and cometh among his people" (Alma 7:7). Jesus lived, He came among His people, He died and triumphed. Truth glorious truth proclaims there is such a Mediator. His atoning sacrifice is the greatest, fixed unchangeable, truth and power in the universe. "God be thanked for the matchless gift of His divine Son."[12]

APPLICATION

In Gethsemane what exactly was Jesus suffering and paying the price for? First and foremost, He suffered for our sins and all of the painful consequences of them. We should note that Christ not only suffered for the sins of those who would embrace and apply His sacrifice, but He also suffered for the unrepentant as well. He suffered for those who would never repent, including those born into mortality who would become sons of perdition. Alone, Jesus went to perdition and suffered what the scriptures refer to as the second death, experiencing spiritual death in its fullest extent.

Such suffering was additional suffering not required by justice. He descended below all things (see D&C 88:6). Why? So, He could comprehend all things "that he may know according to the flesh how to succor his people" (Alma 7:12). There is not one person in the universe who can tell Jesus something about pain and suffering that He does not already fully comprehend.

David A. Bednar explained, "You and I in a moment of weakness may cry out, 'No one understands. No one knows; No human being, perhaps, knows.' But the Son of God perfectly knows and understands, for He felt and bore our burdens before we ever did. And because he paid the ultimate price and bore that burden, He has perfect empathy and can extend to us His arm of mercy in so many phases of our life."[13]

The word "succor" found in Alma 7:12 means "to run to, or run to support; hence, to help or relieve when in difficulty, want or distress; to assist and deliver from suffering."[14] Christ will run to us, and like the father in the parable of the prodigal son, is running even now. The choice is ours to receive His embrace and receive His extended arm of mercy.

In Gethsemane Jesus suffered for our sins. However, the scriptures explain that His suffering extended far beyond sin. Alma taught He would suffer for our "pains, afflictions, temptations and sicknesses" (Alma 7:11–12). Jacob likewise taught that He would suffer for our "pains" (2 Nephi 9:21). Isaiah taught He would suffer for our "griefs, sorrows, transgressions and iniquities" (Isaiah 53:4–5).

The following is an incomplete list of content in the bitter cup that Jesus suffered for:

- Sin and the painful consequences of them.
- Innocent and ignorant transgressions of the law. That includes our mistakes and accidents that are not sin related.
- Temptations.
- Sicknesses.
- Grief and sorrows. Sometimes sorrow is a consequence of our own sins. Sometimes we experience grief and sorrow because of the sins of others.
- Disappointments.
- The inherent natural man in all of us that resulted as a consequence of the Fall.
- Infirmities, inadequacies, weaknesses, and imperfections.

The Savior not only pays the penalty of sin and their consequences, but He also heals and changes the sinner. We might compare the Savior's rescue of us to a man who cannot swim that falls into deep water and nearly drowns. Fortunately, a lifeguard standing by dives into the water and saves him. Following the rescue, the lifeguard stays with the man and teaches him how to swim. In a like manner the Savior jumps into the deep waters of our lives and lifts our souls to safety. Then He stays with us and helps us to overcome the very infirmities that caused our troubles in the first place.

- Guilt. One of the consequences of sinning is guilt (see Mosiah 2:38, Alma 42:18, Alma 36:12–14).

  Stephen E. Robinson explained, "Jesus Christ did not just assume the punishment for our sins—He took the guilt as well. The sin, the experience itself with all the negative consequences and ramifications, and not just the penalty for sin, became His. This is a crucial distinction. In the Atonement, Jesus does not just suffer for our punishment for us, he becomes the guilty party in our place—he becomes guilty for us and experiences our guilt. . . . In Christ there is a real transfer of guilt for innocence. Through the oneness of our covenant relationship, my guilt becomes Jesus' guilt, which he experienced and for which he suffered. At the same time, his innocence and perfection become mine, and I am rendered clean and worthy."[15]

- Inequity, inequality, and unfairness (lack of justice).

  "The Savior has suffered not just for our iniquities but also for the inequality, the unfairness, the pain, the anguish, and the emotional distresses that so frequently beset us."[16]

Elder Richard G. Scott said, "The Atonement will not only help us overcome our transgressions and mistakes, but in His time, it will resolve all inequities of life—those things that are unfair which are the consequences of circumstance or others' acts and not our own decisions."[17]

Boyd K. Packer shared the following: "I recently received a letter from a woman who reported having endured great suffering in her life. A terrible wrong, which she did not identify but alluded to, had been committed against her. She admitted that she struggled with feelings of great bitterness. In her anger, she mentally cried out, 'Someone must pay for this terrible wrong.' In this extreme moment of sorrow and questioning, she wrote that there came into her heart an immediate reply, 'Someone already has paid.'"[18]

We have all heard someone say that life is not fair. During mortality, that is certainly the case for many. Life is full of unjust, unfair circumstances and events. That unfairness appears to be part of the plan of this second estate, part of the testing. Because of the Atonement of the Savior there are delayed, future blessings awaiting the faithful that will one day compensate for the unfairness of life. To a group of suffering, persecuted Saints the Prophet Joseph Smith declared, "All of your losses will be made up to you in the resurrection, provided you continue faithful, by the vision of the almighty I have seen it."[19]

Jeffrey R. Holland likewise promised, "Some blessings come soon, some come late, and some don't come until heaven; but for those who embrace the gospel of Jesus Christ, they come."[20] Some of you or those you know and love have, are, or will face unfair, unjust circumstances. Because of the atoning sacrifice of our Savior there are delayed, compensating blessings being held in reserve that will come in a future day.

I recall a time in my life when I felt a terrible injustice had occurred against me. For months, I was upset and struggled with bitter feelings toward an individual. I knew I needed to forgive. I knew what the gospel taught. But try as I would, I could not let it go. I tried and tried. At times I thought I was making progress, but then I would relapse. Letting it completely go seemed to be an impossibility. I struggled and struggled with it. I suffered; I was wounded. I had many conversations with the Lord about it—long conversations with Him in the mountains as I rode my bike. Then the miracle came. After a few months of torment, miraculously one day it happened. The Atonement became intimate and personal. It became real. The bitterness, the hurt feelings, and anger were suddenly gone; they were all taken from me. It was a gift, it was mercy, it was grace. I find it difficult to explain. I don't understand the sacred mechanics of how it works. It just works. I don't know how it happened, but it happened. The Lord, in His goodness, healed me. He helped me let go of the injustice I could not let go of myself.

Boyd K. Packer insightfully taught, "Restoring what you cannot restore, healing the wound you cannot heal, fixing that which you broke, and you cannot fix is the very purpose of the atonement of Christ. When your desire is firm and you are willing to pay the uttermost farthing, the law of restitution is suspended. Your obligation is transferred to the Lord. He will settle your accounts."[21] Christ can fix the unfixable. He can restore the unrestorable and mend the unmendable. Our obligations can be transferred to the Lord. As we come to Him, He will settle our accounts and plead our cause before the Father saying, "Father, spare these my brethren and sisters who believe on my name, that they may have everlasting life" (D&C 45:4–5).

For the faithful, the promise is that the day will come that "God shall wipe away all tears from their eyes, and there shall be no more death, neither sorrow, nor crying, neither shall there be any more pain" (Revelation 21:4). The resurrected Lord asked a distraught Mary Magdalene, "Woman, why weepest thou"? (John 20:15). In an instant, with one word, those tears were wiped away and her pain and anguish were replaced with joy. To the faithful the Savior will "appoint unto them that mourn in Zion, to give unto them beauty for ashes, the oil of joy for mourning, the garment of praise for the spirit of heaviness" (Isaiah 61:3). Such was the case for Mary. It can likewise be for us.

Regarding the unfairness of life, Dale G. Renlund explained,

> If life were truly fair you and I would never be resurrected; you and I would never be able to stand clean before God. In this respect, I am grateful that life is not fair. . . . Because of the Atonement of Jesus Christ, ultimately, in the eternal scheme of things there will be no unfairness. All that is unfair about life can [and will] be made right. Our present circumstances may not change, but through God's compassion and kindness, and love, we will all receive more than we deserve, more than we can ever earn, and more than we can ever hope for.[22]

As we consider the unfairness of life, we can remember that life was never more unfair, never more unjust, than for Jesus. The greatest trials in life seem to be those which are the most unfair and undeserved. The Apostle Paul invited the Hebrew Saints to "consider him that endured such contradiction of sinners" (Hebrews 12:3). They were to remember that the Savior experienced the contradiction of all contradictions. His was an injustice of infinite proportions.

Back to my initial question. In Gethsemane, what exactly was Jesus suffering and paying the price for? In short, anything that could cause us any type of physical, emotional, mental, or spiritual pain, whether related to sin or not.

THE COVER-UP

Satan lost the battle in Gethsemane and on Calvary. Since then he has been involved in the world's greatest cover-up. Satan does not want the results of those events made public. He does not want the ramifications of those results made known. Satan seeks to get all of us to downplay Christ's atoning sacrifice. He strives to get us to undersell, understate, and underestimate the saving power of the Savior's atoning sacrifice. Zenock's people did just that. Zenock prayed, saying, "Thou art angry, O Lord, with this people, because they will not understand thy mercies which thou hast bestowed upon them because of thy Son" (Alma 33:16). When we, like Zenock's people, fail to believe and apply Christ's redeeming merciful power, Heavenly Father is angry with us. "For what doth it profit a man if a gift is bestowed upon him, and he receive not the gift? Behold, he rejoices not in that which is given unto him, neither rejoices in him who is the giver of the gift" (D&C 88:33). How tragic that God so loved the world that He gave His Only Begotten Son, and the world at large is so blind that it does not care to receive and apply the gift. The world as a whole has difficulty seeing through Satan's cover up.

Truman G. Madsen made this comforting observation: "If there are some of you who have been tricked into the conviction that you have gone too far, . . . that you have had the poison of sin which makes it impossible ever again to be what you could have been—then hear me. 'I bear testimony that you cannot sink farther than the light and sweeping intelligence of Jesus Christ can reach. I bear testimony that as long as there is one spark of the will to repent and to reach, He is there. He did not just descend to your condition; he descended *below* it. (D&C 88:6)"[23] In this life, we will never fully comprehend the events that took place in the Garden of Gethsemane with Jesus that Thursday night. Yet we must try and learn to appreciate and apply His atoning sacrifice more and more.

Gospel scholar Stephen E. Robinson beautifully summarized Gethsemane this way:

> All the negative aspects of human existence brought about by the fall, Jesus Christ absorbed into himself. He experienced vicariously in Gethsemane all the private griefs and heartaches, all of the physical pains and handicaps, all of the emotional burdens and depressions of the human family. He knows the loneliness of those who don't fit in, or who aren't handsome or pretty. He knows what it's like to choose up teams and be the last one chosen. He knows the anguish of parents whose children go wrong. He knows these things personally and intimately because he lived them in the Gethsemane experience. Having personally lived a perfect life, he then chose to experience our imperfect lives.
>
> In that infinite Gethsemane experience, He lived a billion, billion lifetimes of sin, pain, disease, and sorrow. God had no magic wand with which to simply wave bad things into non-existence. The sins that he remits, he remits by making them His own and suffering them. The pain and heartache that he relieves, he relieves by suffering them Himself. These things can be transferred, but they cannot be simply wished or waved away. They must be suffered. Thus, we owe Him not only for our spiritual cleansing from sin, but for our physical, mental and emotional healing as well. For He has borne these infirmities for us also. All that the fall put wrong; the Savior in His Atonement puts right. It is all part of His infinite sacrifice, of His infinite gift.[24]

Elder Boyd K. Packer said, "[The Savior's] atoning sacrifice [which began in Gethsemane] was the keystone in the arch of the great plan of the Father. . . . It is the keystone in the arch of our existence. Without it, life is meaningless."[25] The atoning sacrifice of our Savior not only gives meaning to life, but it also gives life to the ordinances and covenants of the gospel. It gives life to every aspect of the plan of salvation. The Atonement of Jesus Christ is not merely a static force in the universe that simply exists, but is an enabling dynamic power that performs a transformational work within willing individuals. It is an active force within cooperating individuals who see through Satan's cover up that will lift, change, and ultimately redeem them.

ENDNOTES

1. S. Kent Brown, et al. *Beholding Salvation: The Life of Christ in Word and Image* (Salt Lake City: Deseret Book, 2006), 67.

2. Dallin H. Oaks, "Sins, Crimes, and Atonement," CES religious educators, Feb. 7, 1992.

3. W. Cleon Skousen, *Days of the Living Christ* (Ensign Publishing Co., 1992/2018), 654–655.

4. B. H Roberts, "The Seventy's Course in Theology, Fourth Year: The Atonement," *Deseret News*, 1911, 128.

5. Ronald E. Poleman, "Divine Forgiveness," October 1993 general conference.

6. After this life, satisfying justice is a different matter. From the Doctrine and Covenants we learn that those who failed to repent apply the Savior's Atonement during their mortal sojourn will suffer as the Savior suffered to appease justice. That is why the telestial candidates will not be resurrected until after the Millennium. They will be suffering and paying the price for their sins in an attempt to satisfy justice (see D&C 19:15–18).

7. Russell M. Nelson, in Handel's Messiah: Debtor's Prison (video), ChurchofJesusChrist.org/media-library.

8. Marion G. Romney, "The Resurrection of Jesus," April 1992 general conference.

9. Boyd K. Packer, "Washed Clean," April 1997 general conference. Gospel scholar Hugh Nibley likewise explained, "Having redeemed them, and satisfied the demands of justice. Then he says, Now can I get them through? . . . So he goes ahead as our sponsor and clears the legal difficulties. There is serious doubt about whether our admission is really justified, so he generously intercedes for us. He breaks the barrier, and then he faces the problem of our legal right to go on. Do we deserve it? No. His argument on our behalf is for mercy and compassion," (*Teachings of the Book of Mormon*, lecture 35, 85). The Prophet Joseph Smith taught, "The great Jehovah contemplated the whole of the events connected with the earth, pertaining to the plan of salvation, before it rolled into existence. . . . He knew of the fall

of Adam, the iniquities of the antediluvians, of the depth of iniquity that would be connected with the human family. . . . He knows the situation of both the living and the dead, and has made ample provision for their redemption, according to their several circumstances, and the laws of the kingdom of God, whether in this world, or in the world to come" (Joseph Smith and Joseph Fielding Smith, *Teachings of the Prophet Joseph Smith* [Salt Lake City: Deseret Book, 1958/1977], 220).

10. According to Brigham Young, had the Savior failed in Gethsemane and refused to obey His Father He would have become a son of perdition (*Journal of Discourses*, vol. 4, *The Editorium*, 2013, 54). See also *Journal of Discourses*, vol. 8, *The Editorium*, 2013, 240; *Journal of Discourses*, vol. 9, *The Editorium*, 2013, 149; *Journal of Discourses*, vol. 10, *The Editorium*, 2013, 324.

11. Neal A. Maxwell, *Lord Increase our Faith* (Salt Lake City: Bookcraft, 1994), 10.

12. "The Living Christ, The Testimony of the Apostles. The Living Christ, The Testimony of the Apostles," The Church of Jesus Christ of Latter-Day Saints, 2000.

13. David A. Bednar, "In the Strength of the Lord," Brigham Young University Idaho devotional, Oct. 23, 2001.

14. Noah Webster, "Succor." *An American Dictionary of the English Language*, 1828.

15. Stephen E. Robinson, "Guilt for Innocence," *The Gift of the Atonement* (Salt Lake City: Deseret Book, 2002), 74–75.

16. David A. Bednar, "The Atonement and the Journey of Mortality," *Ensign*, Apr. 2012.

17. Richard G. Scott, "Jesus Christ, Our Redeemer," April 1997 general conference.

18. Boyd K. Packer, "The Reason for Our Hope," October 2014 general conference.

19. Joseph Smith and Joseph Fielding Smith, *Teachings of the Prophet Joseph Smith* (Salt Lake City: Deseret Book, 1958/1977), 295.

20. Jeffrey R. Holland, "A High Priest of Good Things to Come," October 1999 general conference.

21. Boyd K. Packer, "The Brilliant Morning of Forgiveness," October 1995 general conference.

22. Dale G. Renlund, "That I Might Draw All Men unto Me," April 2016 general conference.

23. Truman G. Madsen, *Christ and the Inner Life* (Salt Lake City: Bookcraft, 1978), 14.

24. Stephen Edward Robinson, *Believing Christ: The Parable of the Bicycle and Other Good News* (Salt Lake City: Deseret Book), 1992.

25. Gordon B. Hinckley, *Teachings of the Presidents of the Church: Gordon B. Hinckley* (The Church of Jesus Christ of Latter-Day Saints, 2016), 331.

CHAPTER 5

LEAVING GETHSEMANE: THE BETRAYAL

I was priced at . . . thirty pieces of silver" (Zechariah 11:13). Thirty pieces of silver was the price Judas accepted to betray Jesus. It was the going rate for the price of a slave. The chief priests had the entire temple treasury at their disposal. They could have easily given a thousand silver pieces or more for the betrayal. Judas had not come to haggle but to betray. Elder Talmage explained that before Judas sold Christ to the Jews, he first had to sell himself to the devil; he had become Satan's serf, and did his master's bidding.[1] Elder Jeffry R. Holland said, "Never in the history of this world has so little money purchased so much infamy. We are not the ones to judge Judas's fate, but Jesus said of His betrayer, 'Good, were it for that man if he had not been born.'"[2]

John records, "Judas having received a band of men and officers from the chief priests and Pharisees, cometh thither with lanterns and torches and weapons" (John 18:3). They had come to Gethsemane to take Jesus. Judas, standing in Satan's stead, was at the head of this band of men. Or should we say mob? Yes, a mob, which was composed of the chief priest, officers, elders, Pharisees, temple guards, and a contingent of Roman soldiers armed with swords and staves.

The word "band" found in John 18:3 means a "cohort." It is probable that a Roman cohort consisted of some six hundred Roman soldiers. Accompanying the soldiers was a great multitude, perhaps thousands in number.[3] Why so many? They were taking no chances of an uproar. Such an army could not have moved without the prior approval of the Roman procurator, Pontius Pilate.

The Apostle John wrote, "Jesus therefore knowing all things that should come upon him *went forth*" (John 18:4; emphasis added). Matthew likewise taught that after His suffering in Gethsemane, Jesus said to His disciples, "Rise, let us be going; behold, he is at hand that doth betray me" (Matthew 26:46). With Jesus there was no hesitation. With total awareness of what lay ahead, He *went forth,* not waiting for the band of men to approach Him. Jesus fearlessly confronted them.

Commenting on this verse in Matthew, Adam Clarke explained, "That is, to meet them, giving thereby the fullest proof that I know all their designs, and might have, by flight or otherwise, provided for my own safety; but I go willingly to meet that death which their malice designs me, and through it, provide for the life of the world."[4] We should note that the Savior in Gethsemane had just suffered for the sins these individuals were about to commit, including Judas's. He certainly knew what was going to happen.

In Jesus's day, it was the custom to greet friends and guests with a kiss on the cheek. Such greetings were a symbol of respect, particularly between a pupil and rabbi. A kiss communicated both brotherhood and friendship. Judas kissed Jesus to single Him out, so the band of men would know who to arrest. Biblical scholar Alfred Edersheim explained, "The Greek text conveys that Judas not only kissed Him, but covered Him with kisses, kissed Him repeatedly, loudly, diffusively."[5] Such a kiss in public was unusual. The greeting itself was an insult; a disciple was never permitted to greet his teacher before his teacher greeted him. A greeting initiated by a disciple implied that the two were equal. Never were two further apart. Jesus determined to do the will of His Father, the Father of lights. Judas determined to do the will of his father, the father of lies.

Following the kiss, "Jesus said unto him, Friend" (Matthew 26:50). Clarke says this should be translated, "Companion, wherefore against whom art thou come?" Clarke then adds, "How must these words have cut his very soul, if he had any sensibility left!

Surely, thou, who hast so long been my companion, art not come against me, thy Lord, Teacher and Friend!"[6]

"Jesus said unto him, Friend" (Matthew 26:50). Even as Judas betrayed Him, the Savior reached out to him as His friend and His companion. The Savior loved Judas to the very end, giving him every opportunity to turn back from his course. Among the ancient Israelites, a kiss often signified reconciliation between separated or estranged parties. For Judas there would be no reconciliation.

Classical scholar Edith Hamilton observed, "When love meets no return, the result is suffering, and the greater the love the greater the suffering. There can be no greater suffering than to love purely and perfectly one who is bent on evil and self-destruction. That was what God endured at the hands of men."[7] Neal A. Maxwell has added, "Many parents and some spouses love and care but experience unreciprocated love. This is part of coming to know, on our small scale, what Jesus experienced."[8] Jesus was betrayed by one of those closest to Him, by one who He had spent nearly three years with in countless intimate personal settings. Jesus was betrayed by one whom He had repeatedly taught, prayed for, served, and patiently loved (see Luke 22:47, 48). Judas's refusal to receive Christ's love added to His suffering.

THE SAVIOR AND REJECTION

Isaiah wrote, "He is despised and rejected of men" (Isaiah 53:3). As we consider the Savior's mortal ministry, we find again and again the fulfillment of that prophecy. The following are just a few examples:

- Following the first year of His ministry, Jesus returned to His hometown of Nazareth. It was a homecoming of sorts. His fame had preceded Him. Jesus returned to the synagogue where He had worshiped for almost thirty years. Following His teachings, He was surrounded by those of His hometown community, thrust out of the city, and taken to the brow of a hill where they attempted to cast Him down headlong.

- At the conclusion of His 'Bread of Life' sermon, "many of his disciples went back and walked no more with him" (John 6:66).
- The majority of the Apostles fled the night of His betrayal (Matthew 26:56).
- Peter denied knowing Him three times.
- His own brothers and sisters rejected Him (John 7:5, Matthew 13:57).
- The prophet Nephi saw in vision a portion of the Savior's mortal ministry. Nephi wrote, "I beheld that he went forth ministering unto the people . . . and the multitudes were gathered together to hear him: and I beheld that they cast him out from among them" (1Nephi 11:28).
- In this dispensation, Jesus declared, "I came unto my own, and mine own received me not" (D&C 45:8). Jesus not only was completely rejected by the leading, influential Jews of His day, but as Nephi taught, multitudes of the common people rejected Him. Abinadi likewise explained that Jesus was "cast out, and disowned by *his people*" (Mosiah 15:5; emphasis added). Jesus was disowned by the Jews from the House of Israel from whom He came.
- In the future when the Savior returns and stands on the Mount of Olives and delivers the Jews from their enemies, they will see the marks in His hands, feet, and side, and ask, "What are these wounds?" The Savior will reply, "These are the wounds with which I was wounded in the house of my friends" (D&C 45:52, Zechariah 12:10).

"He *is* despised and rejected of men, a man of sorrows, and acquainted with grief; and we hid as it were our face from him; He *was* despised and we esteemed him not" (Isaiah 53:3; emphasis added). A close look at this verse reveals that Isaiah not only used the past tense, "*was* despised," but he also used the present tense, "*is* despised." At times the Savior is still presently despised and rejected. When we sin, when we fail to choose Him, to some degree He is despised and rejected. At times we all hide our faces from Him.

Every human being who has ever been born onto this earth at times forgets and overlooks the Savior. "All we like sheep have gone astray" (Isaiah 53:4). Jesus knows rejection in the ultimate sense.

If we are to become like the Savior, we likewise may experience some rejection before our mortal life is over. As we talk of Christ and take His message to the world, some "will cast us out from among them." What prophet, what missionary has not, on a much smaller scale, at times been "despised and rejected of men?" If the days come when we experience rejection, we can take heart and know that we are in good company; such is the path of Christian discipleship.

Judas not only rejected Jesus but also brought an armed cohort to Gethsemane to kill Him. "Jesus therefore knowing all things that should come upon him, went forth, and said unto them, Whom seek ye? They answered him, Jesus of Nazareth. Jesus saith unto them, *I am he*" (John 18:4–5; emphasis added). The last word, "he," was later added to this verse. It is not used in the earliest translations that are available. The Savior identified Himself to the band of men as "I AM." Jesus used "I AM" as a divine name, equivalent to Jehovah. The title I AM was how the Lord revealed Himself to Moses when Moses received his commission go into Egypt. "I AM" in Hebrew literally means Jehovah. In this instance before His captors the Savior openly declared that He was Jehovah, the God of the Old Testament.

As the band of men approached and heard Jesus boldly declare His divinity, "they went backward and fell to the ground" (John 18:6). Remember, the arresting party possibly numbered 600 or more. Picture that scene in your mind—all 600 men falling backward to the ground as Jesus declared Himself to be Jehovah.

It was not just what Jesus said but most likely how He said it (the Spirit accompanying His words) that made them fall to the ground. The armed cohort stood in awe of Jesus. His divine presence was more than they were ready to face. Farrar wrote, "Those quiet words ['I Am'] produced a sudden paroxysm of amazement and dread. That answer so gentle had in it a strength greater than the eastern wind, or the voice of thunder, for God was in that still voice and it struck them down to the ground."⁹ Jesus made it clear that He could not be arrested unless He permitted it. Clarke explained, "Our Lord chose to give them this proof of his infinite power, that they might know that their power could not prevail against him if he chose to exert his might, seeing that the very breath of his mouth confounded, drove back, and struck them down to the earth. Thus, by the blast of God they might have perished, and by the breath of his nostrils they might have been consumed."¹⁰

As they attempted to apprehend the Savior, Peter "stretched out his hand, and drew his sword, and struck a servant of the high priest's, and smote off his ear" (Matthew 26:51). The Savior responded, "Thinkest thou that I cannot now pray to my father, and he shall presently give me more than twelve legions of angels" (Matthew 26:53). In the first century Roman Judea, the chief subdivision of the imperial army was a legion, a unit composed of up to 6,000–foot soldiers, plus cavalry. Twelve legions would thus equal 72,000 heavenly warriors. It should be remembered that one angel in the book of Kings slew 185,000 Assyrian warriors as they threatened the city of Jerusalem in 701 B.C. (see 2 Kings 19:35). Jesus had infinite power and command at His disposal. Jesus made it clear to His disciples and to all of those present that He could not be arrested or taken without His consent. His life could not be shed unless He willed it. His was to be a voluntary, free will offering.

Gerald N. Lund explained,

> Imagine the Being whose power, whose light, whose glory holds the universe in order, the Being who speaks and solar systems, galaxies, and stars come into existence—standing before wicked men and being judged by them as being of no worth or value! When Judas led the soldiers and the high priest to the Garden of Gethsemane and betrayed [Jesus] with a kiss, Jesus could have spoken a single word and leveled the entire city of Jerusalem. When the servant of the high priest stepped forward and slapped his face, Jesus could have lifted a finger and sent that man back to his original elements. When another man stepped forward and spit in his face, Jesus had only to blink and our entire solar system could have been annihilated. But he stood there, he endured, he suffered, he condescended.¹¹

The Savior meekly submitted to His Father's will and allowed Himself to be taken. Bruce R. McConkie explained that Jesus was then "led away with a rope around his neck, as a common criminal."[12] The use of such a rope fulfilled the type established by the scapegoat in the law of Moses. On the Day of Atonement, the sins of the people were transferred to the head of the scapegoat. The goat was then led with a noose around its neck outside the city walls and set free in the wilderness and left there to perish (see Leviticus 16:21–22).

HIS DISCIPLES FLEE

The record states that as Jesus was taken away, "all of the disciples forsook him and fled" (Matthew 26:56), fulfilling the words Jesus had spoken to His disciples just hours earlier following the Last Supper: "All ye shall be offended because of me this night" (Matthew 26:31). The disciples fleeing also fulfilled the prophecy of Zechariah that the "shepherd would be smitten and the sheep scattered" (Zechariah 13:7). "Thus, of divine necessity, the supporting circle around Jesus gets smaller and smaller and smaller."[13]

Jesus was not the only one in danger that night. The Apostles themselves were also in danger of arrest. It is possible that had any of the Eleven been apprehended with Jesus and made to share the cruel abuse and torturing humiliation of the next few hours, their faith may have failed them, relatively immature and untried as it then was.[14]

As the mob came to arrest Jesus, He said to them, "Let these [my disciples] go their way" (John 18:8). Clarke explained,

> These words are rather words of authority, than words of entreaty. I voluntarily give myself up to you, but you must not molest one of these my disciples. At your peril injure them. Let them go about their business. I have already given you a sufficient proof of my power: I will not exert it in my own behalf, for I will lay down my life for the sheep; but I will not permit you to injure the least of these [their work is not done]. It was certainly the supreme power of Christ that kept the soldiers and the mob from destroying all the disciples present, when Peter had given them such provocation, in cutting off the ear of Malchus.[15]

Elder Jams E. Talmage added, "All the eleven forsook Him and fled. This was not to be accounted as certain evidence of cowardice, for the Lord had indicated that they should go."[16]

That their danger was real is seen in the fact that there was then present in Gethsemane "a certain young man [most likely John Mark], a disciple, having a linen cloth cast about his naked body" (JST, Mark 14:51–52). Judas most likely had first led the band of men to the home of John Mark (or his parents) where the Last Supper had been served. John Mark may have been roused by the armed cohort and then followed them to Gethsemane in an attempt to warn Jesus. He did not arrive in time. When the soldiers laid hold on him and tried to arrest him, he left the linen cloth and fled from them, saving himself out of their hands.

PETER'S DENIAL

Following the Last Supper, during His farewell discourse, Jesus said to His disciples, "Little children, yet a little while I am with you. Ye shall seek me: and as I said unto the Jews, Wither I go, ye cannot come. . . . Simon Peter said unto him, Lord, whither goest thou? Jesus answered him, Whither I go, thou canst not follow me now; but thou shalt follow me afterwards. Peter said unto him, Lord, why cannot I follow thee now? I will lay down my life for thy sake. Jesus answered him, will thou lay down thy life for my sake? Verily, verily, I say unto thee, the cock shall not crow, till thou hast denied me thrice" (John 13:33,36–38). Peter not only was troubled by that prophecy, but he completely rejected it. "But he [Peter] spake the more vehemently, If I should die with thee, I will not deny thee in any wise" (Mark 14:31).

Much has been written and said concerning Peter's triple denial. The debate continues on whether the Savior's comments were either a prediction or an actual command. Denying Christ goes against everything we know about Peter and his character. He was never one to shrink from danger. In Gethsemane as the band of men had approached to arrest the Savior, Peter without hesitation drew his sword and cut off the ear of Malchus, the servant of the high priest (see John 18:10). Despite being severely outnumbered, Peter was willing to take on all comers, in defense of the Master.

Some have suggested that perhaps the Apostles had been encouraged in their flight from the garden. They needed to live; their work was not done. Jesus may have known that Peter's reckless behavior would cost him his life if it were not tempered. Spencer W. Kimball surmised, "It is possible that there might have been some other reason for Peter's triple denial? Could he have felt that circumstances justified expediency?"[17] Elder Jeffrey R. Holland commenting on the event said, "We don't know all that was going on here, nor do we know of protective counsel which the Savior may have given to His Apostles."[18]

Gospel scholars Kelley Ogden and Andrew Skinner have explained, "It is possible to read the Greek text of the Savior's declaration to Peter about the latter's forthcoming denial as a request or instructional command rather than a prediction. . . . The Greek text indicates that Peter may have been told to deny being associated with the Savior."[19] Again, without some specific direction from the Savior, impetuous Peter may have recklessly laid down his life. He needed to live to be a witness of the remaining events in the life of Jesus and to lead the future Church. His work was not done. The statement given to Peter by the Savior to deny Him may have been a command.

On the other hand, maybe Peter in a moment of weakness just fell short. Over the years, as I have studied the account I lean toward that conclusion. It is important to make the distinction that Peter did not deny Jesus in the sense of denying that He was the Christ, the Son of God. Rather, he denied knowing Him, as in associating with Him. In other words, he temporarily denied their friendship.

Of the denial Elder Theodore M. Burton said,

> I personally believe this was the beginning of the conversion of Peter. Up to this time Peter had never questioned his own ability to cleave to truth. He was an honest man by nature and felt the strength that honesty gives a man. Perhaps, as so many of us, he lacked humility. As a result of this experience, however, he learned humility. There is no question of his remorse, for he wept

bitterly at his own weakness. I feel, however, that a great change began to work in Peter, beginning with this knowledge of his own weakness.[20]

In a moment of weakness, Peter fell short. There are numerous lessons we can learn from him. One lesson is that people can change. President Spencer W. Kimball said, "If Peter was cowardly, how brave he became in so short a time. If he was weak and vacillating, how strong and positive he became in weeks and months. If he was unkind, how tender and sympathetic he became almost immediately."[21]

We learn that prophets and leaders of this Church are not perfect. With all of Peter's shortcomings and weaknesses, the Savior still had given Peter all of the keys necessary to lead His Church and kingdom. Despite Peter's imperfections, the Lord trusted him. Like Peter, we do not have to be perfect to be an instrument in God's hands. We just need to be worthy and clean. What qualifies one to be worthy? Repentance. Peter repented.

President Lorenzo Snow taught,

[Peter] proved himself unequal for the trial; but afterwards he gained power. . . . And if we could read in detail the life of Abraham, or the lives of other great and holy men, we would doubtless find that their efforts to be righteous were not always crowned with success. Hence, we should not be discouraged if we should be overcome in a weak moment; but on the contrary, straightway repent of the error or the wrong we have committed and as far as possible repair it, and then seek to God for renewed strength to go on and do better.[22]

President Gordon B. Hinckley similarly taught,

My heart goes out to Peter. So many of us are so much like him. We pledge our loyalty; we affirm our determination to be of good courage; we declare, sometimes even publicly, that come what may we will do the right thing, that we will stand for the right cause, that we will be true to ourselves and to others. Then the pressures begin to build. Sometimes these are social pressures. Sometimes they are personal appetites. Sometimes they are false ambitions. There is a weakening of the will. There is a softening of discipline. . . . And then there is remorse, followed by self-accusations and bitter tears of regret. . . . If there be those throughout the Church who by word or act have denied the faith, I pray that you may draw comfort and resolution from the example of Peter, who, though he had walked daily with Jesus, in an hour of extremity momentarily denied the Lord and also the testimony which he carried in his own heart. But he rose above this and became a mighty defender and a powerful advocate. So, too, there is a way for any person to turn about and add his or her strength and faith to the strength and faith of others in building the kingdom of God.[23]

Additionally, Spencer W. Kimball has written, "I do not pretend to know what Peter's mental reactions were nor what compelled him to say what he did that terrible night. But in light of his proven bravery, courage, great devotion, and limitless love for the Master, could we not give him the benefit of the doubt and at least forgive him as his Savior seems to have done so fully. Almost immediately Christ elevated him to the highest position in his church and endowed him with the complete keys of that kingdom."[24]

The Savior did not condemn Peter but forgave him. So, like the Savior and President Kimball, let's give Peter the benefit of the doubt. His example serves as an encouraging model for all of us.

Years later Luke wrote of Peter, "They brought forth the sick into the streets, and laid them on beds and couches, that at the least the shadow of Peter passing by might overshadow some of them . . . and they were healed every one" (Acts 5:15–16). Commenting on this verse Jeffrey R. Holland has written, "One wonders if there is a single written line in any other record that stands as a greater monument to the faith and power of one mortal man bearing the holy priesthood of God."[25]

Peter was a man with weaknesses and faults like the rest of us. At times he failed. He was foolish, impetuous, overzealous, and even ignorant. He spoke occasionally without thinking. He was certainly fallible. I believe the Gospel writers were inspired and chose to deliberately include his shortcomings in their records. Mark's writings are the memoirs of Peter. Peter commissioned Luke to write. Peter may have instructed Mark and Luke to include his shortcomings in their writings.

At the end of the day, Peter's faithfulness and his faith in Christ was greater than His failings. Through the grace of Christ, through the enabling power of the Atonement, Peter became one of the greatest men who ever walked the earth. Peter's transformation was remarkable. He is one of my heroes. His life gives me hope, that in spite of my numerous shortcomings, over time I can be transformed. Borrowing from the words of the Prophet Joseph Smith, I can become a "smooth and polished shaft in the quiver of the Almighty."[26]

Regardless of what Peter may or may not have done, it is what he went on to do and who he became afterwards that really matters. So, it is in our lives. In our dispensation the Lord once said of Oliver Granger, "When he falls, he shall rise again" (D&C 117:13). When we fall and are overcome in a moment of weakness we, like Oliver, can make the choice to not be overcome with discouragement but *rise again* and seek the mercy and help of the Master. And then like Peter we go on to do good and become a more dedicated disciple. Jesus changed Peter. He can change us too.

Dieter F. Uchtdorf admonished us, "Remember, that disciple-ship is not about doing things perfectly. . . . Even when you fail, you can choose not to give up, but rather discover your courage, press forward and rise up. That is the great test of the journey."[27] Peter would go on to pass that test.

This was not the first time that one of the disciples were afraid to confess Christ before the people. The Joseph Smith Translation of Luke 12:9–11 adds an important insight. In these verses the Savior said to the Twelve:

> But he who denieth me before men shall be denied before the angels of God. Now his disciples knew that he said this because they had spoken evil against him before the people; for they were afraid to confess him before men. And they reasoned among themselves, saying, He knoweth our hearts, and he speaketh to our condemnation, and we shall not be forgiven. . . . But he

answered them, and said unto them, Whosoever, shall speak a word against the Son of man, and repenteth, it shall be forgiven him; but unto him who blasphemeth against the Holy Ghost it shall not be forgiven him.

It appears the majority of the Apostles at one point or another had struggled with public opinion. They were not only afraid to confess Jesus before men but had even spoken evil of Him. The Savior did not condemn them but gave them hope by offering them the gift of repentance. All but Judas would eventually embrace that gift and would change and become mighty defenders of Christ and His cause.

ENDNOTES

1. James E. Talmage, Jesus the Christ (Salt Lake City: Deseret Book, 1915/1982), 592.
2. Jeffrey R. Holland, "None Were with Him," April 2009 general conference.
3. Bruce R. McConkie, *Doctrinal New Testament Commentary*. Vol. 1 (Salt Lake City: Bookcraft, 1965), 781.
4. Adam Clarke, *The New Testament of Our Lord and Saviour Jesus Christ* (Abingdon), 259.
5. Alfred Edersheim, *The Life and Times of Jesus the Messiah*. Vol. 2 (Eerdmans Pub. Co., 1971), 543.
6. Adam Clarke, *The New Testament of Our Lord and Saviour Jesus Christ* (Abingdon), 259.
7. Edith Hamilson, *Spokesmen for God: The Great Teachers of the Old Testament* (W. W. Norton, 1994), 112.
8. Neal A. Maxwell, "O How Great the Plan of Our God!" Address to CES Religious Educators, Feb. 3, 1995.
9. Frederic W. Farrar, *The Life of Christ* (Salt Lake City: Bookcraft, 1995), 584.
10. Adam Clarke, *The New Testament of Our Lord and Saviour Jesus Christ* (Abingdon), 642.
11. Gerald N. Lund, 'Knowest Thou the Condescension of God?" *Doctrines of the Book of Mormon* (Salt Lake City: Deseret Book, 1992), 86. "Fathom, if you can, the powers Jesus had at his command. How pitifully futile the might of Pilate's Roman garrison would have been in the face of the twelve heavenly legions Christ could have summoned but didn't. How easy it would have been for the one who cast out devils to banish the arrogant high priest. How elementary for one who loosed the tongues of the dumb to stop the tongues of false witnesses. Yet he who brought worlds and galaxies into being stood mute

before his mortal accusers. He who stilled the rushing winds and pounding waves of the Sea of Galilee stilled not the stormy cries of 'Crucify him! Crucify him!' He who had escaped unharmed from the angry mob at Nazareth (see Luke 4:29–30) faced the small band of arresting soldiers with a simple 'I am he' (John 18:5). The awesome, infinite power at his command was not unleashed to spare himself the least pain, the smallest discomfort. His will was irrevocably interwoven with that of the Father's, and nothing deterred him from its accomplishment" (Gerald N. Lund, *Selected Writings of Gerald N. Lund* [Salt Lake City: Deseret Book, 1999], 308).

12. Bruce R. McConkie, "The Purifying Power of Gethsemane," April 1985 general conference.
13. Jeffrey R. Holland, "None Were with Him," April 2009 general conference.
14. James E. Talmage, *Jesus the Christ* (Salt Lake City: Deseret Book, 1915/1982), 615.
15. Adam Clarke, *The New Testament of Our Lord and Saviour Jesus Christ* (Abingdon), 642.
16. James E. Talmage, *Jesus the Christ* (Salt Lake City: Deseret Book, 1915/1982), 629.
17. Spencer W. Kimball, "Peter, My Brother," BYU devotional, July 13, 1971.
18. Jeffrey R. Holland, "None Were with Him," April 2009 general conference.
19. D. Kelly Ogden and Andrew C. Skinner. *Verse by Verse, Acts through Revelation* (Salt Lake City: Deseret Book, 2006), 39.
20. Theodore M. Burton, "Convince or Convert?" BYU devotional, Oct. 6, 1964.
21. Spencer W. Kimball, "Peter, My Brother," BYU devotional, July 13, 1971.
22. Lorenzo Snow, "Blessings of the Gospel Only Obtained by Compliance with the Law," *Journal of Discourses*, 20th ed., Vol, 190.
23. Gordon B. Hinckley, "And Peter Went Out and Wept Bitterly," April 1975 general conference.
24. Spencer W. Kimball, "Peter, My Brother," BYU devotional, July 13, 1971.
25. Jeffrey R. Holland, "The Lengthening Shadow of Peter," *Ensign*, Sept. 1975.
26. Joseph Smith and Joseph Fielding Smith, *Teachings of the Prophet Joseph Smith* (Salt Lake City: Deseret Book, 1958/1977), 304.
27. Dieter F. Uchtdorf, "Your Great Adventure," October 2019 general conference.

CHAPTER 6

FROM THE ILLEGAL TRIALS TO THE CROSS

nd Simon Peter followed Jesus, and so did another disciple . . . and went in with Jesus into the palace of the high priest" (John 18:15). Peter and presumably John the Beloved followed Jesus and the arresting party, from a distance. Why was it important that two disciples follow? To fulfill the law of witnesses. These were some of the most important events that would ever occur, there had to be witnesses to record and later declare it.

Following Gethsemane, the Savior was taken and tried before Annas, Caiaphas, the Sanhedrin, Pilate, Herod, and then back to Pilate. It is interesting to note that the Gospel of Matthew implies that Judas was at some of the initial hearings (see Matthew 27:2–3). Judas was apparently concerned with the final outcome of his betrayal.

Jesus's arresters came out against Him, according to the Greek, as "against a robber" (see (Matthew 26:55, Mark 14:48 and Luke 22:52). Robbers were outlaws who were given virtually no legal rights by the ruling establishment. Such was the case for Jesus.

The trials that Jesus was subjected to were marked with injustice, torture, and humiliation. He was repeatedly beaten. He was stripped of His clothing, mocked, and spit upon. With venom in their mouths, His accusers verbally abused and lied about Him. What added to the injustice was that not only was Jesus not afforded His legal rights, but the arrest and trials themselves were completely illegal.[1]

Gerald Lund explained,

The men who had Jesus put to death were the "spiritual leaders" of Judaism. . . . These men used the law, the very law they claimed so scrupulously to obey, as the weapon to kill Jesus. Even as they swelled with righteous indignation and cried that they were protecting the law from this blasphemous man, they violated that law in a dozen ways. . . . Over and over again the leaders of Judaism trampled the law under foot in order to achieve their objective. And yet, even as they did so, they were adhering to other parts of the law with meticulous exactness.[2]

Walter M. Chandler, a member of the New York city bar, in his two volume treatise, *The Trial of Jesus from a Lawyers Standpoint*, has written: "The pages of human history present no stronger case of judicial murder than the trial and crucifixion of Jesus of Nazareth, for the simple reason that all forms of law were outraged and trampled under-foot in the proceedings instituted against him."[3] In reality there were no real trials in the case of Jesus! Once again, there is nothing we can tell Him of injustice and unfairness.

"It might well be stated as a rule of human nature that when a man reaches his greatest extremity, a moment of extreme danger, pain, emotion, or critical need, a point in life which is marked by imminent destruction or death, the true nature of his soul becomes evident. . . . During the most trying and difficult circumstances of life, an individual's words mirror his innermost soul. His speech [reveals] what his character is really like—the quality of his concerns, his compassion, his love—the whole focus or thrust of his life, whether noble or mean, depraved or exalted."[4]

We learn so much about the Savior's character as He is taken and tried and tortured before these wicked men. Through it all Jesus remained meek and submissive. He was poised in the face of provocation. He remained fully composed and He never once lost control of Himself or the situation.

Spencer W. Kimball taught,

In quiet, restrained, divine dignity he stood when they cast their spittle in his face. He remained composed. Not an angry word escaped his lips. They slapped his face and beat his body. Yet he stood resolute, unintimidated. He who created the world and all that is in it, he who made the silver from which the pieces were stamped which bought him, he who could command defenders on both sides of the veil—stood and suffered. What dignity! What mastery! What control! Though pronounced innocent, he was scourged. Unworthy men lashed him. . . . One word from his lips and all his enemies would have fallen to the earth, helpless. All would have perished . . . Yet in calmness, he suffered. . . . With a reed in his hand, a scarlet robe over his shoulders, and a crown of thorns on his head, he was made to suffer indignity: they laughed and mocked and jeered and challenged him. Taking the read from his hand, they would strike him on the head. Yet he stood there, the model of long-suffering.[5]

What would have happened if Jesus was impatient and reacted poorly in just one of these trying situations? What would have happened if the Savior had sinned just once during His mortal life? The entire plan of salvation would have been frustrated and Satan would have won. For justice to be completely satisfied, Jesus needed to be a pure, perfect sacrifice. The Atonement had to be performed by one who was sinless—by one who was perfectly obedient to the laws of God (see 1 John 3:5). Our salvation rested upon His entire life, His every action, His every word, and every thought. Frederic Farrar said, "It is a serious error to separate, or rather isolate, the death of Christ from all His life, as though on His death alone and not on His Incarnation and His whole life depended the work of our salvation."[6]

Bruce D. Porter likewise explained, "The cruelties and indignities suffered by Jesus during the various trials represented a last-ditch effort by Lucifer to cause Christ to stumble. A single misstep—a cross word, an angry outburst, even a moment's indulgence in self-pity or pride—and all was lost. Hence every possible indignity was heaped upon the Savior: false accusations, blasphemous outbursts; a crown of thorns; the horrible scourging . . . the mock robe of royalty; the spitting, taunting, and physical blows of the soldiers. The whole pitiable drama was masterminded by Lucifer in the hope that he might yet find a way to nullify the Redeemer's triumph at Geth-semane."[7] Again and again Jesus was the perfect model of long-suf-fering and patience. In baseball terms it was the ninth inning with two outs and two strikes. Time was running out for Satan to turn Jesus from His foreordained mission.

THREE ILLEGAL JEWISH TRIALS

Jesus was subject to three illegal Jewish trials. First, He was taken before Hanan Annas, an adulterous Jew, a former high priest. The name of Hanan means "merciful"—the exact opposite of the man's real nature. In all of Israel there was not a more wicked man than Annas. He was possibly the wealthiest Sadducee of his day, receiving immense revenues derived from the temple booths. He was the most influential and best-known Jew in all of Israel. Although he was no longer the high priest, he continued to direct all of the major affairs of his people.

He had held the office of high priest for only six or seven years; but it was filled by at least five of his sons, by his son-in-law Caiaphas, and by a grandson. Hanan continued to enjoy all the dignity, power, and influence of the office high priest since those closest to him held the office after him. While they acted publicly, Hanan, behind the scenes, directed the affairs, without either the responsibility or the restraints which the office imposed. Farrar writes, "If there were one man who was more guilty than any other of the death of Jesus, the man was Hanan."[8]

One main reason Hanan Annas and his fellow Sadducees raged against the Savior was that Hanan controlled the temple funds. His-torians claim that moneychangers paid a percentage of their profits to Hanan. Jesus was an economic threat to them. Their craft was in danger. Jesus had hurt the thriving business enterprises that poured the wealth of the world into their pockets. The Savior had cleansed the temple twice now. The "Mahan" principle, "to get gain," by sinful means, first used by Cain was at the heart of the conspiracy (see Moses 5:31).

Susan Easton Black wrote, "Annas was not aloof from the other events that led to the death of Jesus. It is assumed that he went with the guards to the palace of Caiaphas and later with the guards to the Antonia Fortress. It is further assumed that he lent his influence and prestige at each trial in support of the conviction and death of Jesus."[9]

Having failed to elicit any incriminating evidence against Jesus, Annas sent Jesus bound to his son-in-law, Joseph Caiaphas, the high priest. Caiaphas, with the coordinated effort of the Pharisees, Sadducees, and Sanhedrin found false witnesses to testify against Jesus.

The perjured words of the false witnesses included statements such as, "We heard him say, I will destroy this temple that is made with hands, and within three days I will build another made without hands" (Mark 14:58). Although many of the Jewish leaders knew the true meaning of the statement, they claimed ignorance and reasoned the temple had been under construction for forty-six years and was far from finished. This fantastic claim would indicate to the Romans that Jesus would rally the people around Him in a revolt that would destroy the peace of the land. Jesus was charged with sedition. They claimed He was a disturber of the peace.

To all of their false accusations Jesus "held his peace" (Mark 14:61). They could arouse no response from Him. Reduced to utter despair and fury, Caiaphas threateningly exclaimed, "I adjure Thee by the living God to tell us whether thou art the Christ, the Son of God?" (Matthew 26:63). To such a question, Jesus could not be silent. He responded in the affirmative, *"I AM: and ye shall see the Son of Man sitting on the right hand of power and coming in the clouds of heaven"* (Mark 14:62, Mathew 26:64; emphasis added). The Savior chose His words very carefully. He referred to Himself once again as "I AM," testifying of His divinity. At this moment Jesus taught us that there are times, regardless of the repercussions, when we are to lift up our voices and testify of the truth.

Jesus had once again openly declared Himself to be Jehovah, and those present clearly understood it. Caiaphas's immediate response was, "BLASPHEMY!" The Sanhedrin followed with the cry, "He is worthy of death!" (JST, Matthew 26:65–66). Jesus was charged with blasphemy. Falsely claiming the power of God was the most serious charge in Jewish law.

Sadly, many of them had just watched Jesus heal the ear of Malchus and had felt of His power as they fell to the ground when He approached and spoke to them in Gethsemane. Regardless of the recent proof, He was regarded by them as a heretic, and according to their law, was liable to death by stoning. "Thus, one of the greatest ironies in history occurred, for Jesus, the divine Son of God, the one person who could not have been guilty of falsely assuming the power of God, was found guilty of blasphemy! Also, the only person since the fall of Adam who had power over physical death was condemned to die!"[10]

Jesus was then taken before the Sanhedrin for a formal trial. The Sanhedrin, the political and religious ruling body of the day, held almost absolute power among the people. They had their own police force and could arrest on both civil and criminal charges. They could pass and impose judgment for anything that they considered to be wrongdoing. Nevertheless, they had a few restrictions. Only by a full session of the entire Sanhedrin could Jesus be legally condemned to die, and under Roman rule, the Sanhedrin had limited authority to execute a judgment of death.

Jesus was taken through the courtyard to the guardroom. There, they spit in His face, smote Him with rods, and struck Him with their closed fists and with their open palms. Mark records, "And *some* began to spit on him, and to cover his face, and to buffet him, and to say unto him, Prophesy: and the servants did strike him with the palms of their hands" (Mark 14:65; emphasis added). Matthew writes, "Then did *they* spit in his face" (Matthew 26:67; emphasis added). Matthew's account omits Mark's use of the word *some.* Who were the *they* to whom Matthew refers to? The Jewish leaders themselves personally were involved with the physical abuse of Jesus, something neither Pilate nor Herod are reported to have done.

The wicked Sanhedrin invented a demonic sort of game. Covering Jesus's eyes, they hit Him again and again, repeating the question, "Prophesy to us, O Messiah, who is it that smote thee" (Matthew 26:68). This violent episode fulfilled Isaiah's messianic prophecy: "I gave my back to the smiters, and my cheeks to them that plucked off the hair: I hid not my face from shame and spitting" (Isaiah 50:6). Earlier Jesus had taught, "But I say unto you, . . . whosoever shall smite thee on the right cheek, turn to him the other also" (Matthew 5:29). The Savior, being our exemplar, perfectly lived what He had taught.

Ironically, at the very moment when Jesus was mocked by the Sanhedrin and challenged to prophecy, the cock was crowing, and His prophecies were coming true. Peter had just denied Him. As noted, the Savior had earlier prophesied, "Before the cock crow twice thou shalt deny me thrice" (Mark 14:72).

We should note that according to rabbinic law, unclean birds were forbidden in Jerusalem. To touch such birds in the Holy City subjected a Jew to Levitical defilement. Yet the Gospel of John claims that Peter's three denials ended just as the cock crowed. Peter may not have heard a rooster crow. It may have been bugle notes coming from the Antonia Fortress. The notes signaled a change of the Roman guard and the close of the third watch. The third Roman watch was called *cockcrow* and ended at three in the morning.[11]

Just after the cock crowed, the Lord turned from His tormentors and looked upon Peter. "And Peter remembered the word of the Lord, how he had said unto him, Before the cock crow, thou shalt deny me thrice" (Luke 22:61). With one look, one glance of the piercing eye of the Almighty God, Jesus had communicated the sermon of a lifetime to Peter. Peter was not insulated, as we are, by the veil. His failure was immediately rebuked by one divine glance. And what if Jesus were to look on us in our moments of failure? He has declared, "I the Lord cannot look upon sin with the least degree of allowance" (D&C 1:31). If the veil were drawn during our greatest moments of weakness, would we feel any different than Peter? Would we be able to look him in the eye? Would we go out and weep bitterly?[12]

When we sin and fall short, we tend to run and even hide from the Lord. Satan is referred to as "the accuser of our brethren" (Revelation 12:10). Among other things, Satan accuses us of being unworthy of the Lord's mercy, forgiveness, and love. He accuses us of our sins, telling us we have reached the point of no return. His message to us is that it is too late to change course. He wants us to stay hidden. Making eye contact with the Savior can be difficult and uncomfortable when we, like Peter, have fallen short. But that is the very thing the Lord wants us to do. He wants us to own our mistakes, look to Him, and reach out for His help and forgiveness.

When Peter faltered in his attempt to walk on water and was sinking, he made eye contact with the Savior. Peter knew who could save him. He looked up and cried out, "Lord, save me" (Matthew 14:30). Jesus immediately stretched forth His hand and caught him. Regardless of his mistakes and shortcomings, Peter again and again would turn to the Savior. The moment Peter or any of us reach out to the Savior, He is there to catch us. His arm is always stretched out. He stands at the door and knocks at all hours, waiting for us to let Him in.

During the unjust, illegal trials, again and again the Savior was verbally and physically abused. Amidst all of the torture and questioning before the Sanhedrin, "Jesus held his peace" (Matthew 26:63). He remained silent. On charges of blasphemy the Sanhedrin council had condemned Jesus to die. We should note that among the Sanhedrin there were noble exceptions, at least Nicodemus and Joseph of Arimathea, and we hope Gamaliel did not participate in the condemnation.

Whether or not the Sanhedrin legally had the power in that day to take life is not perfectly clear. Elder Talmage and Farrar did not think so. Clarke and others believed that they had no power regarding civil or state matters, but they did when it came to religious matters. Regardless, the Sanhedrin seemed to have little problem taking matters into their own hands when they deemed necessary. They stoned Stephen, Paul, and others when they wished. Why, then, send Jesus to Pilate? Why not just take matters into their own hands and stone Him?

First, the Triumphal Entry had shown that Jesus had many followers, and those followers posed a possible problem for them. The Sanhedrin feared the people and public opinion. A riot might ensue if they took matters into their own hands. Hence the secret arrest at night by an armed band with Roman soldiers and the rushed trials.

Second, if Jesus was handed over to the secular arm of the law and received an official decree of death by the Romans, they could not be stopped. It would serve as a shield for them to hide behind. In addition, the type of death Jesus died was important to Jewish leaders. As we will discuss later on, a mere stoning simply would not do. This may have been the main reason they turned Jesus over to Pilate.

Tried before Pilate

The council therefore bound Jesus and delivered Him over to the Roman governor, Pontius Pilate. They hoped an official decree of death would be ordered. Pilate lived in Caesarea but was visiting Jerusalem during the Passover and staying in the Antonia Fortress.

They brought Jesus to Pilate "straightway in the morning" (Mark 15:1). "It was early" (John 18:28). The gospels mention the time of day Jesus was delivered to Pilate, possibly to infer that the hearing was rushed to avoid attracting the followers of Jesus.

The council issued new charges against Jesus. "We found this man perverting the nation, and forbidding to give tribute to Caesar, saying that he himself is Christ, a king" (JST, Luke 23:2). The charge against Jesus was changed by Caiaphas and the Sanhedrin from blasphemy against God to sedition and high treason against Rome. Their accusations fell on deaf ears. Pilate could see through them.

"Then Pilate entered into the judgment hall again, and called Jesus, and said unto him, Art thou the King of the Jews? Jesus answered him, Sayest thou this thing of thyself, or did others tell it thee of me?" (John 18:33–34). Jesus was in charge of the interview. His question to Pilate was basically, "Are you speaking as a Roman official or are you simply repeating what the Jews have said? Are you asking a political or an ecclesiastical question?"

Pilate answered, "Am I a Jew? Thine own nation and the chief priests have delivered thee unto me: what hast thou done?" (John 18:35). Pilates response, "Am I a Jew," meant, "I am not asking as a Jew, I am asking as a politically appointed Roman official."

"Jesus answered, my kingdom is not of this world, if my kingdom were of this world then would my servants fight, that I should not be delivered to the Jews: but now is my kingdom not from hence" (John 18:36). Jesus made it clear to Pilate that He was there by His own volition.

"Pilate therefore said unto him, Art thou a king then? Jesus answered, Thou sayest that I am a king. To this end was I born, and for this cause came I into the world, that I should bear witness unto the truth. Every one that is of the truth heareth my voice. Pilate saith unto him, What is truth?" (John 18:37–38).

Pilate's last response represents the view of many in the secular world today; that truth is relative; that each individual decides what is right and wrong based on their own moral standard. When it comes to the truth some have become their own highest authority. For them there is no absolute truth. If there is no absolute truth, then there is no absolute truth giver. Therefore there is no ultimate accountability and the plan of salvation is void. Pilate may have been saying, "What is true for me as a Roman leader is different than what is true for you or even your accusers."

Jesus had come into the world to bear witness of a fixed, eternal, unifying truth. Of that absolute truth Jeffrey R. Holland explained,

> In all that Jesus came to say and do, including and especially in His atoning suffering and sacrifice, He was showing us who and what God our Eternal Father is like, how completely devoted He is to His children in every age and nation. In word and in deed Jesus was trying to reveal and make personal to us the true nature of His Father, our Father in Heaven. . . . God in His ultimate effort to have us know Him, sent to earth His Only Begotten and perfect Son, created in His very likeness and image, to live and serve among mortals. . . . In His life and especially in His death, Christ was declaring, This is God's compassion I am showing you, as well as that of my own.[13]

That is why Jesus was born, why He came into the world—to provide and show us the way to His Father. Gospel scholar Paul Keller wrote, "It took the incarnation of Jehovah and His willingness to suffer the atonement to open the veil between the Father and us."[14]

Throughout His mortal ministry Jesus repeatedly bore witness of Himself and of His Father who sent Him. Jesus declared, "I am way the truth, and the life, no man cometh unto the Father but by me" (John 14:6). We likewise have come into the world to bear witness of that immutable truth. The truth that Jesus, through His life and atoning sacrifice, is only way to the Father.

Tried before Herod

Pilate, finding there was no fault in Jesus and learning that Jesus was from Galilee, sent Him to Herod to be tried. Herod was the ruler of Galilee and was visiting Jerusalem at the time of Passover. The angry multitude proceeded from Antonia Fortress to Herod's Palace.

It was Herod who had ordered the head of John the Baptist. He is the one who flaunted both incest and adultery before the nation. He was a Jewish Sadducee with Roman power. Although the people called him King, Rome had conferred no such title upon him.

Herod had heard of the miracles of Jesus and was anxious to meet Him. Herod "questioned him with many words; but he answered him nothing" (Luke 23:9). For Herod the Savior had nothing but disdainful silence. As far as we know, Herod is distinguished as the only being who saw Christ face to face and spoke to Him yet never heard His voice.

Earlier, when Jesus stood before Pilate, "he was accused by the chief priests and elders of many evil things, but he answered nothing in return" (Matthew 27:12). "Then said Pilate unto him, Hearest thou not how many things they witness against thee?" But Jesus held His peace and "answered him . . . never a word; insomuch that the governor marveled greatly" (Matthew 27:13–14).

Time and again, the Savior gave no response to His accusers and torturers, fulfilling the prophecy of Isaiah: "He was oppressed and afflicted, yet he opened not his mouth: he is brought as a lamb to the slaughter, and as a sheep before her shearers is dumb, so he opened not his mouth" (Isaiah 53:7). [15] Peter, who followed and witnessed many of these events, later testified, "Who when he [Jesus] was reviled, reviled not again, when he suffered, he threatened not" (1 Peter 2:23).

Elder Neal A. Maxwell said, "To be wisely silent when we so much wish to be heard is a triumph of meekness over eagerness. Meek Jesus taught us, too, by His sermons of silence."[16] Jesus had mastered meekness and humility and was always in complete control of Himself and the situation. It was a godlike restraint that I can scarcely fathom. We often complain at the slightest inconvenience or discomfort. We tend to cry out at the slightest hurt. On many occasions I have instantly responded to criticism defensively. It was never so with our Savior. He, unlike us, never talked too much. He never wasted a word. Before His accusers Jesus suffered in silence, conserving His energy for Calvary, with a fixed determination to do His Father's will. There are certainly times in our lives when it would be wise to follow the example of Jesus and remain silent.

SUFFERING IN SILENCE

As mentioned in chapter 2, when I was a young full-time missionary Elder Vaughn J. Featherstone of the Quorum of the Seventy visited my mission. During a zone conference, he taught, "When challenges and trials come to us, we are to suffer in silence." Suffering in silence was a principle he had tried to live, and he encouraged us to do the same.

As we look at the last day of the Savior's life, we see how He exemplified the principle of suffering in silence. The Savior taught us that sometimes silence can be the only proper response to trials, tribulations, and hardships. Perhaps it is in those suffering silent moments that we can come to know God best. If we are meek and submissive, the Lord can use those difficult, quiet moments to tutor, refine, and transform us. The command at times is to "be still [to be silent in your suffering] and know that I am God" (D&C 101:16).

Back to Pilate

Herod, finding no fault with Jesus, arrayed Him in a gorgeous robe, mocked Him, and then sent Him back to Pilate. Herod may have been reluctant to prosecute Jesus further because he may have learned that his chief steward (Chuza), his advisor (Manean), and many more of his subjects were the Lord's disciples.

Among those closest to Pilate may have been another disciple or future disciple of Jesus. Tradition holds that the name of Pilate's wife was Claudia Procula. As Jesus returned to Pilate, she sent counsel to her husband. It was a dire warning: "Have thou nothing to do with that just man, for I have suffered many things this day in a vision because of him" (Matthew 27:19).

Tradition has it that Claudia was inclined towards Judaism, and either by then or later was a proselyte to the true Christian faith. She eventually was honored as a Saint by the Greek Orthodox Church.

Bruce R. McConkie wrote, "There are times—not a few in the course of a life—when men would do well to give heed to the wise counsel of their wives. If ever there was such a time in the life of Pilate, this was it. The Lord in his goodness to her—and also, for his own purposes, that another witness might be borne of his Son—had revealed to this woman that Jesus was Lord of all and that calamity and sorrow awaited those who opposed him. Nor was Pilate unsympathetic to her message; in reality it but confirmed his own feelings and desires."[17] This may have been the most important message a wife ever sent a husband.

As Pilate interviewed Jesus again, the Savior made something abundantly clear to Pilate. He declared, "Thou couldest have no power at all against me, except it were given thee" (John 19:11). Once again, what was about to happen to Jesus did not come because Pilate had power to impose it but because the Lord had the will to accept it.

Pilate saw that nothing was working to satisfy the Jewish leaders, and a riot was starting (see Matthew 27:24). The Jewish leaders had been at work, stirring up the crowds, thirsting for blood. The situation had become serious. In frustration, Pilate took action to placate the masses in hopes of calming the brewing violence.

Under the law of Moses, the priests were instructed to take two goats on the Day of Atonement. One was a scapegoat, which was set free into the wilderness. The other was a sacrificial goat, which was killed on the altar, thus symbolically removing the sins of the people (see Leviticus 16:7–22). Following the tradition of the time Pilate was to release and set free one prisoner at Passover. Pilate presented two prisoners before the people to choose from—Jesus and Barabbas.

An ancient variant reading of Matthew 27:16–17 has preserved the full name of the prisoner, Jesus Barabbas. Scholars point out that under these circumstances Pilate was asking, "Which Jesus do you want?"

Jesus Barabbas had been incarcerated for sedition and murder and was sentenced to die. The word "robber" in Greek (*lestes*) in this instance suggests that he was an actual revolutionary. He was an insurgent against the occupying power, Rome. Barabbas had raised an insurrection in Jerusalem, and it appears from Mark 15:7 that lives were lost in the scuffle.

In light of this, it is perhaps not surprising that Jewish leaders preferred the more exciting revolutionary, Jesus Barabbas. He was the type of Jesus the people were hoping for—one who would physically fight to remove the Roman occupiers. The people had a choice between the true Messiah and a counterfeit. During our pre-earth life we were faced with a similar choice, a choice between the true Messiah and a counterfeit.

Ironically Barabbas in Aramaic means "son of the father." Christ, of course, was the true and literal Son of the Father. Barabbas was guilty of sedition and should have been put to death but was ultimately freed. Christ, though innocent, was falsely accused of sedition and sentenced to death. Once again, we see the irony and contradiction of the situation for Jesus. There is nothing anyone can ever tell our Savior about the unfairness of life.

"Pilate saith unto them, What shall I do then with Jesus which is called Christ? They all say unto him, Let him be crucified" (Matthew 27:22).

Of this moment Gordon B. Hinckley said, "I ask anew the question offered by Pilate two thousand years ago, 'What shall I do then with Jesus which is called Christ?' (Matthew 27:22.) Indeed, we need continually to ask ourselves, What shall we do with Jesus who is called Christ? What shall we do with his teachings, and how can we make them an inseparable part of our lives?' . . . What shall we do with Jesus who is called Christ? Learn of him. Search the scriptures for they are they which testify of him. Ponder the miracle of His life and mission. Try a little more diligently to follow his example and observe his teachings."[18]

Barabbas was set free. In one sense, we are all like Barabbas. We are the sinful sons and daughters set free because the true Jesus, the true Son of the Father, was condemned to death for each and every one us.

Even with the release of Barabbas, Pilate was still hesitant to pass the sentence of death upon Jesus. The Jewish leaders were relentless and continued to call for His death. The chief priests knew that Pilate was morally weak, and they seized the moment and used the right words to coerce him. They maneuvered him into an awkward position in relation to the emperor when they challenged him with the outcry, "Whosoever maketh himself a king speaketh against Caesar" (John 19:12). The Sanhedrin played their trump card and had won. In the end, Pilate was more concerned with self-preservation than doing the right thing.

It is ironic that the Roman procurator, a heathen who did not believe in Jehovah or His commandments, asked the Jews to spare the life of their God and King at least four times. The response of the angry crowd was, "We have no king but Caesar" (John 19:15). With this cry Judaism was, in the person of its representatives, guilty of denying God, of blasphemy, of apostasy; the very crimes they claimed were committed by Jesus.[19]

"Then answered all the people, and said, His blood be on us, and on our children" (Matthew 27:25). When the Jews said they and their children would take the blame, it was prophetic. Within a few years Jerusalem, the temple, and most of the city's inhabitants were destroyed.

Of Matthew 27:25 gospel scholar Richard Holzapfel has written, "The cries to crucify Jesus have echoed down through the centuries. However, what is often forgotten is that Matthew (a Jew) is writing about Jews (Jesus included) for a Jewish audience. Perhaps Matthew and his original audience would have understood the doctrinal implication of the crowd's cry, 'His blood be on us, and on our children,' as atonement 'to cover' language. Although they did not understand what they were saying, that is exactly what was going to happen: Jesus' blood would cover the people as a powerful symbol of purification and cleansing."[20] Such a declaration was in a sense an unconscious request for the atoning sacrifice of the Savior to cleanse them.

Having repeatedly declared the innocence of Jesus, Pilate rose from the judgment seat, signifying he would impose no sentence; that there would be no judicial murder and no shedding of innocent blood; that he would free himself from the blood of the Innocent One. Such an act was a Gentile symbol of innocence. According to Bruce R. McConkie, "Pilate with a keen and intuitive insight into the Jewish mind, performed before them their own rite, the Jewish rite that symbolized innocence and freed the soul from innocent blood. He washed his hands."[21] It was a vain pretense of shifting the responsibility from himself.

I have on occasion listened in gospel doctrine classes as some have sympathized and spoken kindly of Pilate, stating he was a decent man and did the best he could under the circumstances. While we must give credit to the procurator for trying to free Jesus, let's be clear on the matter. The act of Pilate washing his hands never freed himself from the awful sin and guilt of sending a God to the cross. Every man is accountable for his own sins, and those of Pilate were deep, red, and evil. He was no longer an agent to himself; he was in bondage to the sins of his past.[22]

Bruce R. McConkie explained, "Pontius Pilate was a murderous, evil despot who ruled with sword. No ruler knowingly and willfully sends an innocent man to death unless prior sins have seared his conscience, tied his hands, and buried his instinct to deal justly. Through all his length of days, Pilate had been and then was an evil man, inured to blood and hardened against violence."[23]

Pilate had the power to stop the illegal and immoral proceedings and yet knowingly delivered the innocent Jesus to be scourged and then crucified. Once again, for Pilate, personal preservation took precedence over principle. We should also note that Pilate remained in complete control of the hearings and never relinquished that control to a subordinate. He was in charge of the entire situation.

More recently Jeffrey R. Holland said, "Pilate's freshly washed hands could not have been more stained or more unclean."[24] Elder Holland hails an earlier statement by Neal A. Maxwell who likewise declared, "Pilate's hands were never dirtier than just after he had washed them."[25] An entire ocean would have not been sufficient to wash away the blood and filth on Pilate's hands.

Testimony from James E. Talmage further explains that "Pilate knew not only that Jesus was innocent of any real crime but also that Jesus was who he said he was. Pilate knew the truth. He really knew!"[26] According to Elder Talmage, Pilate knew that Jesus was the Christ. "In the end . . . we leave Pilate to the Lord as we do all other sinners."[27]

Not convinced of Jesus's guilt but unwilling to let him go, Pilate had Jesus scourged, and then allowed the soldiers to dress Him as a mock king, complete with a crown of thorns and a purple robe—all in an effort to placate the Jewish leaders and the masses that were beginning to riot. "Then Pilate therefore took Jesus and scourged him" (John 19:1). Paul informs us of the traditional number "forty stripes save one" (2 Corinthians 11:24). Minus one in case of a miscount. Thirteen hits across his chest and thirteen hits across each shoulder.

The usual instrument delivering the punishment was a short whip having a wooden handle with several single strands or braided leather thongs that had a lead ball attached to each end. Sometimes pieces of glass or chunks of bone were woven into the thongs. The victim was stripped of all clothing and tied by his wrists to an upright post. The first blows of the thongs cut through the skin only. But subsequent blows cut deeper and deeper into the subcutaneous tissue.[28]

Sometimes by accident, and sometimes on purpose, with terrible barbarity the victim would be struck in the face and eyes. It was a punishment so hideous that, under its lacerating agony, the victim generally fainted and often died. But not Christ. Instead, He "rose from the sufferings of the scourge that he might die an ignominious death upon the cruel cross of Calvary."[29]

Regarding the crown of thorns, Adam Clarke explained,

> It does not appear that this crown was intended to be an instrument of punishment or torture to his head, but rather to render him ridiculous; . . . The crown was not probably of thorns, in our sense of the word: there are eminently learned men who think that the crown was formed of the herb acanthus. [A word used by John] may very well be translated as acanthine crown or wreath, formed out of the branches of the herb *acanthus*, or *bear's foot*. This, however, is a prickly plant, though nothing like thorns, in the common meaning of that word. Many Christians have gone astray in magnifying the sufferings of Christ from this circumstance; and painters, the worst of all commentators, frequently represent Christ with a crown of long thorns, which one standing by is striking into his head with a stick. These representations engender ideas both false and absurd.[30]

The mocking by the soldiers was done in the form of a cruel game called the game of kings. A game piece was rolled, and whatever kingly description it fell on would be acted out against the prisoner in a humiliating way. Jesus was made to look like a king by being given a robe, a crown, and a scepter. He was then mocked, beaten, and spit upon, while they pretended to pay homage to Him. A game board for the game of kings may still be seen in Jerusalem in the Church of Flagellation and the Sisters of Zion.

As part of the game of kings, Jesus's belongings were gambled on, fulfilling the prophecy, "They part my garments among them, and cast lots among my vesture" (Palm 22:18). "And they [the Roman soldiers] . . . parted his garments, casting lots" (Matthew 27:35). Of this moment Dallin H. Oaks taught, "The Roman soldiers of Pilate provided an unforgettable illustration of the different perspectives of the carnal mind and the spiritual mind. During a tragic but glorious afternoon on Calvary, a handful of soldiers waited at the foot of a cross. One of the supreme events in all eternity was taking place on the cross above their heads. Oblivious to that fact, they occupied themselves by casting lots to divide the earthly property of the dying Son of God. Their example reminds each of us that we should not be casting our lots for the things of the world while the things of eternity, including our families and the work of the Lord, suffer for our lack of attention."[31]

Following the scourging and the game of the kings, Pilate attempted to release Jesus one final time. He presented the lacerated, wounded Jesus once more to the people. "Then came Jesus forth, wearing the crown of thorns, and the purple robe. And Pilate saith unto them, Behold the man!" (John 19:5). Pilate most likely hoped that by looking upon the bloodied and beaten Jesus the Jews would have compassion and act accordingly. But it was to no avail. The leading Jews were blood thirsty and past feeling. They would continue to work the crowds. Nothing but a crucifixion would satisfy them. Bruce R. McConkie wrote of this moment,

> In that hour of His extremist humiliation-as He stood in the grandeur of His holy calm on that lofty tribunal above the yelling crowd, there shone all over Him so Godlike a pre-eminence, so divine a nobleness, that Pilate broke forth with that involuntary exclamation which has thrilled with emotion so many million heart—"Behold the Man!" But his appeal only woke a fierce outbreak of the scream, "Crucify! Crucify! Him." . . . Why did these Jews thirst for blood, it was his claim to Messianic divinity. They had kept it from Pilate until his death by crucifixion was approved. At this new declaration, Pilate was startled and fearful.[32]

Whitney L. Clayton explained,

> Pilate's plea ["Behold the Man"] was profoundly ironic. Jesus's physical appearance at that moment was marred, but there never had been until then, and has not been since, any man or woman who more richly deserved to be "beheld." His life was perfect. He was without peer. No one had ever lived as He did. No one ever would. He possessed every virtue in its consummate form. . . . Pilate unknowingly and unintentionally expressed the simple formula for achieving the highest purposes of life. . . . When Pilate asked the Jews to behold the Savior, he pointed them and us toward the One, the only one, who can make our lives abundant and our salvation perfect. What we should remember when we behold Him is that because of Him,

and all He did and all He was and is, we too can triumph. We also can overcome. We can live abundantly in the midst of trials. If we choose to 'behold' Him and accept and apply His saving gospel, He will save us. He will rescue us from the effects of our own fallen natures and foibles, and He will save us from sin, from spiritual mediocrity, and from ultimate, eternal failure. He will purge, refine, beautify, and eventually even perfect us. He will give us joy and peace. He is the key to the abundant life.[33]

Earlier in His ministry the Savior taught, "I am come that they might have life and they might have it more abundantly" (John 10:9). The Savior just doesn't want us to have a good life; He came so we can have an abundant life. As we follow Pilate's admonition to "behold the Man," our lives will indeed be abundant.

FATE OF THE PERSECUTORS

What was the fate of those who were directly associated with sending Jesus to the cross? Judas died in the horrors of a loathsome suicide. Caiaphas was deposed a year later and appears to eventually have committed suicide. Herod Antipas was exiled from Palestine and died in infamy. The house of Annas lost its power and wealth and was destroyed a generation later by an infuriated mob, and his son was dragged through the streets, and then scourged and beaten to death.

Within a year of Jesus's trial, rumor reached Pilate of a threatened Samaritan rebellion against Roman dominion. Pilate violently reacted to the rumor. He marched his soldiers against unarmed Samaritans and won an easy victory. The Samaritans were angered at the bloody loss and complained to Vitellius, the leader of the Syrian province. Vitellius sent Pilate to Rome to answer the Samaritan accusations. Upon reaching Rome, Pilate learned that his foe Caligula had succeeded to the throne. According to tradition, in A.D. 36 Caligula either banished Pilate to Vienna, the south of France, or to a mountain near Lake Lucerne. In exile Pilate wearied of his life and misfortunes, and committed suicide.

The Road to Calvary

The sin offering of the law of Moses was always offered outside the camp of Israel. The Savior was to be taken without the city walls. It was the custom among the Romans to have those condemned to die by crucifixion carry their own cross bar. A sign, either hanging around their neck or carried by one of the soldiers, announced the crimes of the one to be crucified. In addition, a herald went before them, calling out the charges against the condemned men. The distance from the Hall of Judgment to Calvary was about one-third of a mile, and the weight of the cross bar was approximately seventy-five to a hundred pounds.

Under the load of the cross, Christ fell. Simon of Cyrene, by chance (or was it an instance of intervening providence?), had come from the country and was compelled to carry the Savior's cross. The indication is that he was born in Cyrene, North Africa, as part of the Jewish colony there. On this memorable day, he apparently had been working in the fields and was returning to the city. We don't know what words may have been exchanged, if any, between Christ and Simon. What we do know is that Simon's son Rufus later joined the Church and became one of the Lord's disciples (see Mark 15:21; Romans 16:13).

Gospel scholar Andrew Skinner taught, "The power of the event in which Simon had a role . . . ultimately resulted in his own conversion as well as that of his wife, his sons, and possibly future generations."[34] Simon's act of carrying cross of Jesus changed his life forever. Like so many who are truly converted to Christ, he would never be the same.

A marvelous multitude marched with the death party. These were the ten-thousands of Judea and the thousands of Galilee, both men and women. As far as the record recites, none of the men in that mighty mass came to the Savior's defense, but with the women it was otherwise. Women have always played an important role in the Lord's kingdom. These women were among His most faithful followers.

The scriptures say that the Crucifixion took place at Golgotha (Aramaic) or Calvary (Latin). The translation of both means "the skull." Limestone had partially weathered away portions of the stone, creating a grotesque and ominous formation that took the shape of a human skull. It could have also been named the place of "the skull" because of all of the death that took place in that location. The traditional and oldest proposed site of the Crucifixion is the current site of the Church of the Holy Sepulcher. We now go with Christ to the cross of Calvary. His sufferings on the cross extended from about 9:00 a.m. to 3:00 p.m., approximately six hours.

ENDNOTES

1. Of the illegal proceedings Elder James Talmage has written the following:

    - The arrest was illegal since it was affected by night.
    - The private examination of Jesus before Annas or Caiaphas was illegal.
    - The indictment against Jesus was, in form, illegal.
    - The proceedings of the Sanhedrin against Jesus were illegal because they were conducted at night.
    - The proceedings of the Sanhedrin against Jesus were illegal because the court convened before the offering of the morning sacrifice.
    - The proceedings against Jesus were illegal because they were conducted on the day preceding a Jewish Sabbath; also, on the first day of unleavened bread and the eve of the Passover.
    - The trial of Jesus was illegal because it was concluded within one day.
    - The sentence of condemnation pronounced against Jesus by the Sanhedrin was illegal because it was founded upon His uncorroborated confession.
    - The condemnation of Jesus was illegal because the verdict of the Sanhedrin was not unanimous.
    - The proceedings against Jesus were illegal in that (1) the sentence of condemnation was pronounced in a place forbidden by law; (2) the high priest rent his clothes; (3) the balloting was irregular.
    - The condemnation of Jesus was illegal because the merits of the defense were not considered (Talmage, *Jesus the Christ* 598–601).

2. Gerald N. Lund, *New Testament Symposium,* Church Educational System, 1984, 27. As quoted in Ed J. Pinegar, et al. *Latter-Day Commentary on the New Testament: The Four Gospels* (American Fork, UT: Covenant Communications, 2002), 371.

3. Walter M. Chandler, *Trial of Jesus from a Lawyers Standpoint.* Vol. 1 (Books on Demand, 2018), 160.

4. Church Education System, *The Life and Teachings of Jesus and the Apostles.* 2nd ed., The Church of Jesus Christ of Latter-Day Saints, 1978, 185.

5. Spencer W. Kimball, "Jesus of Nazareth," *Ensign*, Dec. 1980.

6. Frederic William Farrar, *The Life of Lives, Further Studies in the Life of Christ* (Cassell and Company, 1900), 515.

7. Bruce D. Porter, *The King of Kings* (Salt Lake City: Deseret Book, 2000), 106.

8. Frederic W. Farrar, *The Life of Christ* (Salt Lake City: Bookcraft, 1995), 639.

9. Susan Easton Black, *400 Questions & Answers about the Life and Time of Jesus Christ* (American Fork, UT: Covenant Communications, 2010), 197.

10. Daniel H. Ludlow, "The Greatest Week in History," *Ensign*, Apr. 1972.

11. Black, ibid., 200.

12. Richards, Bryan, "Commentary on Luke 22:61." *Gospel Doctrine*, gospel-doctrine.com/new-testament/luke/luke-22.

13. Jeffrey R. Holland, "The Grandeur of God," October 2003 general conference.

14. Peterson, Paul H., et al., editors. *Jesus Christ, Son of God, Savior* (Brigham Young University: Religious Studies Center, 2002), 150–151.

15. "This Man of Galilee knew little but misunderstanding and ingratitude and criticism and abuse; but he never complained, and at the end of the day he was as sweet as at dawn. Long before he came somebody had said that when the supreme man arrived he would submit to tribulation without complaining. As men looked upon this Man of Galilee they were reminded of the great line of the prophet, 'As a lamb before the shearer is dumb, so he opened not his mouth. Brethren and sisters, what is the attitude, the spirit of the vilifier, as compared with the spirit of the Christ, the spirit of the leaders of the Church, the spirit of every true Latter-day Saint? It is better to suffer wrong than to do wrong, and if we as Latter-day Saints will but hold to the truth as it has been revealed all will eventually be well" (McKay, David O. Conference Report, Oct. 1931, 13).

16. Neal A. Maxwell, *That Ye May Believe* (Salt Lake City: Bookcraft, 1992), 132.

17. Bruce R. McConkie, *The Mortal Messiah: From Bethlehem to Calvary.* Vol. 4, (Salt Lake City: Deseret Book, 1979), 185.

18. Gordon B. Hinckley, "What Shall I Do Then with Jesus Which Is Called Christ?" *Ensign*, Dec. 1983.

19. Susan Easton Black, *400 Questions & Answers about the Life and Time of Jesus Christ*, (American Fork, UT: Covenant Communications, 2010), 209. Richard Neitzel Holzapfel and Thomas A. Wayment, *Making Sense of the New Testament* (Salt Lake City: Deseret Book, 2010), 243–244.

20. McConkie, ibid., 188.

21. Ibid., 189.

22. Ibid., 171. Elder McConkie's assessment comports with the famous Jewish historian Josephus, who likewise stated that Pilate was noted for cruelty. Philo of Alexandria, a prominent Jewish leader, also wrote that there was nothing good to say about him, for he was "by nature rigid and stubbornly harsh . . . of spiteful disposition and an exceedingly wrathful man . . . the bribes, the acts of pride, the acts of violence, the outrages, the cases of spiteful treatment, the constant murders without trial, the ceaseless and most

grievous brutality" (Ted Schroder, *Buried Treasure: Recovering the Mysteries of Faith* [Amelia Island Pub., 2005], 161–162).

23. Jeffrey R. Holland, "None Were with Him," April 2009 general conference.
24. Neal A. Maxwell, "Why Not Now?" October 1974 general conference.
25. James E. Talmage, *Jesus the Christ* (Salt Lake City: Deseret Book, 1915/1982), 657.
26. Spencer W. Kimball, *The Miracle of Forgiveness* (Salt Lake City: Deseret Book, 1969), 167.
27. Davis, C Truman. "A Physician Testifies About the Crucifixion," *CBN*, The Christian Broadcasting Network, www1.cbn.com/medical-view-of-the-crucifixion-of-jesus-christ.
28. Bruce R. McConkie, "The Purifying Power of Gethsemane," April 1985 general conference.
29. Adam Clarke, *The New Testament of Our Lord and Savior Jesus Christ* (Abingdon), 272.
30. Dallin H. Oaks, *Pure in Heart* (Salt Lake City: Bookcraft, 1988), 116.
31. McConkie, *The Mortal Messiah*, 193–194.
32. Whitney L. Clayton, "Rooted in Christ," *Ensign*, Aug. 2016.
33. Andrew C. Skinner, *Golgotha* (Salt Lake City: Deseret Book, 2004), 111.

CHAPTER 7

THE CROSS OF CALVARY

In the time of Jesus, there was a small cultured town known as Sepphoris, meaning "jewel" or "ornament." It became the Roman capital of Galilee. Jesus's hometown of Nazareth was only a few miles from Sepphoris. At Sepphoris eighty years before Jesus's birth, a Hasmonean army took terrible revenge on a rebel uprising by a massive crucifixion. When Jesus was in His teens, hundreds of rebels from Sepphoris were again crucified. Reports of these crucifixions surely would have reached Jesus. He may even have conversed with witnesses or seen them Himself. The Romans possibly required their subjects, including Jesus's father, Joseph, and his apprentice son to provide some of the crossbars or stakes. In any case, the shadow of the crucifixion reached Jesus early in His life. Did it bring apprehensions to His heart? One can only wonder how early Jesus realized He was to be "the Lamb slain" upon a cross.[1]

Punishment by stoning was the usual method of death used by the Jews in Jesus' day. Once Pilate approved the death of Jesus, the Jewish leaders could have requested a stoning, which was their tradition. According to the Mishnah, strangulation, beheading, burning, and stoning were all approved forms of punishment, but crucifixion was not. Death by crucifixion originated in Mesopotamia by the Persians and was later perfected by the Romans. Why not a stoning for Jesus? Why a crucifixion? One reason was to fulfill prophecy (see Isaiah 22:23–24; 1 Nephi 11, 19:9–14; 2 Nephi 6:9,10:5; Mosiah 15:7). During His ministry Jesus had foretold that He was to be crucified. "Behold, we go up to Jerusalem: and the Son of man shall be betrayed unto the chief priests and unto the scribes, and they shall condemn him to death. And shall deliver him to the Gentiles to mock, and to scourge, and *to crucify him:* and the third day he shall rise again" (Matthew 20:18–19; emphasis added).

When it came to Jesus, a mere stoning would not do. The Jewish rulers deliberately contrived and carefully engineered the Savior's execution. Their purpose was insidious and ingenious—they aspired to both discredit and shame Jesus before His own people. Their plan was inspired by a popular interpretation of Deuteronomy 21:22–23: "And if a man have committed a sin worthy of death and he be put to death, and thou hang him on a tree: His body shall not remain all night upon the tree, but thou shall in any wise bury him that day, *for he that is hanged is accursed of God;* that thy land be not defiled which the Lord thy God giveth for an inheritance."

According to Rabbinical commentaries, to leave a body hanging was a degradation of the human body and therefore an affront to God in whose image man's body was made. In Deuteronomy 21 the Hebrew word *qelalah*, translated "accursed," denotes something or someone delivered up to divine wrath, meaning, God removed those under this indictment from His favor and protection and delivered them over to the powers of hell. Paul also refers to the belief in Galatians 3:13: "Cursed is everyone that hangeth on a tree."

Both the Pharisees and the Sadducees believed that a crucified person fell under this condemnation. The Jewish rulers desperately needed to discredit any belief in the Lord's divinity and specifically engineered His death so that He appeared to fall under the curse of God. The manner of the Lord's death was designed to witness that Hades and not paradise would claim Him.

Isaiah wrote, "Surely he hath borne our griefs, and carried our sorrows: yet we did esteem him stricken, smitten of God and afflicted" (Isaiah 53:4). The desire of Satan and the wicked Jewish leaders was for all of us to esteem the Savior as having fallen under the curse of God, for us to "esteem him stricken, smitten of God and afflicted." The Jewish leaders may have believed that such a fate would finally extinguish the thought that Jesus was a divine teacher.

We should note the irony of their choice. In the attempt to discredit and shame Jesus by crucifixion these leaders were fulfilling prophecy and generating an iconic death that would be recognized by billions with worship and adoration.

One reason the Romans adopted death by crucifixion was that it was a slow, excruciating death with the absolute maximum amount of pain and suffering. The word "excruciating" comes from the Latin *excruciatus*, meaning "out of the cross." In the classic *The Life of Christ*, Fredric Farrar wrote this about the crucifixion:

> A death by crucifixion seems to include all that pain and death can have of the horrible and ghastly—dizziness, cramp, thirst, starvation, sleeplessness, traumatic fever, tetanus, publicity of shame, long continuance of torment, horror of anticipation, mortification of untended wounds, all intensified just up to the point at which can be endured at all, but all stopping just short of the point which would give to the sufferer the relief of unconsciousness. The unnatural position made every movement painful; the lacerated veins and crushed tendons throbbed with incessant anguish; the wounds, inflamed by exposure, gradually gangrened; the arteries, especially of the head and stomach, became swollen and oppressed with surcharged blood; and, while each variety of misery went on gradually increasing, there was added to them the intolerable pang of burning and raging thirst. Such was the death to which Christ was doomed.[3]

His tormentors used mallets to drive nails through Christ's palms and feet, just as David had prophesied: "They pierced my hands and feet" (Psalm 22:16). Nails were also driven into His wrists, as Isaiah had foreshadowed: "And I will fasten him as a nail in a *sure place*" (Isaiah 22:23–24; emphasis added). Those nails were driven into a sure place, securing Christ to the cross. The prophet Helaman taught that Christ Himself is a "sure foundation," not just a good, strong or even a firm foundation, but a sure foundation, "a foundation where on if men build, they cannot fall" (Helaman 5:12). Just as those nails were driven into a sure place and bound Christ to the cross so that He would not fall, we in a like manner through ordinances, covenants, and faith bind ourselves to the Savior. Thus, He can become a sure foundation in our lives so we may never fall.

Just prior to being crucified, there was one custom occasionally practiced by the Romans, which revealed some touch of passing humanity. It consisted of giving the sufferer a heavy blow under the armpit, which hastened death's approach without actually causing death. For whatever reason, it does not appear to have been practiced on this occasion. Another act of mercy consisted of giving the condemned, immediately before his execution, a draught of wine medicated with some powerful opiate. Just prior to the crucifixion "they gave him vinegar to drink mingled with gall: and when he had tasted thereof, he would not drink" (Matthew 27:34).

It was most likely the women disciples, "which also bewailed and lamented him," with the merciful intent of deadening His senses to pain, that offered the Savior the drugged cup (see Luke 23:27). With that act of mercy the women disciples fulfilled the Messianic utterance, "They gave me also gall for my meat; and in my thirst they gave me vinegar to drink" (Psalm 69:21). Jesus tasted but did not drink. He preferred rather to look death in the face. He chose to suffer and die with His mind clear and His senses unimpaired.[4] Tad R. Callister explained, "Jesus took every pain un-anesthetized and in full force. There would be no unconsciousness, no sedatives, no pain killers. His faculties would remain acutely aware of everything until His mission was finished."[5]

When the cross was raised, the leading Jews, for the first time, noticed the inscription at the top: "THIS IS JESUS THE KING OF THE JEWS" (Matthew 27:37). An insult to the Jewish leaders with which Pilate had vented his indignation. Before, in their blind rage, they had imagined that the manner of the crucifixion would be an insult aimed at Jesus. But now as they read the inscription and saw Him hanging between the two thieves, it suddenly flashed upon them that it was a public scorn inflicted upon them.

Pilate probably meant, or partly meant, to imply that this was, in one sense, the King of the Jews—the greatest, the noblest, the truest of His race, whom His race had rejected and crucified. For the Jewish leaders, their hour of triumph had been poisoned.[6]

The inscription was written in Hebrew, Greek, and Latin—as though to symbolize the fact that here was a message for all nations, tongues, and people to consider. The sign on the cross indicated the criminal charges for which the person was being crucified. The inscription read, "The King of the Jews." Jesus was formally condemned for having claimed to be the king of the Jews and not for declaring Himself to be the Jewish Messiah or Jehovah.

Why the Cross?

As terrible as the cross was, as a young teenager I understood that the infinite suffering for our sins and the most intense pain inflicted upon Jesus took place in Gethsemane. For years I'd ask myself, "If that is the case, then why the trials, the scourging, and most importantly, why the cross? Jesus already suffered in Gethsemane for our sins and drank the bitter cup. Was the cross really necessary? Why did He need to go through that?" Over the years, I have tried to find an answer for the question, why the cross?

The Apostle Paul felt that a vital part of the gospel was to preach Christ and the cross. He saw our salvation was tied to it and repeatedly taught it. Paul wrote, "For Christ sent me . . . to preach the gospel: not with wisdom of words [the wisdom of the world] lest the cross of Christ should be made of no effect. For the preaching of the cross is to them that perish foolishness: but unto us which are saved is the power of God" (1 Corinthians 1:17–18).

The prophet Isaiah alludes to one possible reason for the cross: "He shall see the travail of his soul . . . he hath poured out his soul unto death" (Isaiah 53:11,12). Death by crucifixion was a slow process that sometimes took days. Such a death allowed Christ to "pour out his soul unto death." It gave Him time, and with that time control over the giving. The cross allowed Jesus to decide the exact moment in time when to freely lay down His life.

After suffering in Gethsemane, Jesus arose and with His disciples went forth to meet the approaching arresting party. In an attempt to defend Jesus from the mob, Peter unsheathed his sword and cut off the ear of the high priest's servant, Malchus. "Then said

Jesus unto Peter put up thy sword. . . . *The cup with my Father hath given me, shall I not drink it?*" (John 18:11; emphasis added). Thus, we see another answer to my question, why the cross? The bitter cup was not yet empty. The atoning sacrifice of our Lord was not completed in Gethsemane. His suffering for mankind continued.

In two successive revelations given to the Prophet Joseph Smith in June of 1831 at Kirtland, Ohio, the Lord explained, "[Christ] was crucified for the sins of the world" (D&C 53:2, 54:1). The Apostle Peter likewise taught that the Savior "bare our sins in his own body on the tree" (1 Peter 2:24). Nephi explained that "he was lifted up upon the cross and slain for the sins of the world" (1 Nephi 11:33). Of Jesus Paul wrote, "Blotting out . . . that [which] was against us, which was contrary to us, and took it out of the way, nailing it to his cross" (Colossians 2:14). These verses of scripture tie our sins to the cross. On the cross at Calvary, the Savior continued to suffer for all of our sins.

Over the years, leaders of the Church have begun to emphasize the need for a balance, to speak of the importance of both Gethsemane and the Crucifixion and to emphasize that what began in Gethsemane was completed at Golgotha. Not only was Jesus crucified for the sins of the world, but all that Christ had suffered the night before in Gethsemane returned and intensified while He was on the cross. James E. Talmage explained that while on the cross, "the agony of Gethsemane had recurred, intensified beyond human power to endure. In that bitterest hour, the dying Christ was alone, alone in the most terrible reality."[7] Bruce R. McConkie further elaborated, "To this we add, if we interpret the holy word aright, that all of the anguish, all of the sorrow and all of the suffering of Gethsemane recurred during the final three hours on the cross, the hour when darkness covered the land."[8]

For the victory to be complete, the infinite pains of Gethsemane returned at Calvary and intensified. We should note that there was a difference between the first and second time Jesus suffered the pains of Gethsemane. When the Savior entered Gethsemane, He was at His best physically, mentally, emotionally, and spiritually. He had just sung a strengthening hymn, had eaten the Passover feast, and most important, had introduced and partaken of the sacrament. All of this was done in preparation to strengthen Him for the horrors of Gethsemane.

While on the cross when the pains and suffering of Gethsemane recurred, Jesus was certainly not at His best, having already suffered the infinite burden in Gethsemane. His suffering was compounded by the loss of blood, the betrayal, the illegal trials, the mocking, and all the physical abuse and torture associated with them. As mentioned previously, many died from scourging alone. Hypovolemic shock would most certainly have set in.

On the cross Jesus was tired, hurt, hungry, thirsty, and worn. He had walked some six to seven miles and had been awake for over thirty-six hours. He had nails driven through His hands, wrists, and feet and was then tortured with the excruciating pains the cross inflicted. In this depleted and weakened condition, the horrors of Gethsemane not only returned but intensified.

During the final three hours on the cross, when darkness covered the land, the Savior cried out, "My God, my God, why hast thou forsaken me?" (Matthew 27:46). To make matters even worse, the Father completely withdrew His presence from His Only Begotten Son. In this moment, the Savior reached the climax of His greatest suffering.

If there ever was a moment of susceptibility to temptation, it was while on the cross. If ever there was a time when Jesus was vulnerable to the adversary, this was it. This was Satan's chance of all chances to find a chink in His armor. What added to the physical suffering, the intensified bitter cup, and the withdrawal of the Father was the fact that through it all Satan continued to tempt, attack, torment, and torture the Savior to the very end. If you ever think Satan is going to let up or leave you alone, think again. We must always be on guard. Thus, the need to daily take upon us the whole armor of God and continuously hold to the rod of iron.

We know Jesus was mocked numerous times as He hung on the cross. Through the voice of mortals Satan spoke, hoping to turn the Savior from His mission. It was Satan's last desperate effort. Time was running out for him. "The rulers . . . derided him saying, He saved others; let him save himself, if he be the Christ . . . the soldiers also mocked him . . . saying if thou be the king of the Jews, save thyself" (Luke 23:35–37). "They that passed by railed on him . . . save thyself and come down from the cross" (Mark 15:29, 30).

Jesus's ministry began and ended with the same temptations and tactics of Satan. First in the wilderness, Satan challenged Him, "If thou be the Son of God, command that these stones be made bread" (Matthew 4:3). Then three years later on the cross of Calvary, Jesus was told, "If thou be the son of God come down off the cross!" (Matthew 27:40). This was Satan's final attempt to cast doubt into the Savior's mind regarding His own divinity and ability. In both instances Lucifer provoked Him to misuse His divine power.

Could Jesus have turned the stones into bread? Could He have come down off the cross? It is an easy answer. Jesus performed countless miracles during His mortal life. To name a few, He walked on water, controlled the elements, turned water into wine, fed 5,000 with five loaves and two fishes, healed the sick, and raised the dead. These final statements at Calvary were reminders that Jesus certainly could have saved Himself. At any point the Savior could have withdrawn and stopped the suffering. If our Lord had not been endowed with this ability, the crucifixion would have been invalidated. The power of choice was always before Jesus. He was not forced to endure this nightmare. Jesus came to save us yet refused to save Himself. "Greater love hath no man than this, than a man lay down his life for his friends" (John 15:13). The suffering and death of Jesus Christ exhibited the greatest act of love ever demonstrated.

While Jesus was on the cross, the leading Jews asked for yet another sign. Would they have finally believed Jesus had He come down off the cross? Did they believe a few weeks earlier when they watched Jesus call Lazarus forth from the tomb? Is there any reason to suppose they would accept His divinity had He come down from the cross in power? "If they hear not Moses and the prophets, neither will they be persuaded, though one rose from the dead" (Luke 16:31). He would shortly rise from the dead and still they would not be persuaded. Miracles alone do not produce faith unto salvation.

The enemies of Jesus continued to taunt Him to the very end. "He saved others . . . he trusted in God; let him deliver him now" (Matthew 27:42–43). Even His enemies knew He had saved others; they knew He trusted in God. Bruce R. McConkie explained, "This very admission that Jesus trusted in God is itself a pronouncement that his enemies knew he had lived a righteous life and had walked in a pious path."⁹

Forsaken and Alone

As discussed in chapter 3, it appears that the Father's spirit left Jesus for a time in the Garden of Gethsemane. But it apparently returned, possibly to assist Jesus through the difficult, trying hours that followed Gethsemane. As mentioned above, at or just before the ninth hour of the day while on the cross, Jesus suffered the complete loss of the Father's presence. The Father withdrew from Jesus, casting a veil of separation over the Savior. This led Him to cry out, "My God, my God, why hast thou forsaken me?" (Matthew 27:46). To that question there was no immediate answer. Of this moment Erastus Snow explained, "The Father did not deign to answer; the time had not yet come to explain it and tell him. But after a little, when he passed the ordeal, made the sacrifice, and by the power of God was raised from the dead it was all explained and comprehended fully." ¹⁰ Our "whys" and questions to God will not always be immediately responded to either. Only later, through the process of time and experience will things be "comprehended fully."

Gospel scholar Stephen Robinson asked,

> Is it possible that the Heavenly Father had really forsaken him? Could God have abandoned him in this most sacred and terrible hour? Yes, indeed. For Christ had become guilty of the sins of the world, guilty in our place. What happens to the rest of us when we are guilty of sin? The Spirit of God withdraws from us, the heavens turn to brass, and we are left alone to stew in our guilt until we repent. In Gethsemane [and on Calvary] the best among us vicariously became the worst among us and suffered the very depths of hell. And as one who was guilty, the Savior experienced

for the first time in his life the loss of the Spirit of God and of communion with his Father.[11]

King David wrote a messianic psalm about this moment of forsakenness on the cross: "Reproach hath broken my heart; and I am full of heaviness; and I looked for some to take pity but there was none; and for comforters, but I found none" (Psalm 69:20). At this hour and climax of suffering and heaviness Jesus was left completely and utterly alone, He sought for comfort but found none.

"My God, my God, why hast thou forsaken me?" (Matthew 27:46). "Some of them that stood there, when they heard that, said, This man calleth for Elias" (Matthew 27:47). Bryan Richards wrote:

> Like so many utterances of the Savior, this too was misunderstood. A generation which pretended to be so religious did not know the difference between Elohim and Elijah. Even more significantly, they missed the message of those four Aramaic words, "Eli, Eli, lama sabachthani." Not only was this a heartbreaking plea to His Father, Jesus was also referencing the 22nd Psalm by invoking the first line of the chapter. Had those present understood the reference, they could have opened their scriptures and read the Messianic psalm which graphically paints the scene of Christ's crucifixion as foreseen by the prophet-king David.[12]

With great effort Jesus had cried out, "My God, my God, why hast thou forsaken me?" Jesus chose His words carefully. He would fulfill the words of all the prophets who had ever testified of His coming, death, and resurrection, including this one given by David. It was not by chance that He uttered the exact first line of Psalm 22. Jesus knew the prophecy and called attention to it at the very moment it was being fulfilled. With that declaration, Jesus not only fulfilled prophecy but also bore His final witness to all present of His true identity. He was the long-promised Messiah, and this terrible scene had been foretold. Did those who heard the cry also remember the psalm? It surely would have been familiar to some of these students of scripture. The Jewish leaders present had ears to hear but could not hear. They had eyes to see but could not see.

Throughout His life Jesus lived and moved and had His being in the Spirit of God, "for God giveth him not the Spirit by measure, for he dwelleth in him, even the fullness" (JST, John 3:34). It was this fulness of the Holy Ghost that enabled Jesus to enjoy constant communion with His Father. Because of this the Father and Son enjoyed much more than what we might call closeness. Theirs was a divine indwelling relationship. Because he kept the law of God perfectly, Jesus was in the Father and the Father was in Him (see John 14:10; 17:21; 1 John 3:24). Through the Holy Ghost and the Savior's perfect obedience the Father and Son had always been connected. They were one.

Of His mortal ministry the Savior explained, "The glory of the Father was with him, for he dwelt in him" (D&C 93:17). How else did the Father dwell in Jesus? Maybe the same way Christ dwells in us. The light of Christ is in and through all things. He is literally in the physical make-up of our bodies and serves to give us life, light, understanding, protection, and guidance. The light of Christ in our bodies directly connects us to Christ (see D&C 88:11–13). In a like manner, a portion of the Father was in the physical body of Jesus. Remember, Heavenly Father was the literal father of Jesus in mortality, not Joseph. He was therefore directly connected to His Only Begotten Son, giving Jesus life, light, understanding, protection, and guidance. "The glory of the Father was with him for He dwelt in him "(D&C 93:17).

Jesus had anticipated the loss of mortal support, but apparently, He had not comprehended the Father leaving Him at this moment. Just a day earlier during His farewell discourse Jesus said, "I am not alone, because the Father is with me and the Father hath not left me alone" (John 16:32). When the Father withdrew His presence from Jesus on the cross, He severed a lifelong connection and Christ was left completely and utterly alone, experiencing spiritual death in the fullest sense.

Without the Spirit and His Father's sustaining presence, Jesus became completely vulnerable to the attacks of Satan. This final departure of the Father allowed Jesus to "descend below all things." Alone and bruised, Christ went into the deepest abyss of outer darkness and perdition to save each and every one of us from Satan's grasp. The separation from the Father and the Spirit enabled the condescension of the Son of God to be complete. It also allowed the victory to be completely and solely the Savior's.

The crucifixion did not kill Jesus. James E. Talmage taught, "His was to be the choice. His was to be the opportunity. His was to be the challenge to give His life voluntarily. With all of the Father's support withdrawn, with the pains of Gethsemane recurring, our Savior was left unto himself in order that he alone might complete the atoning sacrifice."[13]

The Apostle Paul wrote, "He [Jesus] had *by Himself* purged our sins" (Hebrews 1:3; emphasis added). By Himself, with no one to help, Christ worked out the infinite atonement. When the Savior returns in power a second glorious time, He will declare to the world from His own lips, "I have trodden the wine-press alone . . . and none were with me" (D&C 133:50).

The Savior could not die until He decided to die. For that to occur it may have required life-giving influence of His Father—the Mighty Elohim—to be completely withdrawn from Him. Once the Father's sustaining power departed, Jesus could then determine the actual moment of His death. Gospel scholar Hyrum Andrus supported this possibility. He explained that once the Father departed, "then caused the critical breakdown to occur in His bodily organs and tissues so that, when He willed that He should die, His spirit could readily depart into the spirit world."[14]

As mentioned in chapter 3, according to Brigham Young, in the garden the absence of His Father's sustaining power caused blood to flow from every pore. His withdrawal on the cross may have been necessary to allow the Savior's heart to physically break, causing cardiac rupture. The water and blood that gushed out from His heart when the spear was thrust into His side suggests that His heart literally broke. James E. Talmage explained, "The rupture of the heart causes blood to accumulate in the pericardium where the corpuscles separate from the almost colorless, water serum."[15] The Savior's heart breaking fulfilled the messianic psalm, "Reproach hath broken my heart" (Psalm 69:20).

Just as Jesus was left alone, to some small degree it may be the same for us on occasion. Part of the testing in mortality will be feeling alone and forsaken at times, feeling that the heavens are sealed and that no divine ear is listening.

Elder Neal A. Maxwell, who valiantly lost an eight-year battle with leukemia, taught in the midst of his own suffering: "There is, in the suffering of the highest order, a point that is reached—a point of aloneness—when the individual (as did the Savior on a much grander scale) must bear it . . . alone. Even the faithful may wonder if they can take any more or if they are in some way forsaken. Those who . . . stand at the foot of the cross often can do so little to help absorb the pain and the anguish. It is something we must bear ourselves in order that our triumph can be complete."[16]

Like Elder Maxwell, many of the Lord's servants have felt this aloneness from firsthand experience. I think of an incarcerated prophet in Liberty Jail who once wrote, "O God where art thou?" (D&C 121:1).

Job wrote, "Wherefore hidest though thy face. . . . I cry out. . . . I am not heard. . . . He is not there. . . . I cannot perceive him. . . . Oh, that I knew where I might find him. . . . I cannot behold him: he hideth himself. . . . I cannot find him" (Job 12:24; 19:7; 23:3,9).

Moroni, whose entire nation was destroyed, wrote, "I remain alone to write the sad tale of the destruction of my people" (Moroni 8:3).

The prophet Jeremiah, who was mocked and rejected by his people wrote, "I sat not in the assembly of the mockers, nor rejoiced; I sat alone" (Jeremiah 15:17).

Moses, for a time "was left unto himself" (Moses 1:9).

I think of Lehi, who traveled for the space of many hours [alone] in the darkness" (1 Nephi 8:8).

The Apostle Paul wrote, "They have killed thy prophets . . . and I am left alone, and they seek my life" (Romans 11:3). "[No] man stood with me, but all men forsook me" (2 Timothy 4:16).

King David wrote, "Thou didst hide thy face, and I was troubled" (Psalms 29:7).

When feelings of aloneness come to us we can remember that we are in good company.

Songwriter Michael McLean's father once said, "Isn't it interesting that the Greatest Intelligence in the Universe abandoned His Son at the most pivotal moment in His plan? Could it be that it was at this moment that the Greatest Intelligence of All bore witness to the universe that He had put His faith in Jesus? That He knew Jesus would choose Him no matter what? And could it be that when you think He has abandoned you that He is actually saying, 'I have faith you will choose me even when I'm not there?'"[17]

Christ's marvelous ability to face adversity without the loss of faith in His Father is one of the great lessons we can learn from Him. No son ever trusted his father so completely as did Jesus. His atoning sacrifice was the single greatest act of faith ever demonstrated. And so, when the day comes that you feel the heavens are silent and that you have been abandoned and forsaken, make the choice, like Jesus, to choose the Father. Choose the Father no matter what, and "wait upon the Lord" (Isaiah 8:17).

Isaiah promised, "But they that wait upon the Lord shall renew their strength; they shall mount up with wings as eagles; they shall run and not be weary; and walk and not faint" (Isaiah 40:31). "For since the beginning of the world men have not heard, nor perceived by the ear, neither hath the eye seen, O God, beside thee, what he hath prepared for him that waiteth for him" (Isaiah 64:4). Part of the testing in mortality is learning to wait upon the Lord and have faith in His timing.

Jesus endured and overcame the horrors of Satan, death and sin completely alone, so we don't have to do it alone. Jeffrey R. Holland testified,

> One of the great consolations of this Easter season is that because Jesus walked such a long, lonely path utterly alone, we do not have to do so. His solitary journey brought great companies for our little version of that path—the merciful care of our Father in Heaven, the unfailing companionship of this Beloved Son, the consummate gift of the Holy Ghost, angels in heaven, family members on both sides of the veil, prophets and apostles, teachers, leaders, friends. All of these and more have been given as companions for our mortal journey because of the Atonement of Jesus Christ.[18]

We will never be left entirely alone nor unaided, even if sometimes we may feel like we are. Such moments of testing may in fact be the time when Heavenly Father and the Savior are actually closest to us. Isaiah wrote that Zion would feel forsaken and forgotten by the Lord, and then explained, "But he will show that he hath not. For can a woman forget her sucking child, that she should not have compassion on the son of her womb? Yea, they may forget, yet will I not forget thee. *Behold I have graven thee upon the palms of my hands; thy walls are continually before me*" (Isaiah 49:14–16; emphasis added). The clause "I have grave thee upon the palms of my hands" is an allusion to the ancient practice of tattooing the palm with a symbol or sacred emblem that would serve as devotion and a reminder of one's commitment. This is a graphic way for the Lord to say, "You are constantly before me. I have not forgotten you." Of these Isaiah verses professor Donald Parry wrote, "The words 'thy walls are continually before me' likely refer to the walls of Jerusalem. These walls are ever present in the consciousness of those who dwell in the city. In the same way, an awareness of the people of Israel is ever present with the Lord."[19]

Considering the fact that the Savior has completed His atoning sacrifice, He is certainly not going to turn His back on us now. He will never abandon us. George Q. Cannon explained, "No matter how serious the trial, how deep the distress, how great the affliction, [God] will never desert us. He never has, and He never will. He cannot do it. It is not His character [to do so]."[20] That is an absolute, fixed eternal truth.

Elder Cannon continues, "When we went forth into the waters of baptism and covenanted with our Father in Heaven to serve Him and keep His commandments, He bound Himself also by covenant to us that He would never desert us, never leave us to ourselves, never forget us, that in the midst of trials and hardships, when everything was arrayed against us, He would be near unto us and would sustain us. That was His covenant."[21]

The Lord will never leave us to ourselves or desert us. That is the one great constant in eternity that we can be sure of. As Neal A. Maxwell put it, "God has no distracting hobbies. . . . We are at the very center of His concerns and purposes."[22] Just as the Savior saw and thought of each of us in Gethsemane and on the cross, we continue to be in His uppermost thoughts daily. We are never far from Him.

His Last Moments on the Cross

One of the last things the Savior uttered from the cross was, "I thirst" (John 19:28). Russell M. Nelson noted, "To a doctor of medicine, this is a very meaningful expression. Doctors know that when a patient goes into shock because of blood loss, invariably that patient—if still conscious— with parched and shriveled lips cries for water."[23] The irony is that Jesus, He to whom we all must go to receive the living waters that we may never thirst, now thirsted (see John 4:14; Isaiah 41:17)

This statement caused a soldier or a disciple, possibly one of the women, to soak a sponge in cheap bitter wine/vinegar. They lifted up the sponge on a hyssop branch and offered Jesus a drink. It is interesting to note that the hyssop was the plant mandated by the law of Moses for certain rituals of purification. During the first Passover the Israelites used the hyssop branch to spread the lamb's blood on their doorposts.

As the sponge was pressed to the Savior's lips, He drank. How ironic that the last taste upon the lips of Jesus who drank the bitter cup was bitterness. This fulfilled the final prophecy of His death: "They gave me also gall for my meat; and in my thirst they gave me vinegar to drink" (Psalm 69:21).

During His final three hours on the cross as darkness covered the land and the pains of Gethsemane re-occurred and intensified, the forsaken Jesus held on. Alone, He pressed on until the uttermost farthing had been paid. Gordon B. Hinkley said, "Everything depended on Him—His atoning sacrifice. That was the key. That was the keystone in the arch of the great plan [of] the Father. Terrible as it was to face, and burdensome as it was to realize it, He faced it. He accomplished it, and it was a marvelous and wonderful thing. It is beyond our comprehension. . . . Nevertheless, we glimpse it in small part and must learn to appreciate it more and more."[24]

And so, while on the cross, Christ held on until He completely fulfilled the will of His Father, satisfying the demands of justice in full, fulfilling every prophecy, every jot and tittle, and every nuance of the law. Nothing was left undone. Jesus drank every drop of the bitter cup and gained the complete victory. According to Elder Jeffrey R. Holland, "The goodness in Him allowed faith to triumph even in a state of complete anguish."[25]

At His final moment of victory, the spirit of God surged back into Him to say, in effect, "My Son I am here. You did it." Or as Elder Talmage put it, "Fully realizing that He was no longer forsaken, but that His atoning sacrifice had been accepted by the Father, and that His mission in the flesh had been carried to glorious consummation, He exclaimed in a loud voice of holy triumph: It is finished."[26]

When death approached to relieve Jesus from His horrible position, a ray of hope appeared through the abyss of darkness with which He had been surrounded, and in a spasm of relief, seeing the bright future beyond He said, "It is finished, thy will is done" (JST, Matthew 27:54). "Father, into thy hands I commend my spirit" (Luke 23:46).[27] And "He bowed his head and gave up the Ghost" (John 19:30). The terrible ordeal was over for both the Son and the Father.

Of this moment Elder Holland taught,

> When the uttermost farthing had then been paid, when Christ's determination to be faithful was as obvious as it was utterly invincible, finally and mercifully, it was finished. Against all odds and with none to help or uphold Him, Jesus of Nazareth, the living Son of the living God, restored physical life where death had held sway and brought joyful, spiritual redemption out of sin, hellish darkness, and despair. With faith in God He knew was there, He could say in triumph, 'Father into thy hands I commend my spirit.[28]

"He bowed his head and gave up the Ghost" (John 19:30). John did not write, "He bowed his head and died." What does the phrase he "gave up the Ghost" suggest? Christ's death was voluntary. He died through an act of will, a choice, and He would not make that choice until all was complete. Once again, no one could take His life from Him; He gave it freely. Joseph Fielding Smith explained, "Of all who have dwelt on this earth, the Son of God stands out alone as the only one who possessed life in himself and power over death inherently. Christ was never subject to death, even on the cross, but death was ever subject unto him."[29]

Theologian Alfred Edersheim has written, "His last cry with a loud voice was not like that of one dying. . . . In the language of the early Christian hymn, 'it was not Death which approached Christ, but Christ death: He died without death.' Christ encountered Death, not as conquered, but as the Conqueror."[30]

Wilford Woodruff explained, "Alone, while treading the winepress of the wrath of devils and men, [Christ] gained the keys of death, hell and the grave. These keys were forged while Christ prayed in Gethsemane, endured the acts of malice that followed, and suffered the agony of the cross."[31] Following His death Christ gained the keys of death and hell and became the Savior of the universe.

In the book of Revelation, John sees the Savior and hears Him bear record that He now has these keys: "I am he that liveth and was dead; and behold I am alive forevermore, Amen; and have the keys of hell and death" (Revelation 1:18). Jesus forged those keys in Gethsemane and at Calvary, and following His death He received them from His Father. Jesus now has presiding authority over the grave, the power to bring forth the Resurrection and the power to redeem us from hell. He holds the saving keys of both death and hell.

Lessons from the Cross

As we study the last day of the Savior's mortal life, we gain tremendous insight into His character. While suffering and facing death, the Savior taught us how to live. From Gethsemane to Calvary, as Christ worked out His Atonement, He taught us through both word and example. It was the greatest sermon ever given.

Christ swallowed every drop of the bitter cup without becoming bitter. He not only endured but endured well. Through the horrific ordeal there was no anger, no complaining or blaming. There was no self-pity, no "wo is me," and no turning inward. To the contrary, despite His own suffering, He continually reached out to comfort, help, and serve others. From Gethsemane through the crucifixion, Jesus ministered and sought to bless others to the very end.

- In Gethsemane, Jesus healed the ear of Malchus, the high priest's servant.
- The Savior protected His disciples from the mob who came to arrest Him in Gethsemane. "Let these go their way" (John 18:8).
- As the Savior carried the cross, He took the time to address the suffering of women who followed and said, "Daughters of Jerusalem weep not for me" (Luke 23:28).
- The Savior asked the Father to forgive the Roman soldiers who were crucifying Him. "Then said Jesus, Father, forgive them; for they know not what they do" (Luke 23:34). Many prophets have commented on this moment.

President Joseph F. Smith said, "I say that no man could utter such words as these at such a time; it required the power and spirit, the love, mercy, charity and forgiveness of God himself. I bear my testimony to you that a being who could ask God to forgive men from whom He had received such unmerited cruelty is nothing less than a God. If there was no other proof than this of the divine mission of Jesus Christ, this alone would convince me that Jesus was the Redeemer of the world. He taught and exemplified in His life the very principles that will redeem the world."[32]

Spencer W. Kimball has written, "He had said, "Love your enemies." Now he proved how much one can love his enemies. He was dying on the cross for those who had nailed him there."[33]

Of this moment Elder Holland taught, "For me, there is no greater amazement and no more difficult personal challenge than when, after the anguish in Gethsemane, after being mocked, beaten, and scourged, Jesus staggers under his load to the crest of Calvary and says, *'Father, forgive them; for they know not what they do'* (Luke 23:34). If ever there is a moment when I indeed stand all amazed, it is here, for this is an amazement of a different kind. So much of the mystery of his power and ministry tear at my mind: the circumstances of his birth, the breadth and variety of his ministry and miracles, the self-summoned power of his resurrection—before all of these I stand amazed and say, 'How did he do it?' But here with disciples who abandoned him in his hour of greatest need, here fainting under the weight of his cross and the sins of all mankind which were attached to it, here rent by piercing spikes in his palms and in his wrists and in his feet— . . . the amazement tears not at my mind but at my heart, and I ask not 'How did he do it?' but 'Why did he do it?' It is here that I examine my life, not against the miraculousness of his, but against the mercifulness of it, and it is here I find how truly short I fall in emulation of the Master.'"

Elder Holland continued, "Every generation in every dispensation of the world has had its own multitudes crowding around that cross, laughing and jeering, breaking commandments and abusing covenants. It isn't just a relative handful in the meridian of time who are guilty. It is most of the people, most of the places, most of the time, including all of us who should have known better. Surely the reason Christ said 'Father, forgive them' was because even in the weakened and terribly trying hour he faced, he knew that this was the message he had come through all eternity to deliver. All of the meaning and all of the majesty of all those dispensations—indeed the entire plan of salvation—would have been lost had he forgotten that not in spite of injustice and brutality and unkindness and disobedience but precisely because of them had he come to extend forgiveness to the family of man. Anyone can be pleasant and patient and forgiving on a good day. A Christian has to be pleasant and patient and forgiving on all days. It is the quintessential moment of his ministry . . . I stand all amazed that even for a man like me, full of egotism and transgression and intolerance and impatience, there is a chance. But if I've heard the 'good news' correctly there is a chance—for me and for you and for everyone who is willing to keep hoping and to keep trying and to allow others the same privilege."[34]

And so, we sing the hymn, "I Stand All Amazed." "I stand all amazed at the love Jesus offers me. Confused at the grace that so fully he proffers me. I tremble to know that for me he was crucified, that for me a sinner, he suffered, he bled and died . . . I marvel that he would descend from his throne divine To rescue a soul so rebellious and proud as mine . . . I think of his hands pierced and bleeding to pay the debt! Such mercy, such love, and devotion can I forget? No, no, I will praise and adore at the mercy seat, Until at the glorified throne I kneel at his feet. . . . Oh, it is wonderful, wonderful to me!" (*Hymns*, no. 193).

• While on the cross, the Savior reached out in love to the thief on the cross next to Him, extending comfort and hope, and saying, "Today shalt thou be with me in paradise"(Luke 23:43).

During my mission I vividly recall discussing this verse with some people who were investigating the Church. This statement has been difficult to interpret and has caused many to believe that all that is needed for salvation is a confession of the Lordship of Jesus Christ. Can a person live a destructive life contrary to the teachings of Christ and then confess the name of Jesus just before they die and thereby attain exaltation? While we are not to judge the fate of others, that thought is contrary to reason and contrary to what is written in the scriptures. Exaltation without effort is a doctrine of men and devils. Bruce R. McConkie has noted, "The great doctrinal problem growing out of this episode is concerned with death-bed repentance. Can man, after a life of wickedness, as they stand at death's door, confess the Lord Jesus with their lips and thereby gain salvation in his kingdom? . . . There is no such doctrine in the true gospel of Christ."[35]

Of this moment the Prophet Joseph Smith further explained, "There has been much said by modern divines about the words of Jesus (when on the cross) to the thief, saying, 'This day shalt thou be with me in paradise.' King James' translators make it out to say paradise. But what is paradise? It is a modern word: it does not answer at all to the original word that Jesus made use of. Find the original of the word paradise. You may as easily find a needle in a haymow. Here is a chance for battle, ye learned men. There is nothing in the original word in Greek from which this was taken that signifies paradise; but it was—This day thou shalt be with me in the world of spirits."[36]

I marvel and "stand all amazed" at the compassion the Savior exhibited while on the cross. He thought of others to the very end. In the midst of His own suffering, He reached out to the sin-laden thief on the cross. Regardless of what the man on the cross had done, regardless of his past, regardless of the fact that the man would soon depart from this life, the Savior reached out in love and offered hope. While on the cross, Jesus was also reaching out to you and to me.

Mary and the Cross

One the most touching moments on the cross is when the Savior acknowledged the suffering of His mother and reached out to her and entrusted her to the care of John, His beloved disciple. "When Jesus therefore saw his mother, and the disciple standing by, whom he loved, he saith unto his mother, Woman, behold thy Son! Then saith he to the disciple, Behold thy mother! And from that hour that disciple took her unto his own home" (John 19:26–27).

It appears that Joseph, the husband of Mary, had previously died and that Mary's other sons had not yet joined the household of faith and accepted Jesus. By saying to John, "Behold thy mother," Jesus tenderly committed His mother to John's protective care. Why John? Perhaps because Jesus knew John was going to outlive her. According to Christian history, Mary spent the rest of her life in John's care. [37]

In addition, not only was John at the cross, but John's mother, who is identified as Salome, was also at the cross. According to medieval tradition, Salome (known as Mary Salome) was counted as one of the three Mary's who were daughters of Saint Anne, making her the sister or half-sister of Mary, mother of Jesus. John's mother would have heard her son's special commission from the Savior and may have also helped care for her sister.

Nearly thirty-three years prior to the cross, Mary the Savior's mother was told by the aged prophet Simeon, who held the baby Jesus in his arms at the temple, that a "spear shall pierce through him to the wounding of thine own soul also" (JST, Luke 2:35). That prophecy would be completely fulfilled following the death of Jesus when the soldiers pierced Him with a spear to ensure His death. One can only imagine how deeply Mary's heart was wounded as she watched her son suffer on the cross.

Many of the scattered disciples had by now gathered. Of them Bruce R. McConkie added, "While helpless disciples looked on and felt the agonies of near death in their own bodies."[38] All of their souls were wounded as they watched their Master suffer.

Sister Elaine L. Jack, former Relief Society General President, taught, "At this most dramatic moment of all time, there was [His] mother, Mary. She couldn't soothe his pain . . . , but she could stand by his side."[39] In the Garden of Gethsemane an angel came to comfort, encourage, and stand with the Savior. While on the cross, the Savior did not receive strength from an angel as He did in Gethsemane. However, His angelic mother was there. She stood by Him. If anyone in mortality understood His mission, I believe it was His mother. She knew that her son's hour had come. I picture her standing by her son at the cross, encouraging Him with thoughts or even words, "I love you, I believe in you, I have faith in you, you can do it, hold on!"

Mary stood at her son's side and suffered as He suffered. We, like Mary, may not at times be able to relieve or remove the suffering of our loved ones, but we can be there with them. We can stand by their sides, pray for them, encourage them, and believe in the goodness in them. We can keep our baptismal covenant, "to mourn with those that mourn" (Mosiah 18:9).

Once the Savior gave John the commission to care for His mother, the record says, "From that hour that disciple took her unto his home" (John 19:27). John took Mary away from the cross, away from her suffering son. Why? The Savior may have instructed John to do that. Once again in His most trying moment, the Savior thought of His mother. Maybe He thought she had seen enough, suffered enough, and He didn't want her to watch anymore. So,

He commissioned John right then and there to take her away and comfort and care for her.

There are two contrary traditions as to where Mary lived following the death of Jesus. One is that she remained in Jerusalem and lived in the house of John the Beloved, traditionally on Mount Zion. The other is that she accompanied John on a journey to Ephesus, where she lived to the end of her life.[40]

The instruction to John and Mary from Jesus on the cross applies to all of us. Do we behold our mothers and fathers? Do parents behold their sons and daughters? For years now, I have watched my father with great compassion "behold" and care for his aged mother.[41]

Professor Andrew Skinner wrote, "Golgotha is as profound a story of unsurpassed concern for others in the face of violence and vileness as will ever be found. Even in the throes of death, when he was experiencing the greatest suffering and most underserved treatment ever known, the Savior of the universe was thinking of others—his family, his associates, all of us, and his literal Father."[42]

The Savior thought of others to the very end of His life. From His comments on the cross we learn the essence of His greatness, His merciful and forgiving nature, His concern for others, His endurance in patience, and His supreme goodness. He taught us that during the much more modest Gethsemanes and Golgothas of our lives we should look to others. Thinking and reaching out to those in need in the midst of our own suffering appears to be an element of enduring our trials well.

HEAVENLY FATHER AND THE ATONEMENT

We sometimes forget that Heavenly Father was intimately involved as the Savior worked out the Atonement. As we have mentioned, in Gethsemane it was the Father who told His Son there was no other way. It was the Father who placed the infinite burden upon Christ and refused to remove it. It was the Father who cast a veil between Him and His suffering Son. We cannot begin to fathom what agony and heartache Heavenly Father must have felt as heard

His suffering Son exclaim, "Father, why has thou forsaken me?" How that must have wrenched His heart.

Maybe that is one reason Abraham was asked to offer up his only son, Isaac, so that one mortal father would have an inkling, some insight, into what Heavenly Father did for us. The prophet Abraham's faith was such that he raised the knife in obedience to slay Isaac. To Abraham's and Isaac's great relief an angel came and delivered them both from the test. Let us never forget that Heavenly Father allowed the knife to be raised, but it was not stayed. There was no angel of deliverance. The knife fell and was driven through His pure, perfect, Holy Son, and "the life's blood" of His Beloved Son went out.

Jeffrey R. Holland shared this important insight about the Father withdrawing His presence: "With all the conviction of my soul I testify that . . . a perfect Father did not forsake His Son in that hour. Indeed, it is my personal belief that in all of Christ's mortal ministry the Father may never have been closer to His Son than in these agonizing final moments of suffering."[43] The Father's physical presence and sustaining power may have departed, a veil cast between the two, but certainly Heavenly Father's eyes were upon His perfect, pure, suffering Only Begotten Son—His every thought, His whole heart going out to Him; His own heart breaking as He watched and let the knife fall. Two divine beings suffered that Thursday evening and Friday. How Heavenly Father must have wanted to save His Son from suffering and remove the bitter cup. Let it be remembered just as Jesus could have withdrawn and stopped the suffering, so could have His Father.

Elder Melvin J. Ballard commented, "In that hour I think I can see our dear Father behind the veil looking upon these dying struggles until even he could not endure it any longer; and like the mother who bids farewell to her dying child, has to be taken out of the room, so as not to look upon the last struggles, so he bowed his head, and hid in some part of his universe, his great heart almost breaking for the love that he had for his Son. Oh, in that moment when he might have saved his Son, I thank him and praise him that he did not fail us, for he had not only the love of his Son in mind, but he also has had the love for us in mind."[44]

Could the Father have saved us and performed the Atonement? Heavenly Father gave His Only Begotten Son the power necessary to save us. Hence, the Savior is the Father's representative in performing the Atonement and bringing salvation to mankind.

Since the Fall came by blood, so redemption from the Fall would occur by blood, for "without shedding of blood [there] is no remission" (Hebrews 9:22). To commemorate the preeminence of this sacrifice, God from the time of Adam had required a blood sacrifice. He required His children to offer the firstlings of their flocks. These sacrifices were in similitude of the sacrifice of the Only Begotten of the Father. And being in similitude, their blood, or life, had to be given. For blood is "the life of the flesh." That is, life, or blood, was required to make "an atonement for the soul" (Leviticus 17:11).

In a sense, Jesus did for His Father that which His Father could not do Himself. The Father could not shed His own blood for the sins of mankind. Why? He had no blood to shed. Nor could He lay down His life in the manner Jesus did. The Father was and is a resurrected being whose spirit and flesh are inseparably connected and are never to be divided (see D&C 93:33; 130:22; Alma 11:45).

At the time this was not the case with Jesus. Thus, the great atoning sacrifice was a supreme, vicarious ordinance in behalf of both the Father and all of His children. The Father sent His Beloved Son because He could not come Himself. And this was in accordance with the plan of redemption which had been formulated by the Father from before the foundation of the world was laid. The Atonement was the ordinance of all ordinances performed by Christ and Christ alone.

The Symbol of the Cross

One evening a few years ago, there was a knock at the door of our home. Three of my children raced to the door and opened it. In front of them stood an older gentleman, a complete stranger. He asked if I was home. I came to the door. He said he had a gift for me and handed me a box. I invited him into our house. He asked me to open the present. To my surprise, he had made me three beautiful wooden crosses. He explained that he had attended one of my stake religion classes where we discussed the significance of the cross and he was impressed to make these crosses for me. For years he had been making crosses but usually did not make it known among Church members.

This man's visit prompted a conversation with my children about the cross. What would you have said to them about the symbol of the cross? How do you feel about how our fellow Christians use the symbol of the cross?

Many would respond and say something like what President Gordon B. Hinckley has taught: "Because our Savior lives, we do not use the symbol of his death as the symbol of our faith. But what shall we use? No sign, no work of art, no representation of form is adequate to express the glory and wonder of the living Christ. He told us what that symbol should be when he said, 'If ye love me, keep my commandments.'"[45] I likewise explained to my children that our thoughts rest not upon a dead but a living Christ. My conversation with my children about the cross did not end with just that.

Gospel scholar Robert Millet explained, "Historically we should note that in the first few Christian centuries the cross was not considered a virtuous or admirable symbol but rather a terrifying reminder of what Jesus and many thousands of others had ignominiously suffered. In fact, some scholars report that the cross did not appear in churches as a symbol of veneration until AD 431. Crosses on steeples did not appear until AD 586, and it was not until the sixth century that crucifixes were sanctioned by the Roman Church."[46] Initially the cross was not a positive symbol for any Christian faith.

However, over time, things changed, and the cross came to be used as a positive symbol for most in Christianity. In 1916, a church asked the Salt Lake City Council to allow them to build a huge cross, "the symbol of Christianity," on Ensign Peak. The request read, "We would like to construct it of cement, re-enforced with steel, of sufficient dimensions that it can be readily seen from every part of the city." Surprisingly, the church that made that request was The Church of Jesus Christ of Latter-day Saints. The cross was intended to honor the Mormon Pioneers. Even though the proposal was approved by the city council, the monument was never built. Some within the Church liked the symbol of the cross, but others did not.

The symbol of the cross appeared all over our early Church and communities. It appeared as jewelry often worn by the women of the Church, including Brigham Young's wives and daughters. It appeared in floral arrangements at funerals. It appeared as tie tacks on men's ties and watch fobs on men's vests. The cross was the official LDS Church brand on cattle. Crosses were on church windows, attic vents, stained-glass windows and pulpits. They were on gravestones and quilts. Even two temples, the Hawaiian and the Cardston, Alberta, Canada Temple, were described in a 1923 general conference as being built in the shape of a cross. The cross is in some ways part of our early heritage that we have forgotten about.

Negative feelings about the symbol of the cross began as a grass roots movement that began around the turn of the twentieth century within the Church. Overtime many members' feelings regarding the cross changed. One reason that occurred was the minor conflicts that occurred between The Church of Jesus Christ of Latter-day Saints and other Christian faiths. Eventually, most members including leaders of the Church, quit using the symbol all together.[47]

The Apostle Paul repeatedly preached the cross. He wrote, *"For the preaching of the cross* is to them that perish foolishness; but unto us which are saved it is the power of God"* (1 Corinthians 1:18; emphasis added). Writing to the Galatian Saints, Paul taught, "But God forbid that I should glory, save in the cross of our Lord Jesus Christ" (Galatians 6:14). Paul gloried in the cross.

Kent S. Brown explained, "The cross is the most enduring symbol in Christendom. As a symbol, it points in two directions. First, it looks backward over the events of Jesus' life and ministry that have brought Him to His agonizing crucifixion, seeing Him as Exemplar, Teacher, Nurturer, Son and Brother. In this sense, the cross casts a dark shadow that, ironically, sets into relief the enlightening goodness that radiated from Jesus. Second, the cross looks to the future, beyond His suffering, to the tomb, specifically the empty tomb on Sunday morning, when His resurrection breaks apart the otherwise unbreakable bands of death and pierces the impenetrable barrier that has separated God and His children for eons of time. In this sense the cross is an instrument of healing, now and forever. We thus see the cross in an ever-shining arc of light as the tree of life."[48]

In this Church and kingdom, symbolism plays an important role in learning and understanding the gospel. As we consider and ponder the ordinances of the temple, we find the symbol of the cross. Symbols are multifaceted and often invite layers of meaning. While the cross was an evil instrument of excruciating torture, with Christ the symbol can take on a positive new meaning for us. In 1915, the *Young Women's Journal* of the Church published this statement: "The cross that was then a sign of disgrace has become a symbol of love and salvation." In 1933, the Relief Society magazine published this statement: "Christ changed the cross into a symbol of Glory." Today, the symbol of the cross can likewise remind us and invite us to do many wonderful things. It can invite us to do the following:

- Forgive all men. (D&C 64:10)
- Extend mercy to others—that we may obtain mercy. (D&C 88:40, 3Nephi 12:7)
- Put others before ourselves and serve one another. (Mosiah 2:17)
- Take up our own crosses and follow Him. (Matthew 10:38, Luke 9:23)

    The prophet Jacob from the Book of Mormon wrote, "Wherefore, would to God that . . . all men would believe in Christ, and view his death and suffer his cross and bear the shame of the world" (Jacob 1:8). Jacob invited us to "suffer his cross." We have we been asked to carry and suffer the cross of discipleship, which invites us to "deny ourselves of all ungodliness" (Moroni 10:32). The cross which we are to take up is not one of our own devising, but the cross which God sees fit to lay upon us.

- Endure all things with patience and dignity. (D&C 67:13; 1 Peter 2:23)
- Remember that if Jesus, who was pure and perfect, suffered

trials, tribulation, and injustice, we likewise will be tutored and tested during our mortal sojourn by some degree of suffering.

- Remember that because of it, we will all be lifted up, resurrected, and drawn to the Savior. The cross connects us to Christ. The resurrected Savior said to the Nephites, "My Father sent me that I might be lifted up upon the cross; and after that I had been lifted up upon the cross, that I might draw all men unto me, that as I have been lifted up by men even so should men be lifted up by the Father, to stand before me, to be judged of their works" (3 Nephi 27:13–14).

There is a line in the second verse in the hymn "We Are All Enlisted" that encourages us to "rally round the standard of the cross" (*Hymns*, no. 250).

President Joseph F. Smith reminded us, "Having been born anew, which is the putting away of the old man sin, and putting on the man Christ Jesus, we have become *soldiers of the cross,* having enlisted under the banner of Jehovah for time and for eternity."[49]

All of this supports what President Brigham Young taught future missionaries when he said, "I would say to my young friends . . . that if you go on a mission to preach the gospel with lightness and frivolity in your hearts, . . . and not having your minds riveted—yes, I may say riveted—*on the cross of Christ,* you will go and return in vain."[50]

Frederic Farrar said, "Any contemplation of the Cross which inspires us to do all and bear all for His sake who died for us and rose again is right."[51] I love the symbol of the cross. Over the years it has taken on new meaning for me. The invitation I have found is that we rally around the standard Christ set for us while on the cross, become soldiers of the cross, have our minds riveted on the cross, and like Paul become preachers of the cross.

WHO IS RESPONSIBLE?

The question might be asked, who is responsible for the arrest, mistreatment, conviction, and death of Jesus?

The Roman soldiers who crucified Christ acted under the mandate of a sovereign nation. While on the cross, that is who Jesus forgave (see JST, Luke 23:35). As we have noted, the responsibility certainly falls upon Pilate, Annas, Caiaphas, and other Jewish leaders of His day. Judas also played a key role in His death. However, the Lord has never come out and put the blame on any single person or group of people. Jesus was not a victim. He was foreordained to die; His death was supposed to happen.

In the end, the issue of culpability is placed squarely at our own feet. As the hymn "He Died, The Great Redeemer Died" reminds us, "He shed a thousand drops for you, A thousands drops of precious blood." We are all sinners, and thus it was necessary for Jesus to perform an atonement and die to complete the act of redemption for you and for me. Thus, we are all in a very real way, responsible for the circumstances of that terrible day. Elder James E. Faust said, "One cannot help wondering how many of those drops of precious blood each of us may be responsible for."[52]

He Took My Whipping for Me

There is a story told that in the mountains of Virginia years ago there was a class of boys no teacher could handle. The boys were so rough that the teachers resigned. A young teacher applied for the job. The old school director scanned him up and down and then said, "Young fellow, do you know what you are asking for? An awful beating, that's what. Every teacher we've had up there gives up in defeat." The young teacher replied, "I'll risk it. Let me try."

When he appeared for duty in the little school, one big fellow, Tom, whispered, "I won't need any help; I can lick him myself."

The teacher said, "Good morning. We have come to conduct school." The students yelled a sarcastic "good morning" back at the teacher at the top of their lungs.

"Now, I want a good school," the teacher continued, "but I confess, I don't know how unless you help me. Suppose we have a few rules. You tell me and I'll write them on the blackboard."

One fellow yelled, "No stealing!" Another chipped in, "Be on time!" Finally, ten rules appeared. "Now, said the teacher, "a law is not good unless there is a penalty attached. What shall we do with the one who breaks them?"

"Beat them across the back ten times without his coat on!" came the shout.

"That is a pretty severe punishment, boys. Are you ready to stand by it?" A yell in the affirmative greeted the teacher. "All right," said the teacher, "then school comes to order."

In a day or so "Big Tom" found his lunch was stolen. Upon inquiry the thief was located—a little hungry fellow about ten. The next morning the teacher announced, "We have found the thief and he must be punished according to your rule—ten stripes across the back! Jim, come up here!"

The trembling little fellow came up slowly with a big coat, buttoned and pinned up around his neck. He pleaded, "Teacher, you can lick me as hard as you like but please don't make me take off my coat."

"You helped make the rules," reasoned the teacher. "Take the coat off."

"Oh, teacher, don't make me!" he begged, but the teacher's stern face showed no leniency, so he began to unbutton. And what did the teacher behold? The lad had no shirt on and only strings for suspenders over his bony little body.

"How can I whip this boy?" thought the teacher. "But I must do something if I am going to keep this classes respect."

Everyone was quiet as death. "How come you came to school without a shirt, Jim?" asked the teacher.

"My father died, and we ain't got much. I only have one shirt, and mother's washing it today, so I wore my brother's coat to keep warm."

With a sigh of a heavy heart, the teacher hesitatingly grasped the rod in his hand. Just then "Big Tom" jumped to his feet and said, "Teacher, if you don't mind, I'll take Jim's licking for him."

"Very well, there is a certain law that one can take another's punishment for him. Are you all in agreement?" With the class's consent Tom removed his coat, and after five strokes the rod broke. The teacher bowed his head and thought, "How can I finish this awful task?"

Then he heard the entire class sobbing, and what did he see? Little Jim had reached up and caught Tom with both arms around the neck. "Tom, I'm awful sorry, Tom. I was so hungry. I'll love you till I die for taking my licking for me. I'll love you forever!"

May we love our Savior forever. May we seek to fulfill the scripture and make mention of His loving kindness and goodness "forever and ever!" (see D&C 133:52).

In December of 2018, I was awakened one night from my sleep by the whisperings of the Spirit. The face of one of my patients entered into my mind. The thought came to me that I needed to extend mercy and help him. He needed a fair amount of treatment. It was treatment he could not pay for. The impression was to help him with it. In addition, this young man currently owed my practice a significant amount of money for previous care. It was an amount that would take him a long time to pay. The thought pressed itself that I needed to release him from his debt.

Immediately following the thought of that young man, a much stronger impression came. The thought was regarding the massive, unpayable debt I owed the Savior. It was made clear to me that the money my patient owed to me was nothing, absolutely nothing, compared to the debt I owed my Savior. It was overwhelming. Words are not sufficient to describe what I felt. I learned something of the debt I owe, and it is a debt that I can never repay. A debt the Savior lovingly, freely paid for me, a debt He freely paid for you. In the words of the hymn, "Come Thou Fount of Every Blessing, "O, to grace, how great a debtor daily I'm constrained to be."

Paul reminded the Corinthian Saints, "For ye are bought with a price" (1 Corinthians 6:20). What an expense price! That purchase was paid in full for us in Gethsemane and upon the cross at Calvary. When it comes to our physical and spiritual salvation, we owe Jesus everything. He took our punishment, our licking for us. He gave His all, His everything in order to save us.

As I have attempted to understand and comprehend the events that took place during the last two days in the life of Jesus, I am completely overwhelmed by it all. Words are insufficient to explain what I have felt. I echo the words of S. Dilworth Young, who wrote,

"There are many events in the life of the Lord in which I experience exquisite joy as I read of them, and there are others which bow me down with the tragedy of his suffering and of his sacrifice. . . . I am not capable of fully understanding the suffering of this great first-born Son of God for the sins of the world. . . . I realize that this was endured for me and for you; I bow my head; it is hard to hold back the tears. Even now, 1900 years later, it is as poignant as though it occurred yesterday."[53]

ENDNOTES

1. Truman G. Madsen, *Sacramental Reflections: Feasting at the Lords Table* (Salt Lake City: Deseret Book, 2015), 4.
2. A., Van Orden Bruce, and Brent L. Top, editors. *The Lord of the Gospels* (Salt Lake City: Deseret Book, 1991), 41.
3. Frederic W. Farrar, *The Life of Christ* (Salt Lake City: Bookcraft, 1995), 641.
4. Bruce R. McConkie, *The Mortal Messiah: From Bethlehem to Calvary.* Vol. 4 (Salt Lake City: Deseret Book, 1979), 210.
5. Tad R. Callister, *The Infinite Atonement* (Salt Lake City: Deseret Book, 2000), 131.
6. McConkie, ibid., 214.
7. James E. Talmage, *Jesus the Christ* (Salt Lake City: Deseret Book, 1915/1982), 613.
8. McConkie, ibid., 232.
9. Bruce R. McConkie, *Doctrinal New Testament Commentary.* Vol. 1 (Salt Lake City: Bookcraft, 1965), 821.
10. Erastus Snow, *Journal of Discourses* 21:26.
11. Stephen Edward Robinson, *Believing Christ: The Parable of the Bicycle and Other Good News* (Salt Lake City: Deseret Book, 1992), 119.
12. Bryan Richards, "Commentary on Matthew 27:47," *Gospel Doctrine,* https://gospeldoctrine.com/new-testament/matthew/matthew-27.
13. Church Education System, *The Life and Teachings of Jesus and the Apostles.* 2nd ed., The Church of Jesus Christ of Latter-Day Saints, 1978, 186. See James E. Talmage, *Jesus the Christ* (Salt Lake City: Deseret Book, 1915/1982), 661.
14. Hyrum L. Andrus, *God, Man and the Universe* (Salt Lake City: Deseret Book, 1999), 425.
15. James E. Talmage, *Jesus the Christ* (Salt Lake City: Deseret Book, 1915/1982), 669.
16. Neal A. Maxwell, *All These Things Shall Give Thee Experience* (Salt Lake City: Deseret Book, 1979), 43. C. S. Lewis writing as a devil to another devil (Wormwood) put it this way: "Sooner or later [God] withdraws, if

not in fact, at least from their conscious experience, all those supports and incentives. He leaves the creature to stand up on its own legs—to carry out from the will alone duties that have lost all relish. It is during such trough periods, much more than during the peak periods that it is growing into the sort of creature he wants it to be. Hence the prayers offered in the state of dryness are those which please Him best. . . He wants them to learn to walk and must therefore take away His hand; and if only the will to walk is really there He is pleased with their stumbles. Do not be deceived Wormood. Our cause is never more in danger than when a human, no longer desiring, but still intending, to do our Enemy's [God's] will, looks around upon a universe from which every trace of Him seems to have vanished, and asks why he has been forsake, and still obeys" (C. S. Lewis, *The Screwtape Letters* [C. S. Lewis Pte. Ltd., 1942/1996], chapter 8, 40).

17. Jamie Armstrong, "Michael McLean Opens Up About His 9–Year Faith Crisis and How He Found His Testimony Again," *LDS Living*, Nov. 2016, 26.
18. Jeffrey R. Holland, "None Were with Him," April 2009 general conference.
19. Donald Parry, *Visualizing Isaiah*, Neal A. Maxwell Institute of Religious Scholarship, USA, 2001.
20. George Q. Cannon, "Remarks," *Deseret News*, Mar. 7, 1891, 4.
21. George Q. Cannon, *Gospel Truth: Discourses and Writings of President George Q. Cannon* (Salt Lake City: Deseret Book, 1974), 134.
22. Neal A. Maxwell, "How Choice a Seer!" October 2003 general conference.
23. Russell M. Nelson, "The Atonement," October 1996 general conference.
24. Gordon B. Hinckley, *Teachings of the Presidents of the Church: Gordon B. Hinckley.* The Church of Jesus Christ of Latter-Day Saints, 2016, 325.
25. Jeffrey R. Holland, "None Were with Him," April 2009 general conference.
26. James E. Talmage, *Jesus the Christ* (Salt Lake City: Deseret Book, 1915/1982), 614.
27. John Taylor, *Mediation and Atonement* (Deseret News Company, 1882/1998), 151.
28. Jeffrey R. Holland, "None Were with Him," April 2009 general conference.
29. Joseph Fielding Smith, *Doctrines of Salvation.* Edited by Bruce R. McConkie (Salt Lake City: Bookcraft, 1992), 31.
30. Alfred Edersheim, *The Life and Times of Jesus the Messiah.* Vol. 2 (Eerdmans Pub. Co., 1971), 609.
31. Wilford Woodruff, et al. "Epistle of the General Superintendency," *The Contributor*, June 1888.
32. Joseph F. Smith, *Teachings of the Presidents of the Church: Joseph F. Smith*, The Church of Jesus Christ of Latter-Day Saints, 1998, 4.
33. Spencer W. Kimball, "Jesus of Nazareth," *Ensign*, Dec. 1980.
34. Jeffrey R. Holland, "I Stand All Amazed," *Ensign*, Aug. 1986.
35. Bruce R. McConkie, *Doctrinal New Testament Commentary.* Vol. 1 (Salt Lake City: Bookcraft, 1965), 184.

36. Joseph Smith and Joseph Fielding Smith, *Teachings of the Prophet Joseph Smith* (Salt Lake City: Deseret Book, 1958/1977), 309. Elder Orson F. Whitney has likewise taught, "[Some] uninspired minds have drawn the conclusion that the penitent thief was promised immediate heavenly exaltation, for repenting at the last moment and professing faith in the Redeemer. . . . Jesus never taught such a doctrine, nor did any authorized servant of the Lord. It is a man-made theory, based upon faulty inference and misinterpretation. The Scriptures plainly teach that men will be judged according to their works, and receive rewards as varied as their deeds. It was best for the thief, of course, to repent even at the eleventh hour; but he could not be exalted until prepared for it, if it took a thousand years" (Orson F. Whitney, *Saturday Night Thoughts*, *The Deseret News*, 1921, 290–291.)

37. W. Jeffrey Marsh, *His Final Hours* (Salt Lake City: Deseret Book, 2000), 77.

38. Bruce R. McConkie, "The Purifying Power of Gethsemane," April 1985 general conference.

39. Elaine L. Jack, "Relief Society: A Balm in Gilead," October 1995 general conference.

40. Ronald Brownrigg, *Who's Who in the New Testament*. 1st ed. (Holt, Rhineart, and Winston, 1971), 295.

41. Regarding the Savior's instruction to John to care for His mother, Matthew Cowley shared the following:

You see, John knew what the Master wanted. "Behold your son; son, behold your mother." I don't think we're doing much of that in our Church. Mothers are not beholding their sons. They're beholding some agency or government organization which has nothing to do with their sons. And the sons are not beholding their mothers. And so, as a result we break down the integrity of the family. I was in Canada one day about five years ago. And I went to a home of a bishop for dinner. He wanted me to stay at his home, but he didn't have room. Well, I went to dinner. When the dinner was all set, he went into a little room and carried out a little woman: a lovely little soul, with white hair, and he took her over and placed her down gently in a chair at the table. Then he took a serviette and put it around her neck, pushed the chair up close, and then he went back to the room and came out with his arms around an elderly man: a little white haired man, and then he took him over and gently placed him at the side of the woman. Then he took a serviette and put it around his neck. And then we all sat down. And then he said, "Brother Cowley, this is the reason we don't have room for you. These are the parents of my wife, and we're trying to get even with them, while they're so helpless, for what they did for my wife when she was a helpless child." And before that man and his wife took a spoonful of food, they fed the lovely parents, who couldn't feed themselves. "Woman, behold thy son; son, behold thy mother." Did you ever hear anything more beautiful than that?

In contrast, I went to a home in Salt Lake City to see a relative of mine. It was a home for aged women. When I called on her, she broke down and wept, pleading with me to call on her children to see if one of them wouldn't take her to his home. She died in that home for aged women. She had been a woman of considerable wealth but had given most of what she had acquired to her children. Is there any way we can live better as sons than by accepting the vocation, the call, the summons that John did-to bless those who are near to us, to whom we owe so much?" (Cowley, Matthew. *Matthew Cowley Speaks* [Salt Lake City: Deseret Book, 1954], 306–307).

42. Andrew C. Skinner, *Golgotha* (Salt Lake City: Deseret Book, 2004), 111.

43. Jeffrey R. Holland, "None Were with Him," April 2009 general conference.

44. Melvin J. Ballard, *Crusader for Righteousness* (Salt Lake City: Bookcraft, 1966), 135.

45. Gordon B. Hinckley, "The Symbol of Christ," *Ensign*, Apr. 1990.

46. Robert Millett, "Glorying in the Cross of Christ," *Behold the Lamb of God: An Easter Celebration*, BYU Religious Studies Center, 2008, 125–138.

47. Michael De Groote, "Mormons and the Cross," *Deseret News*, Sept. 10, 2009, https://www.deseret.com/2009/9/10/20339414/mormons-and-the-cross#lds-president-joseph-f-smith-talks-at-funeral-at-brigham-city-tabernacle-amid-cross-shaped-floral-arrangements.

48. S. Kent Brown,, et al. *Beholding Salvation: The Life of Christ in Word and Image* (Salt Lake City: Deseret Book, 2006), 77.

49. Joseph F. Smith, *Gospel Doctrine* (Salt Lake City: Deseret Book, 1986), 91.

50. Brigham Young, "General Instructions to Missionaries Going Abroad," *Journal of Discourses*, vol. 12, *The Editorium*, 2013, 33–34.

51. Frederic William Farrar, *The Life of Lives, Further Studies in the Life of Christ* (Cassell and Company, 1900), 520.

52. James E. Faust, "The Supernal Gift of the Atonement," October 1988 general conference.

53. S. Dilworth Young, "When I Read, I Am There," *Ensign*, July 1973.

CHAPTER 8

THE AFTERMATH OF THE CRUCIFIXION

THE EARTH REACTS TO THE CRUCIFIXION

We know that following the crucifixion in Jerusalem darkness covered the land and "the earth did quake and the rocks were rent" (Matthew 27:51). We also read in the Book of Mormon of tempests, earthquakes, fires, whirlwinds, and other physical upheavals. One of the earthquakes alone lasted for three hours. Following the destruction was three days of darkness in the Americas, all of it attesting to the crucifixion and death of Jesus (see 3 Nephi 8).

Nephi taught, "The rocks of the earth must rend; and because of the groanings of the earth, many of the kings of the isles of the sea shall be wrought upon by the Spirit of God to exclaim: *The God of nature suffers*" (1 Nephi 19:12; emphasis added). President Spencer W. Kimball taught, "These earth spasms were a revolt by the created earth against the crucifixion of its Creator."[1]

Enoch explained more than the earth was affected by the death of Christ. We read that *"all the creations of God mourned; and the earth groaned; and the rocks were rent"* (Moses 7:56; emphasis added). Enoch taught that when Jesus died, *"all eternity shook"* (Moses 7:41; emphasis added).

John Taylor explained,

By reason of some principle, to us unfathomable, His suffering affected universal nature. . . . When he gave up the ghost, the solid rocks were riven, the foundations of the earth trembled, earthquakes shook the continents and rent the isles of the sea, a deep darkness overspread the sky, the mighty waters overflowed their accustomed bounds, huge mountains sank and valleys rose, the handiwork of feeble men was overthrown, their cities were engulfed or consumed by the vivid shafts of lighting, and all material things were convulsed with the throes of seeming dissolution . . . *Thus, such was the torturing pressure of this indescribable agony, that it burst forth abroad beyond the confines of His body, convulsed all nature and spread throughout all space.*[2]

All of the creations in the universe mourned and felt the effects of the Savior's suffering and death that Friday. That is, all but the wicked and rebellious mourned. The entire creation itself, including all of the organized intelligence in matter that makes up the universe, was affected by the death of Jesus Christ. It all acknowledged and honored His atoning sacrifice, with the noted exception of rebellious man.

The Veil of the Temple

In addition to the earthquake and the rocks rending in Jerusalem, "the veil of the temple was rent in twain from the top to the bottom" (Matthew 27:51).

Bruce R. McConkie taught,

Once each year in ancient Israel the high priest passed through the veil of the temple into the Holy of Holies. This solemn act was part of the sacrificial rites performed in similitude of the coming sacrifice of the Son of God, and these rites were performed for the remission of sins. . . . But Christ is now sacrificed; the law is fulfilled; the Mosaic dispensation is dead, the fullness of the gospel has come with all its light and power; and so—to dramatize, in a way which all Jewry would recognize, that the kingdom had been taken from them and given to others—Deity rent the veil of the temple "from the top to the bottom." The Holy of Holies is now open to all, and all, through the atoning blood of the Lamb, can now enter into the highest and holiest of all places. . . . Paul, in expressive language (Hebrews 9 and 10), shows how the ordinances performed through the veil of the ancient temple were in similitude of what Christ was to do, which he now having done, all men become eligible to pass through the veil into the presence of the Lord to inherit full exaltation.[3]

The Talmud describes the temple veil as actually two veils hanging in front of the Holy of Holies. The veils were some sixty feet long, thirty feet wide, and about four inches thick. They were made of fine material and beautifully embroidered with white, scarlet, blue, and gold thread. The veils were so heavy—due to the seventy-two plaited squares sewn onto the fabric—that it took three hundred priests to immerse and clean just one veil before hanging it in the holy temple. If the temple veils were rent as the scriptures attest, an earthquake would not cause them to be "rent in twain," or to be torn from top to bottom. Indeed, everything seems to indicate that although the earthquake might furnish the physical basis, the rent of the temple veil was—with reverence be it said—really made by the hand of God.

When the veils were rent, the Holy of Holies was exposed. The exposure revealed an empty chamber except for a large stone on which the high priest sprinkled sacrificial blood on the Day of Atonement. Rending the veil symbolized the rending of Judaism, the consummation of the Mosaic dispensation, and the inauguration of Christianity under apostolic administration.[4]

The Holy of Holies was exposed and now open unto all. Paul similarly taught the Ephesians, "Christ . . . hath broken down *the middle wall of partition* between us . . . ye are no more strangers and foreigners but fellow citizens with the saints, and of the household of God" (Ephesians 2:13–14, 19; emphasis added). Surrounding the ancient temple was a stone (partition) wall about four and one-half feet high, with inscriptions posted in Greek and Latin warning Gentiles not to pass into exclusively Jewish space. It meant death for a Gentile to pass the barrier. The word "foreigners" was the very word used in the inscription on the partition forbidding Gentiles to approach. Christ had now symbolically broken down or taken away that barrier between Gentile and Jew. The gospel blessings were now available to all.

THE BURIAL

Joseph of Arimathea

Isaiah had prophesied that the Messiah would be "with the rich in his death" (Isaiah 53:9). Joseph of Arimathea would fulfill that prophecy. Joseph was a very wealthy, distinguished member of the Sanhedrin, high in character.[5] However, he had one major character flaw we are aware of. "Being a disciple of Jesus, but secretly for *fear of the Jews*" (John 19:38; emphasis added). Joseph was afraid of public opinion.

When the Sanhedrin were called into session early Friday morning, Joseph absented himself from the council. While we give him some credit for abstaining in the vote that condemned Jesus to die, he certainly could have taken a stronger position and defended Jesus. But, for "fear of the Jews," he remained in the shadows, lacking the moral courage to stand for the right.

Mark recorded, "Joseph of Arimathea, an honorable counsellor, which also waited for the kingdom of God came, and went in boldly unto Pilate, and craved the body of Jesus" (Mark 15:43). The death of Christ stirred the soul of Joseph. Certainly, the Holy Ghost moved upon him and prompted him to act. Flinging secrecy and caution to the wind, Joseph boldly went before Pilate to acquire the body of Jesus. While other disciples were confused, scared, and in hiding, Joseph acted with remarkable boldness and courage.

Joseph was a man of influence. His wealth, social status, and distinguished membership in the Sanhedrin allowed him to obtain an audience before Pilate. I believe the Lord had raised him up for this moment in his life. There certainly was danger in what he did. A petition like this before a Roman ruler, according to gospel theologian Fredric Farrar, had cost men their lives. In addition, Joseph was no longer a secret follower of Christ. There would most likely be severe repercussions from the Jewish leaders and his fellow members of the Sanhedrin.

Why did Joseph desire the body of Jesus? He wanted the Savior to have a proper, clean, private, honorable burial. According to

Jewish law, Jesus did not have the right to an honorable burial. The Sanhedrin council had condemned Jesus to die. The law stated, "They that were put to death by the council were not to be buried in the sepulchers of their fathers, but two burial places were [to be] appointed by the council."[6] If the Sanhedrin had appointed the two burial places as was custom, both burial sites would have been offensive to the followers of Jesus. If Joseph had not intervened, the body of Jesus would most likely have been burned or thrown into a common unmarked, shallow grave and become the property of the Roman government. This was the type of dishonorable burial the leaders of the Jews were hoping Jesus would receive.

To the request of Joseph, "Pilate marveled if he were already dead; and calling unto him the centurion, he asked him whether he had been any while dead" (Mark 15:44). Pilate marveled; Jesus had only been on the cross for approximately six hours.

It was the custom of the time to station soldiers to watch the cross, to prevent the removal of the sufferer while yet alive. This was necessary because of the lingering character of death of those crucified. It was a slow, excruciating process that sometimes did not supervene for days and was at last the result of a combination of starvation, shock, infection, exhaustion, and exposure. The Romans had learned that they needed guards. The possibility of crucified persons being taken down by their loved ones and recovering from the cross was real. Such was the case of one of the friends of the Jewish historian Josephus.

Once the centurion had confirmed that Jesus was dead, Pilate "gave the body to Joseph" (Mark 15:45). By giving the body of Jesus to Joseph, Pilate also may have risked political repercussions from both Rome and Jewish leaders. Normally the Romans left the bodies of their crucified victims on their crosses for days after they had died to decompose and be eaten by animals, which served as an example to keep the people in line.

Pilate went against Roman protocol and allowed Jesus's body to be removed from the cross. In addition, he allowed the body to be given to the care of someone who voted against the decision to put Jesus to death, to someone who loved Jesus. Pilate's actions here are puzzling.

Perhaps he allowed the body to be taken off the cross to avoid further conflict with Jews by making sure concerns over their fast approaching Sabbath were honored. According to Jewish law, the body of an executed criminal could not be left hanging overnight lest the land be defiled (see Deut. 21:22–23). That is most likely why the Jewish leaders wanted the legs of the three crucified persons broken. Their Sabbath was upon them.

While the weight of the body hung from the cross, the suffering individual could only take the shallowest of breaths. In order to breathe, the victim had to straighten his legs against the nails driven through the feet. The Jewish leaders besought Pilate to have the legs of the three crucified persons broken, which quickly would put an end to any life that remained in them. Sometimes this was followed by a sword or lance stroke. The legs of the two thieves were broken, and they would soon suffocate.

However, when they came to Jesus and saw that He was already dead, "they brake not his legs that the scripture [Exodus 12:46] should be fulfilled, A bone of him shall not be broken" (John 19:33, 35). The Mosaic law required that the Passover lamb must have no broken bones, but that its blood be sheds—something every Jewish leader would have known. Maybe their request to break the legs to avoid profaning their Sabbath day was a ruse. They may have wanted Jesus's legs broken to avoid any comparisons to the Pascal lamb. John the Baptist and others had testified to the people that Jesus was very the Lamb of God.

To make certain He was dead, one of the soldiers with a spear pierced Christ's side, and forthwith came there out blood and water (see John 19:34). This fulfilled an additional prophecy of David: "I am poured out like water. . . . My heart is melted in the midst of my bowels" (Psalm 22:14).

Why would Pilate allow the body of Jesus to be given to some-one who loved Him, to someone who would give Jesus an honorable burial? Pilate may have allowed the proper burial to get back at the Jewish leaders who had put him in the difficult political position that led to the crucifixion. Pilate had insulted the leaders with the inscription on the cross. He may have deliberately added to that insult by allowing a proper burial.

It should be noted that Roman law did permit an honorable burial for prisoners convicted of political crimes. Maybe this law opened the way for Pilate to accept the offer of Joseph of Arimathea to bury Jesus. Joseph may have been very persuasive and used this law to his advantage as he spoke with Pilate.

In the end, the answer to the question is that it was Heavenly Father's will that His Son receive a proper burial in a tomb. "The works, and the designs and the purposes of God cannot be frustrated, neither can they come to naught" (D&C 3:10). It was going to happen, and a way was opened up for it to occur. As an instrument in the Lord's hands, Joseph of Arimathea was raised up and prepared for this moment. He used his own personal, unused family tomb located in his garden plot for the burial of Jesus. The Savior's honorable burial was a testimony to all of His innocence. A stinging rebuke and testimony that served to sour the moment for the Jewish leaders.

Nicodemus

The prophecy of Isaiah that the Messiah would be "with the rich in his death" was also fulfilled in the life of Nicodemus, who was apparently a man of enormous wealth. Like Joseph of Arimathea, he was a member of the Sanhedrin and a secret follower of Christ. He had begun to overcome his fear of public opinion and trepidation. Earlier he had courageously defended the Savior before the chief priests and Pharisees, saying, "Doth our law judge any man, before it hear him, and know what he doeth?" (John 7:51). This was a very daring course of action on the part of Nicodemus. It caused his colleagues to ask, "Art thou also of Galilee?" (John 7:52).

Like Joseph, Nicodemus abstained from sharing in the vote to condemn Jesus to death. At the death of Christ, the soul of Nicodemus had also been stirred. The Holy Ghost undoubtedly had been preparing and working upon him as well.

"And when Joseph had taken the body, he wrapped it in a clean linen cloth" (Matthew 27:59). The record reads, "When Joseph had taken the body." Taken the body from where? Taken the body from

Calvary, from off of the cross. It is probable that the cross on which Jesus hung was laid on the ground and the nails were removed by Joseph and presumably Nicodemus to release it from the wood. Then, Joseph and Nicodemus wrapped the body of Jesus in a linen cloth and carried it to the nearby tomb of Joseph.

"It is profoundly sobering to think of Joseph of Arimathea and Nicodemus, two of Jerusalem's most distinguished leaders laboring in the darkening night to loosen the shattered remains of their Master from the horrible spikes."[7] It was a sacred task that was performed with the greatest of care and reverence.

When discovered, these actions certainly would have distanced Joseph and Nicodemus even further from the Sanhedrin. They would now be viewed by their fellow council members as ritually unclean for the next seven days. How ironic that they would be considered unclean for touching the holiest and most sacred of all corpses, the corpse of Jesus.

The death sentence of Jesus had occurred illegally and quickly in order to keep the followers of Jesus from gathering. We can surmise that Joseph and Nicodemus were able to act quickly to obtain the body of Jesus because they had inside information. They were aware of the trials and knew of the death of Jesus because of their associations with the Jewish ruling elite.

Preparations for the burial of Christ had to be hurried. The sun had set, and their Sabbath would have begun. It is important to note that even in the midst of their greatest tragedy, heartbreak and suffering, Joseph, Nicodemus, and the faithful women disciples would strive to strictly observe the Sabbath.

There is a lesson in this for us. Regardless of what we might be going through, these faithful disciples teach us that we are to keep the Sabbath at all times. Our Sabbath observance or non-observance of the Sabbath is an indication to the Lord of how we feel about His death, burial, and resurrection. It serves as an indication of the depth of our conversion and understanding of His atoning sacrifice.

The Sabbath had begun, and all these faithful disciples could do was quickly wash the corpse, roll the fine linen around the Savior's

THE AFTERMATH OF THE CRUCIFIXION

body, wrap His head in a napkin, and lay the body amid the spices within the rocky niche. "And there came also Nicodemus . . . and brought a mixture of myrrh and aloes, about a hundred-pound weight" (John 19:39). Nicodemus had brought embalming spices to the burial to prepare the corpse of Jesus. He brought "a hundred-pound weight." According to Adam Clarke, that amount was enough to embalm 200 corpses.[8] The amount was representative of what was used in Israelite royal burials. Jesus not only received an honorable burial that proclaimed His innocence, but He also received a burial that declared Him to be a king. The Savior, the King of Kings, was "with the rich in His death" (Isaiah 53:9).

After the burial, Joseph and presumably Nicodemus rolled a great stone to the door of the sepulcher and departed (Matthew 27:60).

As a result of obtaining and burying the body of Jesus, the lives of Joseph and Nicodemus would never be the same. They were no longer secret followers of the Savior. At the bare minimum, they were sure to be criticized by their fellow members of the Sanhedrin, cut off from the council, cast out of the synagogue, ostracized from their community, and most likely banished from Jerusalem. Their entire way of life would change—something both men must have known prior to acting. Time was of the essence; they would not wrestle with these thoughts for long. They had been raised up for this moment, and their actions would bless countless lives for ages to come.

During His ministry Jesus had taught, "Whosoever he be of you that forsaketh not all that he hath, he cannot be my disciple" (Luke 14:33). The Prophet Joseph Smith likewise taught: "A religion that does not require the sacrifice of all things never has power sufficient to produce the faith necessary unto salvation. . . . The faith necessary unto the enjoyment of life and salvation never could be obtained without the sacrifice of all earthly things."[9]

I believe Joseph of Arimathea and Nicodemus got to the point in their lives where they loved the Lord more than they cared for the honors of men. In the end, His opinion was the only opinion that mattered to them. They were willing to forsake and sacrifice all earthly things for the Kingdom of God and the Lord they loved. They left their associations and lives of power, wealth and comfort to fully, follow Christ. They fearlessly stepped out of the shadows and made their faith known. It was the type of faith that leads to life and salvation. This singular act of worship and love may have been a turning point for them.

Following the Savior's resurrection, tradition holds that Joseph of Arimathea became the great disciple and missionary who took the gospel to England under the direction of Phillip. Joseph is said to have built Britain's first church and became the first bishop in that country. In time, it is said that his converts to Christianity came to be numbered in the thousands.

Of Nicodemus, Farrar wrote:

> Tradition says that after the Resurrection [Nicodemus] became a professed disciple of Christ, and received baptism from Peter and John; that the Jews then stripped him of his office, beat him, and drove him from Jerusalem; that his kinsman Gamaliel received and sheltered him in his country house till death, and finally gave him honorable burial near the body of St. Stephen. The Talmud teaches, he outlived the fall of Jerusalem, and his family were reduced from wealth to such horrible poverty that, whereas the bridal bed of his daughter had been covered with a dower of 12,000 denarii, she was subsequently seen endeavoring to support life by picking the grains from the ordure of cattle in the streets.[10]

One Legend has it that Nicodemus was eventually martyred for the faith.

During the Savior's ministry, a young man "came running, and kneeled to him, and asked him, Good Master, what shall I do that I may inherit eternal life?" (Mark 10:17). Tradition suggests that the young man was either a ruler, a presiding official in a local synagogue, or a member of the Sanhedrin. A conversation ensued between the two. The young man had tried to keep the commandments the best he could, and he appears to have lived an honorable life. "Then Jesus beholding him loved him, and said unto him, one thing thou lackest, go thy way, sell whatsoever thou hast, and give to the poor, and thou shalt have treasures in heaven: and come, take up the cross, and follow me" (Mark 10:21).

This young man lacked one thing that would make him a complete disciple. He was asked to sacrifice all of his earthly possessions, to forsake the world and follow Jesus. "And he was sad . . . and went away grieved for he had great possessions" (Mark 10:22).

Nicodemus and Joseph were both like this young man and had great possessions. They were, in essence, asked to do the same thing and forsake everything to follow Jesus. At one point they, like the young man, "lacked one thing." With the burial of Jesus completed, they were no longer lacking; they were no longer secret followers of Christ. They left the cares of the world and took up their cross to follow Jesus. We don't have the full story of the young man who came running and kneeled before the Savior. But I like to think that he later reconsidered and, like Nicodemus and Joseph, received the Savior's invitation to forsake the world and follow Him. [11]

THE COVER-UP

While Joseph and Nicodemus were at work obtaining the body of Jesus and burying Him, the leading Jews were not idle.

> Now the next day, that followed the day of the preparation, the chief priests and Pharisees came together unto Pilate, saying, Sir, we remember that that deceiver said, while he was yet alive, after three days I will rise again. Command therefore that the sepulcher be made sure until the third day, lest his disciples come by night, and steal him away, and say unto the people, He is risen from the dead . . . Pilate said unto them, Ye have a watch: go your way, make it as sure as ye can. So, they went and made the sepulcher sure, sealing the stone, and setting a watch. (Matthew 27:62–66)

The wicked leaders broke their Sabbath observance and approached Pilate to obtain permission to place numerous guards around the tomb and to seal it. The Jewish leaders were quite conscious of Jesus's predictions about His own resurrection. Just following the first cleansing of the temple, "the Jews said unto him, what sign shewst thou unto us, seeing that thou doest these things? Jesus answered and, and said unto them, destroy this temple, and in three days I will raise it up. Then said the Jews, Forty and six years was this temple in building, and wilt thou rear it up in three days? But he spake of the temple of his body" (John 2:18–21). As we have discussed, the enemies of Jesus used that statement against Him during the trials as a literal statement. However, as these subsequent actions indicate, many of the leaders understood the true meaning behind Jesus's saying.

The Jews had a corps of Roman troops, consisting of several companies, standing guard for the temple (see Acts 4:1). These companies mounted guard by turns. Pilate allowed some of these companies which were not then on duty to watch the tomb.

The request was not only for guards to just watch the tomb, but also to "command therefore that the sepulcher be made sure" (Mathew 27:64). To seal the tomb more securely they would have added mortar of some sort or possibly a wax seal so that unauthorized entry could easily be detected. Adam Clarke believes that the seal was to prevent the guards from being corrupted so as to permit theft.[12]

The Jewish leaders made it virtually impossible for anyone to come and take the Savior's body away from the tomb unknowingly. Sometimes the enemies of the truth, those who are seeking to destroy it, become the unwitting means of verifying the truth and helping move the work forward—such would be the case in this instance. As we will discuss, these actions serve to support the truth of the resurrection.

As the soldiers were guarding the tomb, "there was a great earthquake: for two angels of the Lord descended from heaven and came and rolled back the stone from the door, and sat upon it" (JST, Matthew 28:2). An aftershock earthquake of the previous Friday struck Jerusalem as two angels came down from heaven. According to Bruce R. McConkie, their heaven-created power caused the earthquake. The angels broke the seal and rolled away the stone from the tomb. The soldiers fell to the ground and for a time were paralyzed. Once they recovered, they fled in fright. The Jewish leaders now had a problem because the soldiers had seen the angels come down from heaven and roll away the stone.

These were unbiased witnesses of yet another miracle connected to Jesus. Their story was irrefutable, and it appears the Jewish leaders did not question or challenge it. It is almost unfathomable to consider the hard-heartedness and wickedness of these leaders. They had been given sign after sign. Many of them had witnessed numerous miracles; the earth itself had just borne witness. Some of them saw Lazarus come forth from the tomb. Jesus had now risen from the dead, yet they refused to consider the evidence. How accurately did the Savior speak of them when he said, "Neither will they be persuaded, though one rose from the dead" (Luke 16:31). They were not interested in the truth. They were hardened and past feeling.

To cover up the truth, the Jewish leaders "gave a large sum of money unto to the soldiers. Saying, say ye, His disciples came by night, and stole him away while we slept" (Matthew 28:13). Getting gain, receiving filthy lucre to distort and cover up the truth were not new tactics of the adversary. These were secret combinations that initially began with Cain and continue today.

Of the cover-up Adam Clarke has written,

> Here is a whole heap of absurdities. 1st. Is it likely that so many men would fall asleep, in the open air, at once? 2ndly. Is it at all probable that a Roman guard should be found off their watch, much less asleep, when it was instant death, according to the Roman military laws, to be found in this state? 3rdly. Could they be so sound asleep as not to awake with all the noise which must be necessarily made by removing the great stone, and taking away the body? 4thly. Is it at all likely that these disciples could have had time sufficient to do all this, and to come and return, without being perceived by any person? And 5thly. If they were asleep, how could they possibly know that it was the disciples that stole him, or indeed that any person or persons stole him?—for, being asleep, they could see no person. From their own testimony, therefore, the resurrection may be as fully proved as the theft.[13]

As Clarke explains so thoroughly here, common sense and reason stood in opposition to their cover up narrative. The Jewish leaders had no viable explanation for the resurrection of Jesus.

DARK DAYS

Immediately following the death of Jesus, the grief and sorrow of the Apostles was beyond words. That Friday and Saturday, I believe, were the darkest of all days for them. They were devastated and stricken with discouragement and gloom. They were left alone, confused, and in a state of despair. Gone were their hopes and forgotten were the promises Christ had made to them. They were not only consumed in their sorrow but were frightened and in hiding. As disciples of Christ, their lives may have been in danger. John records that when they finally assembled, they shut the doors, for fear of the Jews (see John 20:19).

The current status of the Church was in shambles. Nothing could have seemed more hopeless than the cause in which they had been engaged. They could not claim a single synagogue, they were poor, they were few in number and scattered. The Church that Christ had founded seemed doomed to extinction. Their hopes and dreams were buried in a tomb. All appeared to be lost.

However, within a matter of weeks, the Apostles were changed, transformed into confident, fearless, heroic preachers and defenders of the gospel of Jesus Christ. Without hesitation or regard for their own personal safety they began to carry the gospel to all the world. The Church would soon flourish for a season as converts would join in droves. All but John would fearlessly go on to a martyr's death. Why not John? He had obtained the promise of translation, power over death. John would tarry until the Savior would return a second time in glory (see D&C 7:1–4).

What changed and transformed the lives of the Apostles and saved the early Church? First, the Apostles received the gift of the Holy Ghost. The last thing recorded that Jesus did on Resurrection Sunday was to bestow the gift of the Holy Ghost upon His disciples. The Apostle John wrote, "He breathed on them, and saith unto them receive ye the Holy Ghost" (John 20:23). That promised gift would be fully ratified a few weeks later on the day of Pentecost (see Acts 2).

What else changed and transformed the lives of the Apostles? It was the revelation and witness they received that Christ had risen from the grave. During the mortal ministry of Jesus, the Apostles failed to fully comprehend His repetitive teachings regarding His future death and resurrection. Such an event had never happened before; it was unprecedented. As hard as the Apostles tried, they just could not wrap their minds completely around it.

We cannot overstate the importance of Jesus rising from the grave; it is the "weightiest matter" of this gospel.[14] The Resurrection of Jesus Christ was the capstone, the crowning moment of the Atonement. No doctrine in the Christian canon is more important to all mankind than the doctrine of the resurrection. It should be the center of every true Christian's faith. Soon, after the burial, it became the center of the ancient Apostles' faith.

Of Jesus rising from the grave, Jeffrey R. Holland taught, "It was this truth, this reality that allowed a handful of Galilean fishermen turned again Apostles without a single synagogue or sword to leave those nets a second time and go on to shape the history of the world in which we now live."[15] The knowledge of the Resurrection transformed the Apostles. It resolved once and for all the true identity of Jesus. The resurrection of Christ was a testimony that Jesus was who He said He was, a divine being, even Jehovah, the God of the Old Testament. No one ever born into mortality ever had the power in him or herself to come to life again after dying, let alone come forth with a perfect immortal glorified resurrected body, that is, no one but Jesus.

President Howard W. Hunter taught, "Without the Resurrection, the gospel of Jesus Christ becomes a litany of wise sayings and seemingly unexplainable miracles—[nothing] but sayings and miracles with no ultimate triumph. No, the ultimate triumph is in the ultimate miracle; for the first time in the history of mankind, one who was dead raised himself into living immortality. He was the Son of God . . . and his triumph over physical and spiritual death is the good news every Christian tongue should speak."[16]

The knowledge of the Resurrection verified the Savior's message and the cause in which the apostles were engaged. They now knew for certain the course they were pursuing, the path they were on, was in accordance with God's will. The Resurrection was in the words of one eminent writer, "The final absolute seal of genuineness . . . put on all His claims, and the indelible stamp of divine authority upon all His teachings. The gloom of death had been banished by the glorious light of the presences of their Risen, glorified Lord and Savior."[17]

The Apostles learned that because of the Resurrection a number of things were now certain. They came to know that every consequence of the Fall had now not only been overcome but had also been improved upon. The grave had lost its sting; physical death had been conquered; all will live again, and all will receive perfect, immortal, glorified bodies. Spiritual death had likewise been overcome. All will return to the presence of God. For some, that stay will be temporary; for others, it will be permanent based on the conditions of repentance.

Because of the Savior's atoning sacrifice and resurrection, all but the sons of perdition will receive a heaven, a degree of glory. John A. Widtsoe explained, "The meanest sinner, in the final judgment, will receive a glory which is beyond human understanding. . . . The Gospel is a gospel of tremendous love. Love is at the bottom of it. The meanest child is loved so dearly that his reward will be beyond the understanding of mortal man."[18] George Q. Cannon likewise observed: "Each one of us will receive glory far beyond anything that we can possibly conceive of, even if we have been sinners."[19]

The disciples learned that the Savior's resurrection permanently crushed Satan's head. In modern revelation the Savior declared, "I having accomplished and finished the will of him whose I am, even the Father . . . Retaining all power, even to the destroying of Satan and his works at the end of the world" (D&C 19:2–3). Satan will ultimately lose the war he has waged against God and His kingdom. In the end, the kingdom of God that the disciples were striving to build would triumph. The Savior's triumphant resurrection made that outcome certain and that knowledge gave the disciples great confidence and perspective. The empty tomb was the answer to the questions of the ages.

SOME DOUBTED

Matthew 28:16–20 records the Savior's final commission to the Apostles on a mountain in Galilee. We only have a fraction of this important meeting. This was not a surprise appearance. The fact that prior to His death, the Savior had appointed this meeting and chosen the location adds to its significance. Bruce R. McConkie agrees: "Of all the recorded appearances this one was paramount."[20] Those who came, came by invitation. It is thought by some that this is where the Savior appeared to over 500 brethren at once. This Galilean mountain was most likely the location of the Lord's special forty–day ministry with His disciples after His resurrection. Gospel scholar Cleon Skousen's surmises that the actual location of this meeting was Mount Hermon. [21]

During the meeting as the Apostles were receiving their final apostolic commission to build up the kingdom and take the gospel to all of the world, the record says, "Some doubted" (Mathew 28:17). What did they doubt? Maybe, like Mary and the disciples on the road to Emmaus, they did not immediately recognize the resurrected Lord and doubted it was Him.

On the other hand, if they recognized Jesus, I have a hard time believing that any of His disciples at this point doubted that Jesus was their resurrected Lord. They had seen Him, touched Him, eaten with Him, and had been taught by Him on multiple occasions. So, what did they doubt?

They may have doubted their own ability. Some of them may have doubted that they could do what Jesus was now asking them to do. They felt their own weaknesses, inadequacies, and short-comings. Maybe they were overwhelmed by the commission of the apostolic calling. What Apostle has not been overwhelmed by that initial call? Jesus would no longer physically be with them, and He was asking them to go forth and do what He had done. Not only were they to take the gospel to all of the world, but the commission was for them to cast out devils, speak in tongues, lay hands on the sick, and even raise the dead (see Mark 16:17–18). The commission seemed daunting, and some doubted.

The Savior, knowing their doubts, explained, "All power is given unto me in heaven and earth" (Matthew 28:18). Some of the Apostles may not have understood the full implications of the Resurrection. I am not sure we understand the full implications today. The Savior explained He had not been given just some power, but because of His triumph all power had been given to Him. He was like the Father in every way, omnipotent, omniscient, and omnipresent. He had received a fulness of the glory of the Father; He received all power both in heaven and on earth (see D&C 93:16, 17).

The Savior then promised His disciples, "And, lo, *I am with you always*, even unto the end of the world" (Matthew 28:20; emphasis added). Because Jesus rose from the grave the disciples would never be alone. He who holds all power, though unseen, would walk and work with them. With His help, they could not fail. The Savior has given similar promises in our dispensation: "Mine eyes are upon you. I am in your midst and ye cannot see me" (D&C 38:7). "I will go before your face; I will be on your right hand and on your left" (D&C 84:88).

The ancient disciples trusted in these promises and "went forth, and preached everywhere, the Lord working with them, and confirming the word with signs following" (Mark 16:20). Though unseen, it was the testimony of the Apostles that the Lord worked with them. Long ago the Savior said to Enoch during his apostolic commission, "Walk with me" (Moses 6:34). He was now walking with these Apostles.

The knowledge of the resurrection of Jesus changed everything for the Apostles. They went from an uncertain, confused, and divided group into united, powerful witnesses of the Lord and defenders of the faith. They were transformed because of that knowledge. All doubt and fear had been dispelled, and they went forth with great confidence, "the lord working with them." They went on to change the world because of it. Because Jesus had overcome physical and spiritual death and gained the victory over Satan and the world, the Apostles could now do so as well and so can we. Just as He walked with them as they took the gospel to the world, likewise He will walk with us.

A sure knowledge of the Resurrection has the power to affect and change all of us like it did those early Apostles. James E. Faust taught, "Like the Apostles of old, this knowledge and belief [of the resurrection] should transform all of us to be confident, settled, unafraid, and [to be] at peace in our lives as followers of the divine Christ. It should help us carry all burdens, bear any sorrows, and also fully savor all joys and happiness that can be found in this life."[22]

The Apostle Paul, writing to the Corinthian Saints, explained how the knowledge of the Resurrection should affect them: "For this corruptible must put on incorruption, and this mortal must put on immortality . . . then shall be brought to pass the saying that is written, death is swallowed up in victory. O death where is thy sting? O grave where is thy victory? . . . But thanks be to God, which giveth us the victory through our Lord Jesus Christ. Therefore, my beloved brethren, [because of the victory of the resurrection] *be ye steadfast, unmovable, always abounding in the work of the Lord, forasmuch as ye know your labor is not in vain in the Lord*" (1 Corinthians 15:53–58; emphasis added). Because Christ gained the victory and was resurrected, all those who labor for His cause do not do it in vain. Paul and the early Apostles believed that with their whole souls; they knew that because of the Resurrection of Jesus the work they were engaged in was His work, and they were willing to suffer a martyr's death because of it.

May a sure knowledge of the resurrection inspire us as it did those early Apostles. May we like them become "steadfast, immovable, always abounding in the work of the Lord, knowing as we labor for the Master, it is not in vain." And may we, like them, faithfully endure and gain the victory over sin and the world as they did. Just as those early disciples had dark, discouraging days, Elder Joseph B. Wirthlin explained, "Each of us will have our own [dark] Fridays, those days when the universe itself seems shattered and the shards of our world lie littered about us in pieces. We all will experience those broken times when it seems we can never be put together again. But I testify to you in the name of the One who conquered death that Sunday will come. In the darkness of our sorrow, Sunday will come. No matter our desperation, no matter our grief, Sunday will come."[23]

My message to you is hold on. Hold on when your dark Friday comes. Remain true to your covenants, true to the faith, and know assuredly that as the sun rises, Sunday will come. Jesus promised that He would not leave His Apostles comfortless. The resurrected Lord came to them in their darkest hour, and He will come to us. I cherish the words of the Psalm, "Weeping may endure for a night, but joy cometh in the morning" (Psalm 30:5). [24] Christ is our "High Priest of Good Things to Come" (Hebrews 9:11). Because of Him, because of His triumph, good things await the faithful in the future. We can with a "surety hope for a better world" (Ether 12:4). Because of Him joy cometh in the morning. We may have some dark days immediately ahead, but because of Him we have many bright, glorious days eventually ahead.

ENDNOTES

1. Spencer W. Kimball, "General Conference," April 1963 general conference.
2. John Taylor, *Mediation and Atonement* (Deseret News Company, 1882/1998), 148.
3. Bruce R. McConkie, *Doctrinal New Testament Commentary*. Vol. 1 (Salt Lake City: Bookcraft, 1965), 829–830.
4. Susan Easton Black, *400 Questions & Answers about the Life and Time of Jesus Christ* (American Fork, UT: Covenant Communications, 2010), 220.
5. There is a non-scriptural tradition that Joseph of Arimathea was the great-uncle of Jesus. That is, uncle to Jesus's mother Mary, brother to Anna, Mary's mother. Tradition has it that before the Savior began His ministry Joseph had taken Him on journeys outside of Israel, particularly to Great Britain.
6. John Roberts Dummelow, *A Commentary on the Holy Bible by Various Writers* (Macmillan, 1974).
7. W. Phillip Keller, *Rabboni: Which Is to Say, Master* (Kregel Publications, 1998), 280.
8. Adam Clarke, *The New Testament of Our Lord and Saviour Jesus Christ* (Abingdon), 654.

9. Smith, Joseph Jr., *Lectures on Faith*, 6:7.

10. Frederic W. Farrar, *The Life of Christ* (Salt Lake City: Bookcraft, 1995), 197.

11. In our modern era President Gordon B. Hinckley illustrated this teaching of forsaking all for the gospel of Jesus Christ. He shared the following story: "I think of a friend who I knew when I was a missionary in London many years ago. He came to our door through the rains one night. I answered his knock and invited him in. He said, as I remember, 'I have to talk to someone. I'm all alone. I asked what the problem was. He said, When I joined the Church, my father told me to get out of his house and never come back. A few months later my athletic club dropped me from membership. Last month my boss fired me because I am a member of this church. And last night the girl I love said she would never marry me because I'm a Mormon.' I said, 'If this has cost you so much, why don't you leave the Church and go back to your father's home, to your club, to the job that meant so much, and marry the girl you think you love?' He said nothing for what seemed like a long time. Then, putting his head in his hands, he sobbed as if is heart would break. Finally, he looked up through the tears and said, 'I couldn't do that. I know this is true, and if it were to cost me my life, I could not give it up'" (Gordon B. Hinckley, "Living with Our Conviction," *Ensign*, Sept. 2001.

12. Adam Clarke, *The New Testament of Our Lord and Saviour Jesus Christ* (Abingdon), 281.

13. Ibid., 283.

14. In the first chapter we quoted the Prophet Joseph Smith teaching, "The fundamental principles of our religion are the testimony of the Apostles and Prophets, concerning Jesus Christ, that He died, was buried, and rose again the third day, and ascended into heaven; and all other things which pertain to our religion are only appendages to it" (Joseph Smith and Joseph Fielding Smith, *Teachings of the Prophet Joseph Smith* [Salt Lake City: Deseret Book, 1958/1977], 121). Joseph explained further that the resurrection of the dead should be preached among the first principles of the gospel. Joseph informed a group of gathering saints that "the doctrine of the resurrection of the dead and eternal judgment are necessary to preach among the first principles of the gospel of Jesus Christ" (Ehat and Cook, *Words of Joseph Smith*, 4). In a letter that is dated March 22, 1839, Joseph wrote, "We believe in the doctrine of faith, and of repentance, and of baptism for the remission of sins, and the gift of the Holy Ghost by the laying on of hands, and of the resurrection of the dead, and of eternal judgment" (Joseph C. Smith, *The Personal Writings of Joseph Smith*. Edited by Dean C. Jessee (Salt Lake City: Deseret Book, 2002). Paul likewise explained that the "first principles [of the gospel] (Hebrews 5:12) should include . . . baptism, laying on of hands [for the gift of the Holy Ghost], and of *resurrection of the dead* and of eternal judgment." (Hebrews 6:2; emphasis added). Both Paul and Joseph Smith taught that the resurrection of the dead should be taught with the first principles of the gospel.

15. Jeffrey R. Holland, "The First Great Commandment," October 2012 general conference.
16. Howard W. Hunter, *Teachings of the Presidents of the Church: Howard W. Hunter*, The Church of Jesus Christ of Latter-Day Saints, 2015, 106.
17. David O. McKay, *Treasures of Life* (Salt Lake City: Deseret Book, 1962), 15–16.
18. John A. Widtsoe, *The Message of the Doctrine and Covenants* (Salt Lake City: Bookcraft, 1969), 167.
19. George Q. Cannon, *Gospel Truth*. 1st ed. Vol. 1 (Zion's Book Store, 1957), 121.
20. Bruce R. McConkie, *Doctrinal New Testament Commentary*. Vol. 1, (Salt Lake City: Bookcraft, 1965), 866.
21. "There was one mountain which was already very sacred to the apostles and that was the Mount of Transfiguration. Both the scriptures and the circumstances indicate that this was clearly Mount Hermon. . . . Mount Hermon looms into the sky 9,166 feet and is the highest and most majestic mountain in all northern Palestine. Lying in its lower foothills, was the resort community of Caesea-Philippi where the disciples had stayed at the time of transfiguration. Since the apostles apparently had to be given a course of rigorous spiritual training during the next few weeks, it would have been convenient to reside in the town at night and then climb into the secluded, quiet precincts of the mountain for their heavenly instructions during the daytime" (W. Cleon Skousen, *Days of the Living Christ* [Ensign Publishing Co., 1992/2018], 577).
22. James E. Faust, "The Supernal Gift of the Atonement," October 1988 general conference.
23. Joseph B. Wirthlin, "Sunday Will Come," October 2006 general conference.
24. I am reminded of a group of suffering, distraught Nephites who learned of the Resurrection. Their "mourning was turned to joy, and their lamentations into the praise and thanksgiving unto the Lord Jesus Christ, their Redeemer" (3 Nephi 10:10). We all have or will experience dark a Friday in our lives after the death of a loved one. Gordon B. Hinckley declared, "Whenever the cold hand of death strikes, there shines through that gloom and the darkness of that hour the triumphant figure of the Lord Jesus Christ. . . . He is our comfort, our only true comfort, when the dark shroud of earthly night closes about us as the spirit departs the human form" (Gordon B. Hinckley, *Teachings of the Presidents of the Church: Gordon B. Hinckley*, The Church of Jesus Christ of Latter-Day Saints, 2016), 328.

CHAPTER 9
THE ULTIMATE TRIUMPH

WOMEN DISCIPLES

As the Sabbath concluded, the first to go and visit the tomb were Mary Magdalene and the other faithful women who had watched Jesus's body be laid to rest. After observing the Sabbath day, they returned to more thoroughly anoint and embalm Jesus's body with the spices and ointments that they had prepared. Adam Clarke surmised, "[They] prepared spices and ointments . . . to embalm him, which sufficiently proves that they had no hope of his resurrection the third day."[1] Like the Apostles, they too were devastated. In their moment of grief, they too had forgotten the promises of His Resurrection.

According to Jewish tradition, the soul hovered around the body until the third day. Then it finally parted from its earthly tabernacle. The women possibly also went to the tomb to fulfill the Jewish custom, which was to visit the tomb of a deceased person within three days in order to check the condition of the corpse.

Early Sunday morning in the darkness, Mary Magdalene and a group of women journeyed toward the tomb. "Their total may well have been in the dozens or scores."[2] As they were traveling a discussion ensued. "And they said among themselves, Who shall roll us away the stone from the door of the sepulchre?" (Mark 16:3). How were they going to remove the sealed stone? They may have also wondered how they were going to get past the guards. These were two problems that did not seem to have a solution, two difficulties that may have seemed like impossible barriers to overcome. Yet these women went forth with the hope that they would somehow get to the body of Jesus. When they arrived, they found that those barriers had been removed. The angels had broken the seal, removed the stone, and the guards had fled. There is a lesson in this for us.

I am reminded of what the Savior once told His questioning disciples, "With God all things are possible" (Mark 10:27). Similarly, an angel once explained to Mary, "For with God nothing shall be impossible" (Luke 1:37). The Lord had said to a childless Abraham and Sarah, "Is anything too hard for the Lord? (Genesis 18:14). The answer to that question is a resounding "no!" When we go as far as we can go, and do all that we can do, if it is the Lord's will, a way will open. Such was the case with these women. In a matter of minutes, the Lord resolved both obstacles. The Lord honored the intentions and efforts of these women. He will likewise honor our efforts to do good.

THE ROLLED STONE

Why was it necessary for the angels to roll the stone away and open the door of the tomb? Was it so Jesus, like Lazarus, could exit with His new physical body? No, resurrected beings have the power to pass through solid objects. This is something Joseph Smith learned at the age of seventeen when Moroni appeared and left his room three times in one night. Joseph Fielding Smith explained, "Resurrected bodies pass through solid objects. Resurrected bodies have control over the elements. How do you think the bodies will get out of the graves at the resurrection?"[3]

The stone was rolled back so the disciples could look inside and enter and see for themselves that the tomb was empty and gain a testimony that Jesus had been resurrected. In addition, there is a symbolic meaning: just as the door of the tomb was now open, the door connecting spirit paradise and spirit prison had at last been opened. The great gulf between them had been bridged. The gospel was now being taken to those in prison, and the prisoners could now be set free. The keys and power to take the gospel to the spirits in prison and set them free were given to Jesus shortly after His death. Brigham Young explained, "Those keys were delivered to him in the day and hour that he went into the spirit world, and with them he opened the door of salvation to the spirits in prison."[4]

We have been discussing the greatest story ever told. We now come to the climax of Jesus's Atonement, the Resurrection. Our English word for resurrection derives from two Latin terms, re ("again") and surgere ("to rise"), and literally means "to rise again." Jesus would fulfill His promise of all promises and rise again.

"And behold, there was a great earthquake: for two angels of the Lord descended from heaven and came and rolled back the stone from the door and sat upon it" (JST, Matthew 28:2). The Joseph Smith Translation clarifies that it was two angels that removed the stone, not just one. It may have been necessary to have two angels involved to satisfy the ancient law of witnesses. Early Christian tradition identified the angels as Michael and Gabriel.

"And the angels answered and said unto the women, Fear not ye, for we know that ye seek Jesus, which was crucified. He is not here: for he is risen, as he said, Come, see the place where the Lord lay" (JST, Matthew 28:5–6). **"He is not here: for he is risen!"** It was the greatest announcement ever given to mortals. The following is a small sample of what modern-day apostolic witnesses have said regarding this glorious declaration:

Marion G. Romney declared, "These words, eloquent in their simplicity, announced the most significant event recorded in history."[5]

Gordon B. Hinckley stated, "These simple words, 'He is not here, but is risen'—have become the most profound in all literature."[6] On another occasion he said, "Of all the victories in human history, none is so great, none so universal in its effect, none so everlasting in its consequences as the victory of the crucified Lord, who came forth in the resurrection that first Easter morning."[7]

Ezra Taft Benson said, "There is nothing in history to equal that dramatic announcement."[8]

Howard W. Hunter testified, "The resurrection of Christ is, the single most fundamental and crucial doctrine in the Christian religion, the one thing that cannot be overemphasized, nor . . . disregarded, and the ultimate triumph as well as the ultimate miracle."[9]

Eldon N. Tanner likewise declared, "Jesus Christ's Resurrection was the greatest event that has ever taken place in the history of mortal man."[10] Christianity is founded on the greatest of all miracles, the resurrection of our Lord.

During His mortal ministry Jesus taught, "I lay down my life, that I might take it again. No man taketh it from me, but I lay it down of myself. I have power to lay it down, and I have power to take it again" (John 10:17–18). By virtue of His parentage, Jesus had at birth received the power to reunite His body with His spirit following His death. From His Father He received the power to resurrect Himself. Of the Resurrection, Lehi taught, "He [Jesus] layeth down his life according to the flesh, and taketh it again by the power of the Spirit" (2 Nephi 2:8). Jesus both laid down His life and took it up again under His own volition. The Atonement could only have been performed by one who had power over life and death.

As mentioned in chapter 8, Christ forged the keys of death and hell in Gethsemane and on the cross, and later received them from His Father. Those keys included the keys of the Resurrection. They were not given to Jesus until He was resurrected. Joseph Fielding Smith explained, "On the third day after the crucifixion he took up his body and gained the keys of the Resurrection, and thus has power to open the graves of all men, but this he could not do until he had first passed through death himself and conquered."[11]

THE FIRST WITNESSES

As the women heard the declaration of the angel "they remembered his words" (Luke 24:8). The women began to remember what Jesus had taught them during His ministry about His eventual death and resurrection. Initially after His death, most if not all of the disciples, had failed to fully understand and comprehend it. "For as yet they knew not the scripture that he must rise again from the dead"

(John 20:9). Once the women heard the angels, they remembered the Savior's teachings. Who was helping these women remember? Certainly the Holy Ghost was involved in bringing these teachings to their remembrance (see John 14:26).

The angels instructed the women to "go quickly and tell his disciples that he is risen from the dead and behold he goeth before you into Galilee; and there shall ye see him" (Matthew 28:7). Before Jesus died, He had appointed a meeting in Galilee where He would meet the brethren. "But after I am risen again, I will go before you into Galilee" (Matthew 26:32). The angels asked the women to remind the brethren of that appointment. The approximate distance from Jerusalem to Galilee is a hundred miles. The Apostles had a hundred-mile journey ahead of them and needed to get moving. Once instructed, the women "departed quickly and did run to bring his disciples word" (Matthew 28:8).

As the women were on their way to find the disciples, "behold, Jesus met them, saying, All hail, And they came and held him by the feet, and worshiped him" (Matthew 28:9). These women became eyewitnesses to the Savior's Resurrection. They were among the first, following Mary Magdalene. The women found the disciples and testified to them they had seen angels, that the tomb was empty, and that they had seen the resurrected Lord.

It appears that it was important for the disciples to first hear the testimony of these women regarding the risen Lord, for "faith comes by hearing the word of God, through the testimony of the servants of God; that testimony is always attended by the Spirit of prophecy and revelation."[12]

Mary, Peter, and John

Mary Magdalene was the first witness of the resurrected Lord. She was one of the first to arrive at the tomb Resurrection morning. Biblical scholar and historian Alfred Edersheim surmised, "It may have been, that there were two parties, starting from different places to meet at the Tomb, and this also accounts for the slight difference in the details of what they saw and heard at the Grave."[13]

Mary, upon seeing the empty tomb, appears to have immediately left the other women. "She runneth, and cometh to Simon Peter, and to the other disciple whom Jesus loved, and saith unto them, they have taken away the Lord out of the sepulcher, and we know not where they have laid him" (John 20:2). Apparently from her statement, Mary had not heard or understood the divine message from the two angels. Once Mary found Peter and John and delivered her message, the three of them traveled to the empty tomb. By the time they reached their destination, the other women, obedient to the instruction of the angels, had departed to find the disciples.

"So they ran both together and the other disciple did outrun Peter and came first to the sepulcher. And he stooping down, and looking in, saw the linen clothes lying, yet went not in" (John 20:4–5). John was the first to make it to the empty tomb. He looked into the sepulcher but waited until Peter arrived and then followed Peter into the tomb. Why did John wait? Seniority is honored among ordained Apostles even when entering and leaving a room. Another possibility is that John hesitated not wanting to desecrate the sacred spot even by his presence.

"Then cometh Simon Peter following him, and went into the sepulcher, and seeth the linen clothes lie. And the napkin, that was about his head, not lying with the linen clothes, but wrapped tighter in a place by itself. Then went in also that other disciple, which came first to the sepulcher, and *he saw and believed*" (John 20:6–8; emphasis added). When John entered the tomb, he saw and believed. What did he see and believe?

The Savior's resurrected body had passed through His burial clothes without disturbing them. "The strips of cloth were left in such a way as to show that his resurrected body had passed through their folds and strands without the need of unwinding the strips."[14] Lazarus needed help removing his burial clothes, but Jesus did not. He had gone right through them. This was explicit evidence of Jesus's Resurrection.

Years ago, as I looked at the sacrament table during a sacrament meeting the thought came to me that we can associate the Savior being wrapped in linen to the ordinance of the sacrament.

When we look at the sacrament table and see the white linen cloth covering the sacrament emblems, we can remember not only the burial of Christ but also His Resurrection—how Jesus was not only buried and wrapped in linen cloth but how He also arose and passed through the cloth without disturbing it.

John and Peter also saw that burial napkin that had been wrapped around the head of Jesus (used to hold the jaw in place) was folded and neatly lying in a place by itself.[15] No thief would have taken time to fold the burial clothing. Jesus had come forth from the dead in an orderly, dignified fashion. Following His Resurrection Jesus had taken the time to fold the napkin. John saw it and may have believed that it was the Savior who had done the folding.

On a regular basis, endowed members of the Church fold sacred temple garments. Following certain ordinances in the temple, endowed members often fold their own temple clothing, the clothing that many are traditionally buried in. As we fold sacred clothing we can remember how Jesus had come forth from the grave and folded His burial napkin. We can ponder the significance of His Resurrection and be grateful for what He did.

The Holy Ghost

In those quiet, sacred moments of reflection in the tomb, John and possibly Peter were at last coming to understand the Resurrection. I believe these two Apostles would first, to some degree, receive their witness from the Holy Ghost. Why would it be important for them not just to see the risen Lord but to also obtain a witness from the Holy Ghost? The most lasting and powerful witness would come to them from the convincing power of the Holy Ghost.

Joseph Fielding Smith explained, "When a man has the manifestations from the Holy Ghost, it leaves an indelible impression on his soul, one that is not easily erased. It is Spirit speaking to spirit, and it comes with convincing force. A manifestation of an angel, or even the Son of God himself, would impress the eye and mind, and eventually become dimmed, but the impressions of the Holy Ghost sink deeper into the soul and are more difficult to erase"[16]

President Smith also has written, "Through the Holy Ghost the truth is woven into the very fiber and sinews of the body so that it cannot be forgotten."[17] Through that gift we likewise can receive a perfect assurance of the Resurrected Lord. It can be as sure for us as though we have seen and felt the wound marks ourselves.

Mary, the First Witness

After Peter and John departed from the garden tomb Mary Magdalene returned and lingered.

> But Mary stood without at the sepulchre weeping: and as she wept, she stooped down, and looking into the sepulcher. And seeing two angels in white sitting . . . they say unto her, Woman, why weepest thou? She saith unto them, Because they have taken away my Lord, and I know not where they have laid him. And when she had thus said, she turned herself back, and saw Jesus standing, and knew not that it was Jesus. Jesus saith unto her Woman, why weepest though? Whom sleekest thou? She, supposing him to be the gardener, saith unto him, Sir, if thou have borne him hence, tell me where thou hast laid him, and I will take him away.
>
> Jesus saith unto her, Mary. She turned herself and saith unto him, Rabboni; which is to say, master. Jesus saith unto her, Touch me not; for I am not yet ascended to my Father: but go to my brethren and say unto them, I ascend unto my Father, and your Father, and to my God, and your God. (John 20:11–17)

Mary was the first eyewitness of the Savior's literal resurrection. Once the Savior called Mary by name, she immediately recognized His voice. From this experience we learn that Divinity is personal. The Savior, the Good Shepherd, knows the names of all of His sheep. With one word, the Savior changed Mary's tears of sorrow into tears of joy.

The Joseph Smith Translation of verse 17 reads, "Jesus saith unto her, Hold me not." Commenting on this Bruce R. McConkie explained, "Various translations from the Greek render the passage as 'Do not cling to me' or 'Do not hold on to me.' Some give the meaning as 'Do not cling to me any longer' or 'Do not hold me any longer.' Leaving the inference that Mary was already holding him. There is valid reason for supposing that the thought conveyed to Mary by the Risen Lord was to this effect: 'You cannot hold me here, for I am going to ascend to my Father.'"[18]

According to some scholars, the present tense of the Greek "me mou haptou" used in John 20:17 should be translated, "Don't keep touching me" or "do not hold me back." The implication is not that Mary could not or should not touch Jesus before He ascended to His Father, but rather because He was ascending, their paths were soon to separate. Just a short time later the other faithful women were allowed to hold the Savior's feet as they worshiped Him.[19]

Immediately following Mary's encounter with the resurrected Lord, she went to the disciples and gave her witness. "Mary Magdalene came and told the disciples that she had seen the Lord, and that he had spoken these thing" (John 20:18). This fulfilled the Messianic scripture, "I will declare thy name unto my brethren; in the midst of the congregation will I praise thee" (Psalm 22:22).

In early Christianity, this earned Mary the title "the apostle to the apostles." She was not a member of the Twelve but "one sent forth" to witness the good news of the Resurrection. She was not only the first person to see the resurrected Lord, but the first mortal to bear her witness of it to others. I think it significant that Mary Magdalene and the other elect women had been chosen first to witness the miracle of the Savior's Resurrection, even before the priesthood leaders. These women were certainly among His most faithful, loyal followers. Their primary concern and focus was their Master whom they loved, followed, and worshiped, and they were rewarded accordingly.

It should be noted that at the time, "in Jewish culture women could not be witnesses. Generally, a woman's testimony, was [considered] along with that of a slave, and was not admissible evidence in court, unless it dealt with a woman's issue."[20]

These first witnesses of the Resurrection of Jesus demonstrate the equality of women and men. In this Church and kingdom, we have prophets and prophetesses, priests and priestesses, kings and queens, and gods and goddesses. Jesus has always been a champion for women and for all of us. He will ensure that all will eventually have an equal opportunity to receive a fulness of blessings.

How did the disciples initially respond to the testimony of the women? "Their words seemed to them as *idle tales* and they believed them not" (Luke 24:11; emphasis added). "The disciples believed not" (Mark 16:9–11). "Afterward he appeared unto the eleven as they sat at meat and upbraided them with their unbelief and hardness of heart, because they believed not them which had seen him after he was risen" (Mark 16:14).

The Resurrection was unprecedented. Nothing like it had ever happened before. The Savior's death had just occurred, and the Apostles were in mourning and overcome with grief. The news of Him rising seemed to them as fantasy or an idle tale. Oh, how things would soon change. In an attempt to save the primitive Church, Peter later wrote to the Saints, "For we have not followed cunningly *devised fables*, when we made known unto the power and coming of our Lord Jesus Christ, but we were eyewitnesses of his majesty" (2 Peter 1:16; emphasis added). The Resurrection was not a devised fable, or fairy tale, but a reality, a reality that all of these disciples would soon discover, a reality they would all (except John) lay down their lives for.

Professor Richard D. Draper taught, "On that Sunday, the disciples were downhearted, frightened men. It seems it would have been easier for them to believe that Jesus had died and stayed dead. Yet their conversion to the reality of Christ's Resurrection strengthens their witness for those who otherwise might disbelieve that vital truth. Each Gospel writer makes it clear that the disciples were not swept into belief because they wanted to be. Rather, they believed in spite of their own inclinations to the contrary."[21]

Gospel scholar Kent S. Brown likewise surmised, "Perhaps the strongest reason to believe His followers testimonies has to do with their plain reluctance at first to believe what they were [hearing], seeing and touching. The Resurrection was not an event they would have made up, for they quickly dismissed the earliest reports which came from the women."[22]

It is important to note that then, as now, the Lord attempted to first establish the truth for these disciples by testimony. Although initially rejected, I believe the seeds of hope and faith were planted in their hearts by the testimony of these women.

Peter

Mary and the women were the first witnesses of the risen Lord. Who would be next? Both Luke and Paul inform us that the risen Lord appeared to Peter on Resurrection Sunday (see Luke 24:34, 1 Corinthians 15:5). This was most likely His third appearance. It may have been then, that Jesus's special appearance to Peter was associated in some way to the principle of keys. Peter was His chief Apostle and would soon be leading the Church.[23]

THE ROAD TO EMMAUS

Christ's fourth appearance was to Cleopas and another disciple, presumably Luke, as they traveled from Jerusalem to Emmaus. As they journeyed, the resurrected Lord joined them and withheld His glory from the two disciples.

The distance was "about threescore furlongs" (Luke 24:13), approximately seven miles. They walked and talked for at least two hours together. It appears their perception of what and who the Messiah would be was skewed. Jesus was the Lamb of God; He came as the Suffering Servant. These disciples, like so many, had hoped that Jesus would have been a political and military leader and deliverer. "We trust that it had been he which should have redeemed Israel" (Luke 24:21). They had not comprehended that Jesus had indeed not only redeemed Israel but the universe and all the inhabitants in it.

As they walked and talked, Jesus "expounded unto them in all the scriptures the things concerning himself" (Luke 24:27). I think it is significant that the Savior used the scriptures to teach them. Shortly after this, the Savior used the scriptures to teach the Nephite leaders (see 3 Nephi 23). Just as the Savior used the scriptures to teach of His divinity, so should we. When giving a talk or teaching a lesson, I believe in most cases the scriptures should be used. There is no satisfactory substitute for them. They serve as a voice of authority, and invite the Spirit. Bruce R. McConkie explained, "Those who preach by the power of the Holy Ghost use the scriptures as their basic source of knowledge and doctrine."[24] When we use the scriptures, we sometimes tend to summarize or paraphrase verses. There is power in reading verses verbatim and then, like the Savior, expounding upon them.

Luke wrote of the experience, "And their eyes were opened, and they knew him; and he vanished out of their sight. And they said one to another, Did not our heart burn within us while he talked with us by the way, and while he opened to us the scriptures" (Luke 24:31, 32). As important and wonderful as it was for these two disciples to see the resurrected Savior with their eyes, the greater, sustaining witness came by the power of the Holy Ghost through the use of the scriptures. It is our privilege to receive similar knowledge and manifestations from the Holy Ghost as we study the scriptures.

In our day President Henry B. Eyring testified, "I am a witness of the Resurrection of the Lord as surely as if I had been there in the evening with the two disciples in the house on the Emmaus road. . . . I so testify as a witness of the risen Savior and Redeemer."[25]

Thomas

Just a word or two regarding the Apostle Thomas. He has been widely criticized because of his initial response to the testimony of his brethren. "Except I shall see in his hands the prints of the nails and put my finger into the print of the nails, and thrust my hand into his side, I will not believe" (John 20:25). As a result of that reaction he has received the infamous title Doubting Thomas. We should point out that Thomas reacted in the same way as the others had when they had first heard the witness of the women. Nothing short of tangible proof would suffice any of them.

Bruce R. McConkie explained, "Thomas apparently did not understand or believe that Jesus had come forth with a literal, tangible body of flesh and bones, one that could be felt and handled, one that bore the nail marks and carried the spear wound, one that ate food and outwardly was almost akin to a mortal body. Obviously, he had heard the testimony of Mary Magdalene and the other women, of Peter, and of all the Apostles. It is not to be supposed that he doubted the Resurrection as such, but rather the literal and corporeal nature of it. Hence his rash assertion about feeling nail prints and thrusting his hand into the Lord's side."[26]

When Thomas beheld the resurrected Lord and received a first-hand witness, "Thomas answered and said unto him, My Lord and my God" (John 20:28). "Thomas was the first that we know of who gave the title of God to Jesus; and, by this glorious confession, made some amends."[27]

Toward the end of the mortal ministry of Jesus, it became extremely dangerous for Jesus to walk openly among the Jews. His enemies were constantly plotting to take His life. They had their spies everywhere looking for opportunities to take Him. It was especially dangerous for Jesus to appear in Jerusalem and nearby cities. Just weeks before His death, Jesus planned to travel to Bethany, which was close to Jerusalem. It appears that some of the disciples, knowing the dangers were hesitant to make that journey. "Then Thomas . . . called unto his fellow disciples, Let us also go, that we may die with him" (JST, John 11:16). Thomas loved and was devoted to the Savior.

Numerous early Christian writings state that after the Resurrection Thomas preached the gospel throughout Syria, Mesopotamia, and India. Tradition holds that Thomas died a martyr. He was run through with a lance on the coast of Coromandel, in East India around 72 A.D.

We need to be careful not to be critical of these disciples. I do not believe it is possible for us to overemphasize the sorrow and grief they experienced. Sometimes the death of someone we deeply love can overwhelm us and skew our thoughts for a time. To think that just after a day and a half, as we measure time, their Master had risen from the dead was inconceivable. Nothing like this had ever happened before. The concept of an actual resurrection defied all their logic and experience. The disciples were invited to believe in something that had no historical precedent. In addition, as previously noted in chapter 8, the promised gift of the Holy Ghost that would enlighten their understanding and bring all things to their remembrance was not ratified until a few weeks later on the day of Pentecost.

APPEARING IN GALILEE

We are going to fast forward to the Savior's seventh appearance. As mentioned, before His death Jesus had scheduled an appointment with the Apostles in Galilee. That meeting would be fulfilled as the Savior appeared first to seven of the Twelve at the Sea of Galilee and then later on a mountain where Jesus had appointed a special meeting (see John 21). "This [final] appearance of the resurrected Jesus, as far as the record shows, seems to have been made to issue the final ministerial call to the Apostles and to instruct them in their duties."[28]

As the disciples were waiting for Jesus to come to Galilee, they went back to the one thing they really knew how to do well. They went fishing. You know the story. The disciples had been fishing all night without success. When the morning had come Jesus called to them from the shore and said unto them, "Cast the net on the right side of the ship, and ye shall find. They cast the net therefore and they were not able to draw it for the multitude of fishes" (John 21:6).

LOVEST THOU ME?

This was not the first time this miracle had been performed for the disciples. They knew immediately that the man on the shore of Galilee was Jesus. A crucial conversation then occurred between Jesus and Peter:

> So, when they had dined Jesus saith to Simon Peter, Simon, son of Jonas, lovest though me more than these? He saith unto him, Year, Lord; thou knowest that I love thee. He saith unto him,

feed my lambs. He saith to him again the second time, Simon, son of Jonas, lovest thou me? He saith unto him, Yea, Lord; thou knowest that I love thee. He saith unto him, feed my sheep. He saith unto him the third time, Simon, son of Jonas, lovest though me? Peter was grieved because he said unto him the third time, lovest thou me? And he said unto him, Lord, thou knowest all things, thou knowest that I love thee, Jesus saith unto him, feed my sheep. (John 21: 15–17)

In verse 15 the Savior had asked Peter, "Lovest thou me more than these?" More than what? More than all of the fish they had just caught. More than fishing? More than the world? More than these other disciples?

Although the English text uses "feed" three times in these verses, the Greek word for feed in verse sixteen implies "shepherding." Clarke explained that the Greek translation signifies "to tend a flock, not only to feed, but to take care of, guide, govern, and defend."[29]

The Greek verb "lovest" in verse 17 asks for a higher degree of commitment, an increased level of devotion than the verbs used earlier. As dedicated as Peter was, in this last verse Christ is asking even more from him—to take his commitment to a higher level. It seems most appropriate that one of the great reminders in this final chapter of John's account is that Christ loves us where we are, even if that is not yet where we ought to be. And because Christ loves us, He constantly invites us to come to Him, to increase our commitment to Him, to engage in His work, and to change and become better disciples.

Jesus then took this very setting to prophesy as to how much sacrificial, Christlike love and commitment Peter would one day be called upon to display. "When thou shalt be old, thou shalt stretch forth thy hands, and another shall gird thee and carry thee wither thou wouldest not. This spake he, signifying by what death he should glorify God. And when he had spoken this, he saith unto him. Follow me" (John 21:18–19).

The verb translated as "gird" in Greek in verse 18 means to "tie up or on," referring to the act of having one's arms tied to a crossbeam prior to being crucified. The Lord's message to Peter was that if he loved Him, if he were to truly feed His sheep, it would one day lead to his death on the cross, just as it had led to His own. The Saviors final closings words in verse 19 to Peter were, "Follow me." Put in context with verse 18, the message was clear: "Peter, follow me to the cross." That prophecy would be fulfilled some thirty-four years later.

Elder Jeffery Holland taught: "My beloved brothers and sisters, I am not certain just what our experience will be on Judgment Day, but I will be very surprised if at some point in that conversation, God does not ask us exactly what Christ asked Peter: 'Did you love me?'"[30] The Lord's message to Peter and to all of us in this encounter is that we show our love to the Savior by feeding His lambs and by feeding His sheep. His lambs could be considered the youth of the Church and the young new converts. His sheep encompass everyone else.

Our commission is to feed His lambs and sheep. I believe we are to first take that invitation literally and feed the Lord's sheep physically. The newly resurrected God and Redeemer of the universe had just taken the time to physically feed His hungry disciples on the seashore. He cared for their physical needs. Throughout His ministry Jesus physically fed people, He had fed thousands and thousands of them. In the Old Testament, Jehovah had day in, and day out fed the children of Israel with manna for forty years.

Two of my heroes in the Old Testament are the prophet Abraham and his wife Sarah. In Genesis 18, three men show up at their tent door. The men are invited to wash themselves and rest, while Abraham and Sarah prepared a great feast for them. This was not an uncommon occurrence in their home. An ancient document recorded that Abraham was known as "the Father of guests." It is written that he would not eat the morning meal or an evening meal without a guest. The Midrash says that "Abraham our father used to bring them into his house and give them food and drink and be friendly to them . . . and [then] convert them in a joint effort with Sarah." The ancient record reads that "Abraham used to convert the men and Sarah the women."[31]

For them, sharing the gospel was a family affair. Abraham would write about the souls they had won (see Abraham 2:15). Their highest priority in life seemed to be winning souls to Christ. One ancient document states that their converts came to be numbered in the tens of thousands.[32] Together, they brought countless souls to Jehovah by first feeding them physically and then spiritually.

When I was a young teenager my grandparents served a mission in Africa. As missionaries, they often first showed up at the homes of the people they were teaching with a bag of groceries. Then they would attempt to teach them the gospel. Their example made a lasting impression upon me. They, like Abraham and Sarah, fed the Lord's sheep in more than one way.

Our Church leaders have taken this commission very seriously and through humanitarian efforts and the Church Welfare Program feed millions of people each year. We likewise can reach out to the poor, to those who are struggling in the faith, to those who don't have the gospel, and feed them. We can feed our neighbors, our friends, and our extended family members. We can also feed the missionaries. Like Abraham and Sarah, we can invite people into our homes and feed them, and the day will come when the Savior will say, "For I was an hungered and ye gave me meat; I was thirsty, and ye gave me drink: I was stranger and ye took me in" (Matthew 25:35).

The invitation to "feed my sheep" is also for us to focus our attention on the spiritual well-being of those within our sphere of influence and feed them. We are to feed them with the word of God. We are to feed them with the Book of Mormon, the most correct book of any book on earth. We are to feed them with the words of our living prophets, the most important word of the Lord. In modern-day revelation, the Lord makes it clear that we have a special mandate and obligation to feed the Lord's sheep with the revelations revealed through the Prophet Joseph Smith (see D&C 31:4, 43:7, 49:4).

It is difficult to feed the Lord's sheep unless we have been fed first. We cannot lift another unless we are first standing on higher ground. We cannot light a fire in the soul of another until a fire is first burning in our own soul. The Lord's command is for us to "treasure up in your minds continually the words of life" (D&C 84:85). As we constantly feed our spirits, we, like the prophet Jeremiah, will be able to say, "His word was in my heart as a burning fire shut up in my bones" (Jeremiah 20:9).

COMMITTED FOREVER

Of the resurrected Lord's appearance to His seven disciples on the sea of Galilee Jeffrey R. Holland taught:

> His Apostles did witness Him in His resurrected state, but that [initially] added to their bewilderment. As they surely must have wondered, "What do we do now?" . . . In effect Peter said to his associates: "Brethren, it has been a glorious three years. None of us could have imagined such a few short months ago the miracles we have seen and the divinity we have enjoyed. We have talked with, prayed with, and labored with the very son of God Himself. We have walked with Him and wept with Him, and on the night of that horrible ending no one wept more bitterly than I. But that is over. He has finished His work, and He has risen from the tomb. He has worked out His salvation and ours. So, you ask, what do we do now? I don't know more than to tell you to return to your former life, rejoicing. I intend to go fishing."
>
> [As mentioned, at least seven of the apostles go fishing, and then meet and eat with the Savior.] After a joyful reunion with the resurrected Jesus, Peter had an exchange with the Savior that I consider the crucial turning point of the apostolic ministry generally and certainly for Peter. . . . Looking at their battered little boats, their frayed nets, and a stunning pile of 153 fish, Jesus said to His senior Apostle, "Peter do you love me more than you love all this? Peter said, "Yea Lord; thou knowest that I love thee. The Savior responds to that reply . . . and says again, "Peter, do you love me?" Undoubtedly confused a bit by the repetition of the question, the great fisherman answers a second time, "Yea, Lord; thou knowest that I love thee."
>
> "The Savior . . . asks for a third time, "Peter do you love me?" By now surely Peter is feeling truly uncomfortable. . . . Whatever

his feelings, Peter said for the third time, "Lord . . . thou knowest that I love thee. To which Jesus responded . . . perhaps saying something like: "Then Peter, why are you here? Why are we back on this same shore by these same nets, having this same conversation? Wasn't it obvious then and isn't it obvious now that if I want fish, I can get fish? What I need, Peter are disciples—and I need them forever. I need someone to feed my sheep and save my lambs. I need someone to preach my gospel and defend my faith . . . . So, Peter, for the second and presumably the last time, I am asking you to leave all this and go teach and testify, labor and serve loyally until the day in which they will do to you exactly what they did to me.[33]

That day, that discussion on the shore of Galilee with the resurrected Christ changed Peter's life forever. Elder Holland believed that is the moment when Peter became the great Apostle. Why? That day I believe was the moment Peter completely committed and dedicated his entire life, his all, to the Lord and to His sheep forever. That was the moment Peter fully embraced his life's work and commission. He completely forgot about himself and went to work.

From that day on for Peter there would be no going back to fish, no second guessing. His course became fixed. On the shore of Galilee, he put both of his hands to the plow and never looked back. The Savior would never again need to ask him to get engaged in His work. His heart, might, mind, and strength became completely focused and dedicated to one thing—feeding the Lord's sheep. Building the kingdom of God had become the ultimate priority and focus of his life.

Three times Peter had proclaimed his love to the Lord on the seashore. Peter went on to prove that love by feeding the Lord's sheep day in and day out for the rest of his life. He was now all in, to the very end. No sacrifice would be too great for him to serve the Master he loved. No assignment, no mission would be too great to serve the Master who had sacrificed His all on our behalf. Peter became one of the greatest men that ever walked the earth. The gift of the Holy Ghost and his knowledge and understanding of the Savior's atoning sacrifice and Resurrection transformed him.

Time, experience, trial, and suffering tutored him. To the Saints Peter wrote from personal experience, "That the trial of your faith, being much more precious than gold that perisheth, though it be tried with fire, might be found unto praise and honor and glory at the appearing of Jesus Christ" (1 Peter 1:7). "Beloved, think it not strange concerning the fiery trial, which is to try you, as though some strange thing happened unto you" (1 Peter 4:12).

Elder Carlos E. Asay explained, "The mettle of the man Peter did not come automatically and without effort. Peter was subjected to trials and temptations and all else commonly referred to as the refiner's fire. The heat of opposition did not consume him; it served only to burn out the impurities and weaknesses and leave refined and pure metal. Peter emerged from the furnace of affliction as a polished, strong sword of righteousness. His iron strength of character carried him through to the end of his mission."[34]

According to the early Christian writer Hegesippus, Peter was martyred as follows:

> When he was old, Nero planned to put him to death. When the disciples heard of this, they begged Peter to flee the city (Rome), which he did. But when he got to the city gate, he saw Christ walking toward him. Peter fell to his knees and said, "Lord, where are you going?" Christ answered, "I've come to be crucified again." By this, Peter understood that it was his time to suffer the death of Jesus, which would glorify God. So, he went back to the city. After being captured and taken to his place of martyrdom, he requested that he be crucified in an upside down position because he did not consider himself worthy to be crucified in the same position as his Lord.[35]

Peter, like Paul, had fought a good fight, had finished his course, and had kept the faith (see 2 Timothy 4:7).

Joseph B. Wirthlin testified, "I do not suggest the road will be easy. But I will give you my witness that those who in faith leave their nets and follow the Savior will experience happiness beyond their ability to comprehend."[36]

May we like Peter find that happiness. May we leave our nets and dedicate our lives, our all to the cause of Christ. Like the Apostles of old, may the knowledge and belief in the Resurrection transform all of us into confident, fearless disciples of Christ. Disciples who love the Lord. Disciples who know and feed the Lord's sheep. Disciples who leave their nets and do it forever and never look back. Disciples who are concerned with the "weightiest matters of law." Disciples who know the story of Christ better than they know anything else. Disciples who remember the greatness of the Holy One of Israel (see 2 Nephi 9:40).

May our voice and testimony of Christ stand as an independent witness with the "great . . . cloud of witnesses" (see Hebrews 11:1) who have gone before us. So that our children and grandchildren might know what source to look for a remission of their sins (see 2 Nephi 25:26). I conclude with the final admonition Mormon gave to his son Moroni: "Be faithful in Christ. . . . May his sufferings and death, and the showing his body unto our fathers, and his mercy and longsuffering, and the hope of . . . eternal life, rest in your mind forever" (Moroni 9:25).

ENDNOTES

1. Adam Clarke, *The New Testament of Our Lord and Saviour Jesus Christ* (Abingdon), 498.
2. Bruce R. McConkie, *The Mortal Messiah: From Bethlehem to Calvary.* Vol. 4, (Salt Lake City: Deseret Book, 1979), 265.
3. Joseph Fielding Smith, *Doctrines of Salvation.* Vol. 2 (Salt Lake City: Bookcraft, 1954), 228.
4. *Journal of Discourses*, vol. 3, *The Editorium*, 2013, 370.
5. Marion G. Romney, "The Resurrection of Jesus," April 1982 general conference.
6. Gordon B. Hinckley, *Teachings of the Presidents of the Church: Gordon B. Hinckley*, The Church of Jesus Christ of Latter-Day Saints, 2016, 130.
7. Gordon B. Hinckley, "The Son of God," *Ensign*, Dec. 1992.
8. Ezra Taft Benson, "The Greatest Event in History," April 1964 general conference.
9. Howard W. Hunter, "An Apostle's Witness of the Resurrection," April 1986 general conference.
10. N Eldon. Tanner, "Remarks," April 1969 general conference.
11. Joseph Fielding Smith, *Doctrines of Salvation.* Vol. 1, (Salt Lake City: Bookcraft, 1954), 128.
12. Joseph Smith, *History of the Church.* Edited by B H Roberts. Vol. 3 (Salt Lake City: Deseret Book, 1842/1976), 379.

13. Alfred Edersheim, *The Life and Times of Jesus the Messiah*. Vol. 2 (Eerdmans Pub. Co., 1971), 630.

14. Bruce R. McConkie, *The Mortal Messiah: From Bethlehem to Calvary*. Vol. 4 (Salt Lake City: Deseret Book, 1979), 268.

15. One Christian writer has explained, "When the servant set the dinner table for the master, he made sure that it was exactly the way the master wanted it. The table was furnished perfectly, and then the servant would wait, just out of sight, until the master had finished eating, and the servant would not dare touch that table until the master was finished. If the master was done eating, he would rise from the table, wipe his fingers, his mouth, and clean his beard, and would wad up that napkin and toss it onto the table. The servant would then know to clear the table. For in those days, the wadded napkin meant, 'I'm done.' But if the master got up from the table, folded his napkin, and laid it beside his plate, the servant would not dare touch the table because the servant knew that the folded napkin meant, 'I'm not finished yet.' The folded napkin meant, 'I'm coming back!'" (Tim McConnell, "Why Did Jesus Fold the Napkin in the Tomb?" Apr. 21, 2017, https://www.citizen-times.com/story/life/2017/04/21/devotional-why-did-jesus-fold-napkin-tomb/100612470/.

This appears to be the opinion of many, including some within the Church. While teaching, I have on a few occasions had class members make this very point about the folded napkin and Jesus returning. While this sounds wonderful, I have yet to find any historical evidence that supports it being a true Jewish custom. To the contrary, many have debunked the notion.

16. Joseph Fielding Smith, *Answers to Gospel Questions*. Vol. 2 (Salt Lake City: Deseret Book, 1958), 151.

17. Joseph Fielding Smith, *Doctrines of Salvation*. Vol. 1 (Salt Lake City: Bookcraft, 1954), 48.

18. Bruce R. McConkie, *The Mortal Messiah: From Bethlehem to Calvary*. Vol. 4 (Salt Lake City: Deseret Book, 1979), 264–265.

19. James E. Talmage had a different interpretation of verse 17. He taught, "One may wonder why Jesus had forbidden Mary Magdalene to touch Him, and then, so soon after, had permitted other women to hold Him by the feet as they bowed in reverence. We may assume that Mary's emotional approach had been prompted more by a feeling of personal yet holy affection than by an impulse of devotional worship such as the other women evidenced. . . . We have to infer that no human hand was to be permitted to touch the Lord's resurrected body until after He had presented Himself to the Father. It appears reasonable and probable that between Mary's impulsive attempt to touch the Lord, and the action of the other women who held Him by the feet as they bowed in worshipful reverence, Christ did ascend to the Father, and that later He returned to earth to continue His ministry" (James E. Talmage, *Jesus the Christ* [Salt Lake City: Deseret Book, 1915/1982], 682).

20. Dawn Hall Anderson, et al., editors. *Every Good Thing: Talks from the 1997 BYU Women's Conference* (Salt Lake City: Deseret Book, 1998).

21. Richard D. Draper, "The Reality of the Resurrection," *Ensign*, Apr. 1994.

22. S. Kent. Brown, et al. *Beholding Salvation: The Life of Christ in Word and Image* (Salt Lake City: Deseret Book, 2006), 95.

23. Church Education System, *The Life and Teachings of Jesus and the Apostles.* 2nd ed., The Church of Jesus Christ of Latter-Day Saints, 1978, 200. See also Bruce R. McConkie, *Doctrinal New Testament Commentary.* Vol. 1, (Salt Lake City: Bookcraft, 1965), 851.

24. Joseph Fielding McConkie, *The Bruce R. McConkie Story* (Salt Lake City: Deseret Book, 2003), 301.

25. Henry B. Eyring, "'Come unto Me,'" April 2013 general conference.

26. Bruce R. McConkie, *Doctrinal New Testament Commentary.* Vol. 1 (Salt Lake City: Bookcraft, 1965), 860.

27. Adam Clarke, *The New Testament of Our Lord and Saviour Jesus Christ* (Abingdon), 659.

28. Bruce R. McConkie, *Doctrinal New Testament Commentary.* Vol. 1 (Salt Lake City: Bookcraft, 1965), 861.

29. Adam Clarke, *The New Testament of Our Lord and Saviour Jesus Christ* (Abingdon), 662.

30. Jeffrey R. Holland, "The First Great Commandment," October 2012 general conference.

31. E. Douglas Clark, *The Blessings of Abraham: Becoming a Zion People* (American Fork, UT: Covenant Communications, 2005), 86–87. Talmudic tradition holds that the name *Abraham* (which means, "father of multitudes or nations") is really the father of proselytes" (Ginzbert, *Legends of the Jews,* 5:233).

32. Ibid. In our dispensation I am reminded of Heber C. Kimball and his wife Vilate. They were like Abraham and Sarah, inviting all who were in need into their home and feeding them. During times of famine they always kept an open house at their home in Salt Lake City and fed from twenty-five to one hundred people at their table, daily, besides making presents innumerable of bread, flour and other necessities (see Orson Whitney, *Life of Heber C. Kimball* [Salt Lake City: Bookcraft, 1967], 402).

33. Jeffrey R. Holland, "The First Great Commandment," October 2012, general conference.

34. Carlos E. Asay, *The Seven Ms. of Missionary Service.* (Salt Lake City: Bookcraft, 1996), chapter 4.

35. John Foxe, *Foxe's Book of Martyrs.* Bridge Logos Publishers, 2001, 7.

36. Joseph B. Wirthlin, "'Follow Me,'" April 2002 general conference.

APPENDIX

LIST OF EYEWITNESSES OF THE RESURRECTED CHRIST

1. Mary Magdalene outside the Garden Tomb on the morning of Jesus's Resurrection. (John 1–18)
2. Other women somewhere between the Garden Tomb and Jerusalem. (Matthew 28: 1–9)
3. Cleopas and another disciple [Luke] on the road to Emmaus on resurrection day. (Mark 16, Luke 24:13–32)
4. Simon Peter on resurrection day. (Luke 24:34, 1 Corinthians 15:5)
5. Ten of the Twelve in a closed room somewhere in Jerusalem on resurrection night. (Luke 24:36–53, John 20:19–24)
6. Eleven of the Twelve in a closed room in Jerusalem one week after the Resurrection. (Mark 16:14, John 20:26–31)
7. Seven of the Twelve at the Sea of Galilee (Tiberias), the third visit to the group. (John 21:1–14)
8. Eleven of the Twelve on a mountain in Galilee by previous appointment of the Savior. (Matthew 28:16–20)
9. More than five hundred brethren at once, probably on the mountain in Galilee with the eleven Apostles. (1 Corinthians 15:6)
10. James (1 Corinthians 15:7)
11. Eleven Apostles at Jesus's ascension near Bethany forty days after the Resurrection. (Mark 16:14,19, Luke 24:50–51; Acts 1:3–11)

12. Saul of Tarsus on the road to Damascus, Syria. (1 Corinthians 9:1; 15:8)
13. The Nephites (2500) in the land of Bountiful in America near the temple about 34 A.D. (3 Nephi 11)
14. John the Revelator on the Isle of Patmos sometime between 81 A.D. and 96. (Revelation 1:9–18)
15. The Nephite Twelve. (3 Nephi 27)
16. Lost Tribes of Israel soon after the Savior's visitation to the Nephites. (3 Nephi 16:1–4; 17:4)
17. Mormon. (Mormon 1:15)
18. Moroni. (Ether 12:39)
19. Joseph Smith in the Sacred Grove near Palmyra, New York, in the spring of 1820 (April 6).
20. Modern-day prophets: Martin Harris, Oliver Cowdery, Newel K. Knight, Lyman Wight, Orson F. Whitney, Heber J. Grant, John Taylor, George Q. Cannon, George F. Richards, Joseph F. Smith, David O. McKay, LeGrand Richards, David B. Height, Melvin J. Ballard, and many others. Harold B. Lee once testified, "I found myself viewing the scenes with a certainty as if I had been there in person."[1] David B. Height testified, "I was shown a panoramic view of His earthly ministry . . . and resurrection."[2]

THE PHYSICAL RESURRECTION WAS REJECTED BY MANY EARLY CHRISTIANS

The early Apostles continually battled against anti-resurrection thinking that kept pushing its way into the Church. Paul asked the Corinthians; "Now if Christ be preached that he rose from the dead, how say some among you that there is no resurrection of the dead?" (1 Corinthians 15:12). A few years later, John warned that "many deceivers are entered into the world who confess not that Jesus is come in the flesh" (2 John 1:7).

Paul found it necessary to cite multiple witnesses of the Resurrection to combat the growing heresy (see 1 Corinthians 15:5–8).

The apostolic fathers writing at the close of the first century fought against the same tendency.

The doctrine of a physical resurrection was not popular. Many of the second century converts to Christianity were Hellenists, and they could not imagine a God contaminated by association with the flesh.

By the time of Augustine, the doctrine had become a major point of contention within the Christian community. Augustine wrote, "There is not an article of the Christian faith which has encountered such contradiction as that of the resurrection. . . . Nothing has been attacked with the same pertinacious, contentious contradiction, in the Christian faith as the resurrection of the flesh."[3]

Greek philosophy was the main contribution to the rejection of this belief. Greek philosophers had a deep and abiding distrust of things of the flesh, and that distrust has continued into modern Christianity. To this day, a large number of Christians reject the doctrine of the physical resurrection. For example, a popular college text used in many introductory New Testament classes in the United States proclaims, "We need to keep in mind that the empty tomb was an ambiguous witness to the resurrection. It attests the absence of the body, but not necessarily the reality or presence of the risen Jesus."[3]

ENDNOTES

1. Harold B. Lee, *Teachings of Presidents of the Church: Harold B. Lee* (The Church of Jesus Christ of Latter-Day Saints, 2000).
2. David B. Haight, "The Sacrament—and the Sacrifice," October 1989 general conference. See also David B. Haight, *A Light unto the World* (Salt Lake City: Deseret Book, 1997), 4.
3. Augustine, *On the Psalms,* Psalm 89. 32, in P.L. 37:1134.
4. Robert A. Spivey and D. Moody Smith, *Anatomy of the New Testament: A Guide to Its Structure and Meaning* (Macmillan, 1989), 239.

ABOUT THE AUTHOR

Dr. Jeffry NeVille has practiced dentistry in Layton Utah for sixteen years. He has a bachelor's degree from the University of Utah in Medical Biology and a Doctor of Medical Dentistry degree from Nova Southeastern University. From 2008 to 2020 he taught Institute of Religion courses at the LDS Business College. He currently teaches Institute courses for Weber State University. Brother NeVille has served in the Church of Jesus Christ of Latter-day Saints as an Elders Quorum President, Young Men's President, Sunday School President, Ward Mission leader, Gospel Doctrine Instructor, and Stake Institute instructor. He and his wife Gracelyn are the parents of five daughters.